GRAVE UNDERTAKINGS

Elizabeth Township
Volume 1

Gravestone Inscriptions

Of

Old Warwick Township

In

Lancaster County

Pennsylvania

By

Martha J. Xakellis

printed by
CLOSSON PRESS
1935 Sampson Dr., Apollo, PA 15613
© Copyright, July, 1989
Martha J. Xakellis
ISBN #1-55856-019-X

GRAVE UNDERTAKINGS

Elizabeth Township

Volume 1

INTRODUCTION

I live in northern Lancaster County and am the Membership Secretary of the Lancaster County Historical Society. I became interested in preserving the information on gravestones when I was asked by the late Hunter Rhineer to read the stones in the Penryn Union Cemetery when he found out that I could read the German inscriptions. While I was reading the stones, I found that I was able to read stones that others had labled "not readable"! Using a list for this cemetery that was printed in 1928, I checked my listing and found that many errors and misreadings had occurred and, of course, all those buried since 1928 had not been listed. With this I became quite excited about doing the same for all cemeteries and family graveyards in what was old Warwick Township, which is now comprised of four townships. They are Elizabeth, Clay, Penn, and Warwick, and I have opted to handle them on an individual basis. To make a long story short, I now have Elizabeth Township completed.

Each cemetery has been assigned a number which corresponds with the number used by Hunter Rhineer in his book "Churches and Cemeteries of Lancaster County, Pennsylvania; A Complete Guide". Larger cemeteries will be divided into numbered sections to generally locate stone position. This section number will appear in brackets [ ]. (G) indicates that the stone was inscribed in German. Every effort was made to accurately copy the names and information that appeared on the stones. Due to age and sometimes the type of stone used, it was not always possible to do this. A question mark (?) will appear if this was the case. If nothing was there, as for an age or a date, nothing was on the stone. Each time a surname is listed means a separate headstone. When more than one person is listed on a stone, the surname will be listed only once. All information is as it was carved on the stones. Names were not always spelled the same, but when they were of the same family, they are listed together. Date of birth was the guideline for listing names with husbands and wives together and then children. Thus look for alphabetical listing, then dates.

Earlier readings, if available, were used to check my readings. If names were in an earlier list and not there when I read the stones, this was noted. This was especially true for the family graveyards. Some have been taken care of over the years, but many more are disappearing. Grass and brush grow around the stones and encourage small animals to make their homes there. The tunneling causes the stones to fall over and gradually they are covered. Sometimes the stones come to light again when the land is cleared for farming and the farmer's plow will uncover some of these stones.

I have tried to be as accurate as possible with these inscriptions of Elizabeth Township. And I hope that they are of use to you in finding your ancestors.

Martha J. Xakellis   1989

2

MAP OF ELIZABETH TOWNSHIP

On the map below you will find the cemetery locations marked by a number in a circle. This number appears in the index along with the name of the cemetery. Not all these cemeteries can be easily seen from the road. The small family graveyards are usually up on a hill in the middle of a field. A crop growing in the field will completely hide them. The short introductory paragraph with each cemetery will help pinpoint it's location.

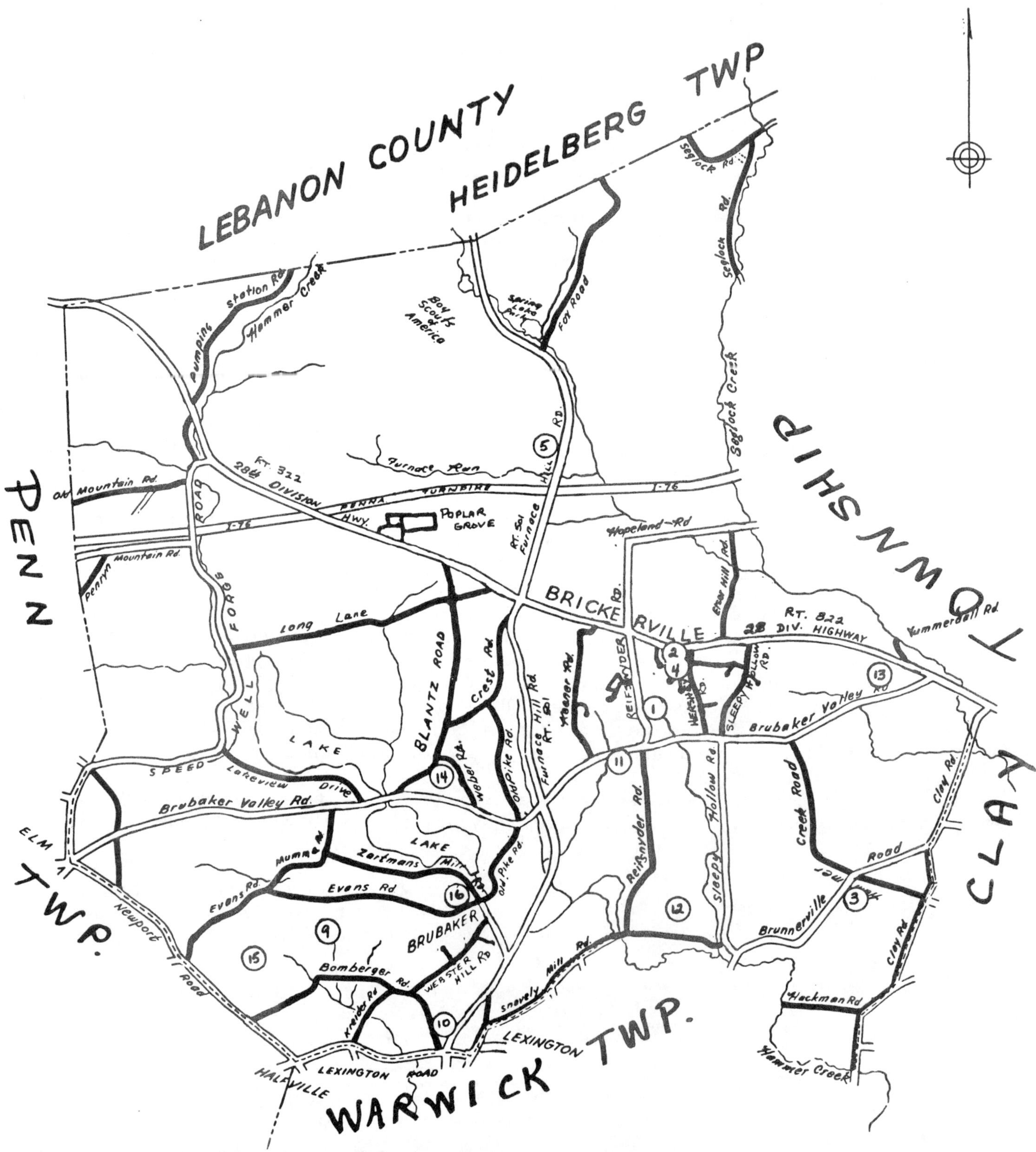

OLD ZION REFORMED CHURCH #1

BRICKERVILLE, LANC. CO.

Founded 1747

Annual Service 2nd Sunday P.O. of September

Thus is inscribed the stone over the door on the west end of this brick church located on Reifsnyder Road south of Route 322. Painted on the balcony facing the 'hour-glass pulpit' is "Emanuel Deyer, October den 2#, 1813". The following are readings of the tombstones that are in the cemetery as of November 1985. Those in German have been translated. Spellings of names are as they appear on the stones.

NAME	AGE	BORN	DIED
APPEL, Henry	89-04-01	03/05/1792	07/06/1881
APPEL, Anna Maria nee Weidman w/o Henry Appel	53-03-27	08/31/1793	12/27/1846
ABEL, Susana d/o Henrich & Maria Abel	04-03-20	12/20/1818	04/09/1823
APPEL, Johannes	About 67 yr. 6 mn.	08/--/1758	02/28/1826
APPEL, Elisabeth nee Weber w/o Johannes Appel	84-06-02	11/25/1761	05/27/1846
APPEL, Johanne	21-00-18	11/18/1789	12/06/1813
APPEL, Samuel	54-01-15	08/29/1794	10/14/1848
Initial Stones: P.B., A.B.			
BEAMESDERFER, John G. s/o Cyrus & Sallie Beamesderfer		08/21/1872	06/11/1873
BEAMESDERFER, Willie s/o Cyrus & Sallie Beamesderfer	12-05-11	03/02/1874	08/18/1886
BIRKENBINE, David	29-10-11	08/27/1801	07/08/1831
BIRKENBINE, William s/o David & Maria Birkenbine	01-11-00	11/18/1829	11/17/1831
BLICKENSDERFER, Maria Ann, Born in Lexington	01-09-25	04/14/1826	02/08/1828
BLICKENSDERFER, Henrich, Born in Lexington	Covered	09/14/1828	12/21/1828
BORRY, Priscilla	60-09-09	06/20/1844	03/29/1905
BOWMAN, Ada	08-11-20	03/07/1868	02/27/1877
BUCHTER, Josiah	77-02-22	01/01/1805	03/23/1882
BUCHTER, Elizabeth w/o Josse	83-02-13	12/05/1806	02/18/1890
CARPENTER, Ann nee Helman w/o Georg Carpenter	50-10-29	09/21/1789	08/20/1840
CARPER, William V.		06/06/1904	
CARSON, William		1879	1956
Jennie M.		1881	1954
CARSON, Glenn V.		1905	1968
Margie M.		1910	
Glenn E., Son		1937	1958
CARSON, Doris M.		1931	1932
DULABAN, Sobeya d/o Johan & Wife	10-08-14	09/15/1835	05/29/1846
DULEBAN, Elias s/o Christian & Margaret Duleban	00-02-10		02/13/1847
DULLABAN, Henrich	00-16-23	05/08/1829	10/01/1830
EISENBERGER, Patricia A.		06/30/1939	
Robert H.		08/10/1941	08/20/1983
EITNIER, John	80-10-29	12/24/1804	11/03/1885
EITNIER, Elenora w/o John Fitnier	85-05-02	04/24/1808	09/26/1893
EITNIER, Leah	76-02-00	05/20/1816	07/20/1892
EITNIER, Lightner R. s/o Urias E. & Fanny Eitnier	08-05-27	01/07/1855	07/03/1863
EITNIER, Infant s/o Thomas & Barbra Eitnier	00-00-20		06/28/1892
ENCK, Johannes Jacob	62-05-??	08/03/1724	01/24/1787
ENCK, Johannes	41-??-??	12/16/1734	02/01/1776
ENCK, Barbara	63-??-??	05/14/1740	08/15/1803

NAME	AGE	BORN
ENCK, George	30-08 mn.	
	less 1 d.	09/11/1772 - 05/10/1803
ENCKE, Maria Christina	12-08-2 wk.	03/09/1775 - 01/15/1787
ENCK, Barbara NEE Enck(in)	18-03-??	01/22/1776 - 04/02/1794
ENCK, Elisabeth nee Herchelroth	61-11-15	12/25/1768 - 12/10/1830
ENCK, Johanna	40-11-05	10/11/1764 - 09/16/1805
ENCK, David	03-09 mn.	
	less 1 d.	12/02/1799 - 09/01/1802
ENCK, Jacob	02-08-00	12/03/1792 - 09/04/1795
ENCK, Elisabeth	08-03-02	12/03/1796 - 08/27/1803
ENCK, Georg		02/27/1798 - ??/23/18??
ENCK, Catharine w/o John Enck	45-10-08	01/16/1794 - 11/24/1839
ENCK, Johannes	80-11-09	05/09/1790 - 04/18/1871
ENCK, George	82-00-24	09/29/1822 - 10/23/1904
ENCK, Anna w/o George Enck	76-11-11	01/24/1902
ENCK, Henrich s/o George & Anna Enck	01-11-22	12/18/1848
ENCK, William s/o George & Anna Enck	00-05-24	06/13/1849
ENCK, William	90-02-04	10/23/1817 - 12/27/1907
ENCK, Caroline w/o William Enck	73-04-17	01/19/1822 - 06/06/1895
ENCK, Mary d/o William & Caroline Enck	00-05-27	09/18/1850
ENCK, Infant s/o William & Caroline Enck	00-00-12	08/16/1856
ENCK, Infant s/o William & Caroline Enck	00-00-22	05/10/1859
ENCK, Isaac	77-09-00	01/09/1828 - 10/09/1905
ENCK, Sarah w/o Isaac Enck	66-01-26	11/02/1824 - 12/28/1890
ENCK, Mary E.		01/14/1841 - 11/16/1929
John		09/08/1843 - 01/04/1928
ENCK, Mary Alice d/o John & Mary Enck		08/17/1873 - 11/12/1876
ENCK, Eleonora d/o John & Mary Enck	02-08-10	01/28/1871 - 10/18/1873
ENCK, Henry	84-09-27	04/13/1842 - 02/10/1927
Louisa	76-06-23	11/08/1843 - 06/01/1920
ENCK, Mary M.	83-01-02	11/02/1855 - 12/04/1938
ENCK, Alice w/o John A.	20-11-01	07/22/1877 - 06/23/1898
ENCK, Calvin (This stone was on a pile at edge of woods behind utility shed.)		12/09/1882 - 01/15/1903
ESCHELMAN, Eva w/o Abraham Eschelman	69-05-19	06/06/1770 - 11/25/1839
Initial Stones: L.E., C.E.		
FEIERSTEIN, Georg	49-07-04	04/07/1782 - 11/11/1831
FEIERSTEIN, Johannes	03-08-00	01/07/1807 - 09/--/1810
FEUERSTEIN, Georg	??	02/27/1810 - 09/--/1818
FEUERSTEIN, Sophia	03-08-00	01/21/1820 - 09/--/1824
Initial Stone: G.F.		
GELBACH, Samuel	01-11-24	09/04/1822 - 08/28/1824
GARTNER, Elisabet	02-04-05	03/10/1771
GREGORY, Mary Alice		1929 - 1979
HABECKER, Reuben K.	63-11-13	09/17/1843 - 08/30/1907
HABECKER, Catharine	82-07-29	07/09/1844 - 03/08/1927
HACKMAN, Ester	78-03-25	01/24/1901
HEINEY, Eli CO. H. 203 REG. PA. VOL.	64-08-10	01/21/1893
HERCHELROTH, Catharine nee Quickel	82-00-14	09/03/1745 - 09/17/1827
HIPPERT, Monroe s/o Joel & Sarah Hippert	16-03-25	12/17/1869 - 04/02/1886
HIPPERT, Sarah w/o Joel Hippert	43-04-12	09/01/1839 - 01/13/1883
HOLLINGER, Georg	76-06-00	04/06/1757 - 10/06/1833
HOLLINGER, Margarethe	68-01-09	02/25/1761 - 04/03/1829

NAME	AGE	BORN	DIED
HOLLINGER, Elmer E.	72-04-27	04/07/1862 - 09/04/1934	
HOLLINGER, Joseph	23-06-11	06/01/1791 - 12/11/1814	
HOLLINGER, Margareta	19-07-02	11/20/1792 - 06/22/1812	
HOLLINGER, David	37-03-21	12/23/1796 - 04/14/1834	
HOLLINGER, Maria	3w. 4d.	08/15/1809 - 09/09/1809	
HOLLINGER, Henrich	02-11-15	06/28/1820 - 06/??/1823	
HUBER, Johannes	22-07-01	03/04/1782 - 10/05/1802	
Initial Stone: M.H.			
KEHLER, Margrethe nee bacertin (as on stone) "Lived in married life 11 month, 6 days."	25-04-02	02/09/1765 - 04/06/1792	
KISSINGER, George s/o John & Mary Kissinger	00-00-25	09/07/1886 - 10/01/1886	
KREITER, David	45-06-23	10/05/1799 - 04/28/1845	
KREITER, Veronica w/o David Kreiter	47-09-01	03/02/1806 - 12/03/1853	
KREITER, Elias	10-rest buried.	01/06/1832 - 05/09/1842	
KREITER, Jacob	01-00-26	03/07/1841 - 04/02/1842	
LAWBER, Martin	19-08-??	02/08/1776 - 10/15/1795	
LAWBER, Jacob	6y. 2m. 2wk. 3d.	11/26/1778 - 02/12/1784	
LABER, Jacob	00-05-06	03/31/1797 - 09/06/1797	
LABER, Margred	00-05-06	09/23/1799 - 02/28/1800	
LENHERT, Phillip	75th. yr.	01/03/1841	
LENHERT, Barbara w/o Phillip Lenhert	80-09-18	01/10/1766 - 10/28/1846	
LENHERT, Philip	88-04-00	09/15/1801 - 01/15/1890	
LENHERT, Elizabeth w/o Philip Lenhert	83-19-10	01/29/1806 - 12/09/1889	
LENHERT, Amanda d/o Philip & Elisabeth Lenhert	00-08-12	06/06/1844 - 01/18/1845	
LENHERT, Elizabeth B.	75-11-22	05/07/1838 - 04/29/1914	
LEANHART, Annie	68-06-28	12/18/1844 - 07/16/1913	
LUTZ, Salome d/o William & Salome Lutz	03-09-08	06/17/1838 - 04/25/1842	
MARKERT, J. E. Russell		02/09/1912 - 07/05/1984	
Dorothy M.		01/06/1914	
MARKERT, Jack R.		11/09/1939 - 03/11/1980	
Empty Space			
MEISKEY, Henry	61-04-09	07/15/1821 - 11/24/1882	
MEISKEY, Lydia w/o Henry Meiskey	54-09-28	02/16/1828 - 12/14/1882	
MEISKEY, Christian s/o Henry & Lydia Meiskey	12-05-23	03/07/1853 - 08/30/1865	
MEISKEY, Mary d/o Henry & Lydia Meiskey	00-11-13	10/12/1867 - 09/25/1868	
RACK, Maria Elisabeth nee Appel w/o Jacob Rack	74-14-24	01/05/1783 - 12/29/1854	
RACK, Lydia nee Dodendorf w/o George Rack	26-03-24	12/31/1819 - 04/24/1846	
RACK, Lidia Barbara d/o Georg & Lidia Rack	04-03-00	04/24/1846 - 07/24/1847	
RACK, Susanna Elisabeth d/o Georg & Lidia Rack	18-04-20	03/23/1842 - 08/11/1860	
RESSLER, Samuel	59-00-15	05/16/1835 - 05/31/1894	
RESSLER, Priscilla w/o Samuel Ressler	73-02-10	08/04/1836 - 10/14/1909	
RUCK, George	83-10-27	09/16/1813 - 08/13/1897	
ROCK, Catharine w/o George Rock	72-04-15	04/12/1818 - 08/27/1890	
ROLLIN, Mildred L.		01/16/1928	
Albert F.		02/20/1926 - 02/23/1982	
ROYER, James Alan		1948 - 1974	
Empty Space			
SAYLOR, Harriet w/o John K. Saylor	52-08-28	09/28/1829 - 06/26/1882	
SAYLOR, Catharine Ann	00-02-06	11/07/1854 - 01/13/1855	

NAME	AGE	BORN	DIED
SAYLOR, Mary Ann	00-07-23	01/14/1852 - 09/07/1852	
SEHLABACH, Philip	64yr. 4mn. 3 wk. 6d.	04/06/1759 - No Date	
SHRINER, Catharine nee Lenhert	64-07-08	02/17/1833 - 09/25/1897	
SINGER, John K.		05/17/1863 - 02/02/1953	
Lizzie M. w/o John K. Singer		03/22/1862 - 01/17/1940	
SINGER, J. LeRoy		05/01/1894 - 01/15/1953	
SINGER, Margaret M.	25-00-26		04/05/1910
SINGER, E. Gertrude	18-04-07		12/18/1904
SINGER, Kermit E.		09/17/1901 - 10/26/1937	
SNYDER, Guy S.		1909 -	
Dorothy E. Wilson w/o Guy S. Snyder		1910 -	1953
SNYDER, Myrtle nee Bushong		11/28/1919	
SPANGENBURG, Scott D.		05/27/1961 - 03/20/1981	
STEINMETZ, Samuel	45-11-26	03/16/1870 - 03/12/1916	
STEINMETZ, Christianna		1872 -	1943
STICKLER, Hedie (This stone was found in a closet inside the church and is now propped outside the main door.)	00-05-20	12/07/1822	
STROHM, Bruce Edward		09/26/1962 - 11/03/1984	
STUDENROTH, Henrich s/o Jo___ & Anna Maria Studenroth	33-00-00	01/12/1756 - 01/12/1809	
STUTENROTH, Susannah w/o Heinrich Stutenroth	82-10 12	03/14/1764 - 01/26/1847	
STUTENROTH, Johannes	34-00-27	12/03/1785 - 01/01/1820	
STUTENROTH, Heinrich s/o Heinrich & Susannah Stutenroth	59-00-04	01/20/1788 - 01/24/1847	
STUTINROTH, Nancy w/o Georg (Stone broken and reset, also badly eroded.)			01/03/1856
STUDENROTH, Susanna	09-04-12	02/01/1792 - 04/12/1802	
STUDENROTH, Elisabeth	07-01-16	02/13/1795 - 03/29/1802	
STUDENROTH, Anna Maria	05-09-03	10/16/1797 - 07/09/1803	
STUTENROTH, Margaret	16-11-21	06/15/1804 - 05/24/1821	
STUDENROTH, Levi	07-07-20	02/05/1814 - 09/25/1821	
STUTENROTH, Jacob	62-06-23	07/10/1819 - 02/03/1854	
STUTENROTH, Johannes	01-10-22	12/01/1819 - 10/23/1821	
STUDENROTH, Maria w/o Edward Studenroth	22-09-16	06/25/1818 - 04/11/1841	
TODD, Emma S. w/o Elmer Todd		05/31/1877 - 10/08/1958	
Elmer D.		12/15/1885 - 11/13/1955	
TREISCH, Melinde d/o John & Elizabeth Treisch	16-09-28	09/12/1842 - 07/10/1859	
TSCHUDY, John Peter s/o David & Catharin Tschudy	00-05-08	04/06/1859 - 09/12/1859	
ULRICH, Jacob	71-01-21	08/15/1791 - 01/08/1863	
ULRICH, Susan w/o Jacob Ulrich	77-05-10	06/10/1792 - 11/20/1869	
ULRICH, Jacob	81-03-04	12/25/1819 - 03/29/1901	
ULRICH, Annie Zimmerman w/o Jacob Ulrich	71-00-25	08/22/1819 - 09/17/1890	
ULRICH, William	23-01-02	10/05/1823 - 11/07/1846	
ULRICH, Mary E.		1918	
John H.		1909 -	1984
WALTER, Isaac	88-08-09	03/14/1846 - 11/23/1934	
Harriet Enck w/o Isaac Walter	81-02-27	07/13/1847 - 10/10/1928	
Ada S. d/o Isaac & Harriet Walter		03/14/1869 - 09/06/1946	
WALTER, Jacob s/o David & Catharine Walter	00-00-03	09/25/1851 - 09/28/1851	
WEBER, Margaret	71-08-11	07/30/1751 - 04/11/1823	
WEBER, Johan Georg	70-10-23	02/15/1748 - 01/07/1818	
WEWER, Johanes	30-00-25	10/12/1790 - 11/07/1820	

NAME	AGE	BORN	DIED
WINDBIGLER, Henry	64-10-07	12/16/1768	– 10/23/1833
WINDBIGLER, Henry s/o Wm. W^{BLR}.	00-00-21	10/21/1832	
ZENTMYER, Edward John s/o B.E. & C. Zentmyer		10/30/1851	– 01/03/1854
ZIMMERMAN, Rebeca d/o Jacob & Elisabeth Goshert			
w/o George Zimmerman		04/01/1828	– 04/15/1855

MISCELLANEOUS

1. Red sandstone lump next to Samuel Galbac?.
2. Jacob s/o ______ & Cath____.
3. Broken off at base. No Stone. Located next to the above Jacob s/o ____ & Cath___.

NOTES:

1. A question mark means unreadable. A dash or nothing means that this was not inscribed on the stone.
2. The names Laber, Lawber, Borry, Barra, Barry could all have come from DeLaBirri, DeLaBary, or DeLaber.
3. In an earlier transcription by Gerberich he noted that the stones of John Z. Enck and Calvin Enck were "at the edge of the woods, considerably north of the graveyard". I noted that Calvin's stone was at the edge of the woods. Later I found that John's stone had been recycled and used for Christianna Steinmetz. John's inscription is as follows: "Father", John Z. Enck, Born February 19, 1853, Died April 12, 1909, Age 56 years, 1 month, and 23 days.

   Gerberich in his list also had Henrich Feierstein born 1799 and died 18??, and Wayne and Jacob Eitnier infant sons of Esaias & Ann Mary Eitnier with a date of 1863. These two stones were not there or could be in the miscellaneous.

Transcribed December 1985 by Martha Xakellis

EMANUEL LUTHERAN CEMETERY #2
ST. JOHN'S LUTHERAN CEMETERY #4

Because these two cemeteries adjoin each other and persons of the same family are buried in both cemeteries, one listing was made with a number reference to help in finding the approximate location of the stone. At the present time Emanuel Lutheran Cemetery is by far the larger of the two cemeteries with St. John's Cemetery a bit less well-cared for. Although this large burial ground is now designated as two cemeteries, it could possibly have been three at one time. I have found nothing at this time to back up my feelings about this other than F.E. Schnerer in his 1904 listing of persons buried in the Old Cemetery at Brickerville who were born before 1800, describes "the cemetery situated within this tract, it is almost square, containing about three acres" and "during the year 1819, the burial ground was enclosed by a stone wall at considerable expense of which only the wall along the Horseshoe Turnpike remains. The wall along the western boundary, was removed about seventeen years ago (1887), some of the stones being used to wall the cellar of the Lexington hotel." This is the area marked on the map as Section 1. In Section 3 there is a Steinmetz Family monument on which Hiram Steinmetz who died in 1918 is given credit for a cemetery with the following inscription on his stone. "He was the founder of this cemetery." And as if to give backing to this, nearby the Laber Family burial plot is surrounded by a very sturdy wrought iron fence with a gate in the middle of the west side. An iron pipe fence stretches across Sections 2, 3, and 5 with stone posts flanking the driveway entrance between Sections 2 and 3. This center section of this large burial ground seems to have a different character than either the square tract of the Old Cemetery or the newer St. John's Cemetery which was started in 1895.

Section 1 is mostly Old Cemetery with only a small strip along the driveway having current burials. As you look across towards the older stones, you can see where the ground rises and you can almost see the old stone wall that once was erected there. The old stones are mostly set in long curb-like bases. Mr. Clyde Metzler, head of the Emanuel Lutheran Cemetery Association in 1987, remembers that when he was a young boy (about 10-12 years of age) the men of the church cleaned up the Old Cemetery and reset the stones in these bases. He remembers it being in pretty bad shape before the work was done. He is now 80 years of age. Mr. Metzler said that burying in the Old Cemetery ceased when too often a new grave would be dug in what was assumed empty ground and a previous burial would be found. Soldiers of the Revolutionary War were buried here in unmarked graves.

GEORGE W. STEINMETZ.
Died July 21, 1910.
Aged 83 years 4 months
& 13 days
He was the founder of this cemetery
HIRAM E. STEINMETZ
Died Feb. 2, 1918
Aged
88 y. 4 mo. 13 d.

Map of Emanuel Lutheran and St. John's Lutheran Cemeteries with Numbered Sections

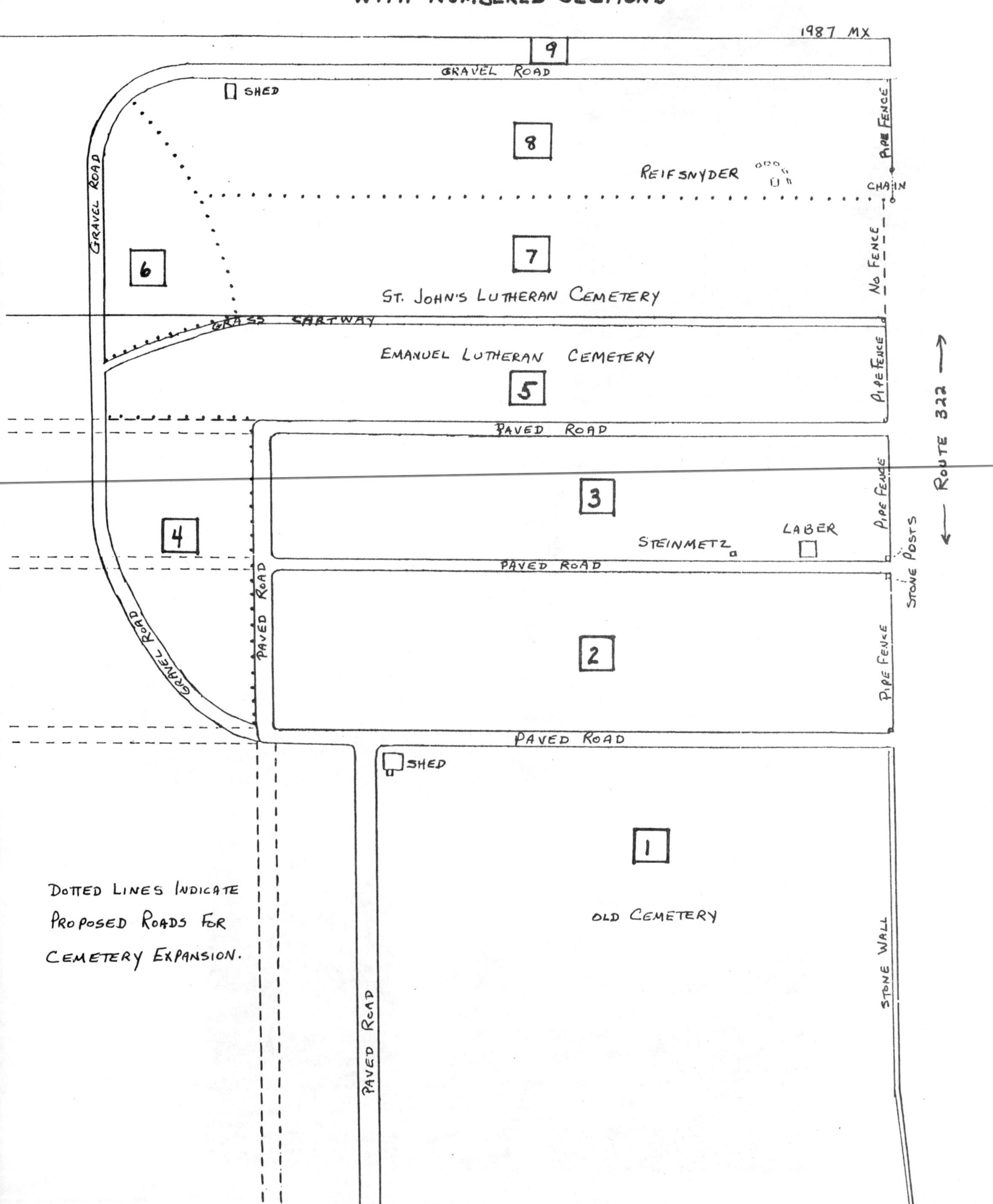

<u>Names ON F.E. SCHNERER'S LIST For Which There Were No Stones In 1986</u>

The following are taken from F.E. Schnerer's List as it appeared in the Ephrata Review on September 23, 1904; September 30, 1904; October 7, 1904; October 14, 1904; October 21, 1904; November 4, 1904; and November 11, 1904.

HEYL, HENRICK   "Hier liegt begraben Henrich Heyl seine Haus Frau Annan Maria eine geborne Schumachern (Shoemaker), geboren in Europ zu Ror_ch bey Sinsheim im Jahr 1701. Hat in der Ehe (wedlock) gelebt 5 Jahr 10 mon. und verschied D. 22 Sepember 1732. ihres alter-" That part is broken off. The above is a brown sandstone, with a seraph carved on. [Note: I believe this to be Anna Maria's stone rather than Henrick's. mx)

LUTZ(IN), ELISABETH   "ist gestorben" This is a red sandstone, is broken, and have been unable to find the part that is broken off; can therefore not give year that she died, for only part of the figures appear.

MILLER(IN), GERTRAUT   "Hier ist begraben Gertraut Millerin (Miller), ist geboren den 15ten August, 1717, und lebet in der Ehe mit ehrem Man 38 Jahr, und starb den 16ten September 1788, Sie hat ihre alter auf 71 Jahr un 1 tag gebracht."

STOBER, VALENTINE   "Born May II, 1712, died XIV January, 1778, aged LXV years, VIII months and XII days. (Mr. Stover's name also appears among the list of those who signed as members of the church in 1743.) It is a red sandstone and is broken.

<u>MISCELLANEOUS</u>

[1]   Stone missing in curbstone base between Margaret d/o Samuel & Susanna Enck and Lea Elizabeth d/o Levi & Lea Enck.

[1]   Unreadable name on small stone that states "A son born & Died September 9, 1860" located between Michael Saylor & Sarah McClaughlin. Sarah's stone and small stone are similar in stone material and shape, and both have a dove at the top. Could be Sarah's child?

(G) [1]   Very worn stone on which can be deciphered [E_____ son of] and [11 tage]. It is located between Elias Wechter and William Roether s/o Daniel and Maria.

[1]   Stone missing-broken off at base, located between Henrich s/o Johanes & Magdalena Steiner and Anna Marie d/o Will. & Sarah Steiner.

(G) [1]   Red sandstone of average size, very worn. Can decipher [Hier R___, DE____]. On reverse are initials P.E. and text which is largely unreadable. This could be Peter Elser son of Peter & Catharine Elser, June 11, 1793, 2 years, 5 months, 19 days.

[1]   White marble mended with iron straps many years ago and has since deteriorated badly. Can decipher [Sept. 10,], [Jan. or Jun.], and age of [87 years, ?? months, 28 days]. These dates match dates in F.E. Schnerer's List for Anna Maria Erb, Sept. 10, 1797 - Jun. 8, 1885, 87 years, 8 months, 28 days. She was the wife of Isaac and her maiden name was Zerfass.

[1]   Small red sandstone that the front has split away in layers. It is not near other stones.

[1]   Larger red sandstone split away in layers located next to Anamaria Wemer(in). It is almost totally gone now.

(G) [1]   Medium red sandstone badly worn. Can deciper [HI] [RU__T] [ANNA HETRI__] [14, 1809] [18 tage].

[2]   Small white stone with no inscription located next to Warren W. Eckert.

[2]   Ground level flat stone. "At Rest" Could be Elizabeth Betz footstone?

[2]   Empty socket in curb base. Other two stones in this base are Frances Blantz and Henry Blantz.

[3]   White stone on red sandstone base. It was found placed on a curb base between the stones of Henry and Hannah Mellinger. It does not seem to belong there. It is an Infant daughter, born & died January 6, 1878. The last names ends T__N.

[5] Small white stone in red sandstone base with inscription "Infant At Rest".   It is
            near the Bingaman stones.

Here begins the listing of the stones found in the cemeteries.   The number in the
brackets is the section as shown on the map.   If a question mark is used it means that
that the information could not be deciphered.   If nothing is there, as for an age or date,
nothing was on the stone.   Each time a surname is listed means a separate headstone.   When
more than one person is listed on a stone, the surname will be listed only once.   A (G)
indicates that the stone is inscribed in German.

		NAME	AGE	BORN	DIED
	[6]	ADAMS, Elmer K.		1887 –	1980
		Lillie M.		1887 –	1961
	[6]	ADAMS, Charles L.		1908 –	1983
		Irene T.		1912 –	1977
	[3]	ANDERSON, Harry A.		12/28/1893 –	01/03/1973
		Iva K.		12/10/1888 –	05/01/1986
	[5]	ANSEL, Cora S. d/o Henry & Addie A. Ansel	05-01-03	10/05/1848 –	11/08/1863
	[5]	ANSEL, Harvey s/o Henry & Addis Ansel	01-??-10	05/21/1868 –	01/31/1870
	[3]	APPLE, John	58-00-29	06/01/1815 –	06/30/1873
	[3]	APPLE, Lavina w/o John Apple	69-09-23	08/15/1819 –	06/08/1889
	[5]	ARMER, Joanne		1950 –	1950

INITIAL STONES: [5] S.B., [5] S.B.

		NAME	AGE	BORN	DIED
	[2]	BAILOR, Wayne B. "T/4 POST OPERATING CO WW II"		07/10/1915 –	
		Christine E.		12/14/1919 –	08/13/1977
(G)	[1]	BALMER, Benjamin s/o Michael & Maria Balmer	59-03-11	02/25/1783 –	06/08/1842
(G)	[1]	BALMER, Elisabeth w/o Benjamin Balmer	76 years	08/--/1784 –	03/28/1860
(G)	[1]	BALMER, Samuel s/o Benjamin & Elisabeth Balmer	33-07-24	06/24/1808 –	02/21/1841
		(Age and dates as carved on stone.)			
	[1]	BALMER, John s/o Benjamin & Elisabeth Balmer	35-07-24	02/20/1816 –	09/13/1851
	[1]	BALMER, Elizabeth w/o John Balmer	86-07-17	04/25/1819 –	12/12/1905
	[1]	BALMER, Anna w/o Benjamin Balmer	39-08-15	07/22/1819 –	04/06/1859
(G)	[1]	BALMER, Elisabeth d/o Benjamin & Anna Balmer	02-06-18	05/06/1856 –	11/25/1858
	[1]	BALMER, Rolandus F. s/o Benjamin & Anna Balmer	18-03-13	03/29/1849 –	07/12/1867
	[7]	BALMER, Wm. M.	63-06-07	04/17/1840 –	10/24/1903
	[7]	BALMER, Sarah F. w/o William M. Balmer	63-01-19	09/20/1842 –	11/09/1905
(G)	[1]	BALMER, Sybilla d/o William & Norah Balmer	01-07-06	06/09/1865 –	01/15/1867
	[7]	BALMER, Wayne C.		1871 –	1937
		Maggie W.		1874 –	1945
	[7]	BALMER, Harvey Z.		1881 –	1961
		Rebecca E.		1888 –	1978
	[7]	BARINGER, Ralph E.		07/09/1917 –	07/10/1980
		Mabel E.		08/04/1920 –	
(G)	[1]	BIMMESDORFER, Johannes	83-01-08	03/24/1712 –	05/03/1794
(G)	[1]	BIEMERSDOERFER, Elisabeth	86-04-28	09/14/1727 –	02/11/1814
(G)	[1]	BIEMESDERFER, Geo.	85-06-21	12/23/1768 –	07/14/1854
(G)	[1]	BIEMESDERFFER, Elisabeth NEE Schie(in)	60-07-26	02/10/1774 –	10/05/1834
	[1]	BIEMESDERFER, John	79-10-03	09/08/1798 –	07/11/1878
	[1]	BIEMESDERFER, Anna Mary w/o John Biemesderfer	87-03-26	11/03/1800 –	02/29/1888
	[1]	BEAMESDERFER, Catharine	89-07-02	06/08/1803 –	01/10/1983
	[8]	BIEMESDERFER, John W.		09/21/1870 –	10/07/1962
		Mary Ella, his wife		11/21/1872 –	06/01/1918
		Cora B., his wife		04/09/1878 –	03/03/1963
	[2]	BEAMESDERFER, Walter (Kroninger Funeral Home marker)		1881 –	1949

		NAME	AGE	BORN	DIED
	[2]	BEAMESDERFER, Mayme "Mother"		04/03/1886	03/18/1933
	[2]	BEAMESDERFER, Lester L.		1904	19
		Margaret L.		1905	1969
	[2]	BEAMESDERFER, Robert B. s/o Lester L. & Margaret L.	00-01-20		03/20/1927
	[6]	BAIR, Bernetha M.		1914	1981
	[1]	BEAR, Robert		1915	1980
		Ethel		1919	
	[1]	BEAR, Devoe		1936	1984
		Janet M.		1941	
	[1]	BEARD, Robert	72-06-29		07/29/1840
	[1]	BEARD, Martha w/o Robert Beard	83-09-05	01/31/1766	11/05/1849
	[3]	BEARD, Charles K.		1879	1947
		Mamie S. Husson, his wife		1885	1974
	[3]	BEARD, Howard K.		1883	1962
		Catherine L. NEE Bamberger		1883	1962
	[3]	BECK, Samuel	73-01-28	11/10/1801	01/08/1875
	[3]	BECK, Catharine w/o Samuel Beck		07/16/1800	03/13/1878
	[7]	BECK, Elmer I.		08/21/1881	12/22/1965
		Mary A. NEE Eckert		01/04/1882	12/30/1962
	[7]	BECK, Miriam E. d/o Elmer I. & Mary A. Beck		03/31/1911	10/08/1912
	[7]	BECK, John L.		08/15/1916	03/03/1939
	[3]	BECKER, Henry B.	29-04-13	07/12/1861	12/25/1890
	[3]	BECKER, Mary M.	50-10-05		05/04/1911
	[2]	BECKER, Lillie M. "Mother"	90-03-16	07/28/1870	11/14/1960
	[3]	BECKER, Harry S.	28-07-16		05/15/1919
		Sallie A.		No Dates	
	[2]	BECKER, Leroy H.		10/06/1895	03/07/1984
		Carolyn E.		06/05/1911	01/29/1972
	[3]	BECKER, Freeman H.	81-04-29	01/01/1902	05/30/1983
		Florence S.		11/30/1904	1987
	[1]	BIEHM, Vienna	73-00-14	10/06/1843	10/20/1916
(G)	[1]	BEINBAURER(N), Christina	01-03-11	01/23/1774	05/03/1775
	[5]	BENDER, Myles G. "SP-3 HQ. CO. 9TH INF. REGT. KOREA"		1932	1957
	[3]	BENTZ, Christian	63-10-25	12/17/1797	09/12/1861
	[3]	BENTZ, Sarah w/o Christian Bentz	77-10-17	07/04/1804	05/21/1882
(G)	[3]	BENTZ, Infant s/o Christian & Sarah Bentz	17 days		04/04/1821
(G)	[3]	BENTZ, Harrietta d/o Christian & Sarah Bentz	02/08/01	05/09/1822	01/10/1825
(G)	[3]	BENTZ, Infant s/o Christian & Sarah Bentz (Stone reset-birth date buried)			10/07/1834
(G)	[3]	BENTZ, Infant d/o Christian & Sarah Bentz	2 days		01/08/1836
(G)	[3]	BENTZ, Christian s/o Chr[n] & Sarah Bentz	06-03-15		06/20/1850
	[1]	BENTZ, Elmer s/o Franklin & _______ Bentz		Born & Died	03/18/1801
	[1]	BENTZ, George (Stone very worn)	82-??-??	09/10/1808	10/19/1890
	[1]	BENTZ, Amelia w/o George Bentz d/o Isaac & Mary Erb	62-06-19	01/07/1816	07/26/1878
(G)	[1]	BENTZ, Urias s/o Georg & Amilia Bentz	00-10-17	02/27/1843	01/17/1844
(G)	[1]	BENTZ, Josiah s/o Georg & Amalia Bentz	00-01-27	11/06/1844	01/02/1846
(G)	[1]	BENTZ, Cecelia d/o Georg & Amalia Bentz	02-02-21	01/26/1851	09/15/1853
	[1]	BENTZ, Zachary Taylor s/o George & Amelia Bentz	04-04-19	08/03/1853	12/22/1857
(G)	[1]	BENTZ, Isabella d/o Sam'l. & Elisabeth Bentz	00-02-02	06/15/1864	08/17/1864
	[2]	BETZ, Elizabeth		1876	03/17/1918
	[2]	BICKELMAN, Mason (Rohlands Service marker)		1923	1985
	[5]	BINGEMAN, Daniel	62-02-10	12/04/1829	02/24/1892
	[5]	BINGEMAN, Susan w/o D. Bingeman	73-11-05	02/05/1832	01/10/1906
(G)	[5]	BINGEMAN, Mary Ann d/o Daniel & Susanna Bingeman	10-05-25	03/06/1852	08/31/1862
	[5]	BINGAMAN, Samuel B.	61-03-10	10/04/1855	01/14/1917
	[5]	BINGAMAN, Emma R. NEE Painter	70-03-02	05/05/1854	08/07/1924

	NAME	AGE	BORN	DIED
[5]	BINGEMAN, Milten s/o Samuel & Emma Bingeman	02-06-08	03/08/1876 - 09/16/1878	
[5]	BINGEMAN, Narman P. s/o Samuel & Emma Bingeman	00-11-25	10/06/1892 - 10/01/1893	
[2]	BINGEMAN, Benjamin F.		02/08/1875 - 12/29/1952	
	Mary Alice		06/04/1875 - 01/29/1896	
[5]	BINGEMAN, Harvey P.	57-01-14	1881 - 1939	
[1]	BISHOP, John C.	27-06-18	12/25/1813 - 07/13/1841	
[3]	BISHOP, David "Father"		09/12/1856 - 03/14/1940	
[3]	BISHOP, Lizzie "Mother"		11/06/1863 - 10/03/1932	
[2]	BISHOP, John Huber	25-09-13	03/07/1909	
[1]	BISSINGER, William (Replacement stone-earlier list shows age			
	and dates of 1-9-13, 5/5/1870 - 02/17/1872)		02/18/1872	
[1]	BISSINGER, John (as above with 4-9-25, 9/16/1866 - 7/11/1871)		07/11/1871	
[3]	BIXLER, Benj. F.		01/03/1857 - 03/22/1909	
	Mary E.		09/13/1858 - 07/28/1934	
[3]	BIXLER, Lizzie L. d/o Benj. F. & Mary E. Bixler	02-01-29	01/27/1888 - 03/26/1890	
[3]	BIXLER, Infant d/o B.F. & Mary E. Bixler	Stillborn	10/31/1899	
[1]	BLANTZ, John	80-09-17	04/13/1790 - 01/30/1871	
[1]	BLANTZ, Anna	82-01-09	06/20/1785 - 07/29/1867	
[1]	BLANTZ, Jacob	80-08-16	07/15/1811 - 04/11/1892	
[1]	BLANTZ, Julia Ann	84-09-12	04/16/1815 - 01/28/1900	
[1]	BLANTZ, Lydia Ann d/o Jacob & Julia Ann Blantz	08-03-19	12/11/1854 - 03/30/1863	
[2]	BLANTZ, Benjamin (With footstone - B.)	70-08-23	11/25/1814 - 08/18/1885	
[1]	BLANTZ, John "CO. K. 5TH Pa. Heavy Art."		10/08/1836 - 08/18/1910	
[1]	BLANTZ, Elvina Steffy w/o John Blantz		07/29/1847 - 11/12/1930	
[1]	BLANTZ, Peter F. s/o John & Elvina Blantz	03-07-28	09/11/1866 - 05/09/1870	
[2]	BLANTZ, Henry		1841 - 1923	
[1]	BLANTZ, Peter B.	74 years	03/15/1921	
[2]	BLANTZ, Frances		1851 - 1936	
[8]	BLANTZ, Samuel		1851 - 1925	
	Mary Amanda, his wife		1857 - 1921	
[5]	BLANTZ, Susan S. w/o Peter Blantz	43-00-24	04/20/1863 - 05/14/1906	
[5]	BLANTZ, John F.	20-02-17	05/02/1864 - 07/19/1884	
[8]	BLANTZ, John		1875 - 1941	
	Virgie		1885 - 1935	
	Marshall		1903 - 1927	
[8]	BLANTZ, Aaron		1887 - 1968	
	Mary		1888 - 1960	
[8]	BLANTZ, Infant s/o Aaron & Mary Blantz		09/26/1925	
[6]	BLANTZ, Leroy (Buch Funeral Home marker)		1908 - 1971	
[6]	BLANTZ, Leroy, Jr. (Beck Funeral Home marker)		1931 - 1960	
[7]	BLECKER, Wilbert H. "Son" (See Albert & Ida Keyton)		1903 - 1933	
[1]	BOLLINGER, Elizabeth w/o Amos Bollinger			
	d/o David & E. Zahm	32-09-15	10/02/1825 - 07/17/1858	
[3]	BOLLINGER, Abram E.		10/08/1897 - 10/09/1974	
	Mae P.		02/24/1902 - 01/06/1987	
[3]	BOLLINGER, Howard P. s/o Abram & Mae Bollinger	03-03-11	10/11/1925 - 01/22/1929	
[3]	BOLLINGER, Earl P. Twin s/o Abram & Mae Bollinger	02-00-23	02/05/1928 - 02/28/1930	
[3]	BOLLINGER, Ray Daniel s/o Ray P. & Geraldine G.	1 day	1962	
[1]	BOMBERGER, Allen H. "Husband"		1909 -	
	Nora R. "Wife"		1909 - 1980	
	A. Althea "Wife"		1916 -	
[2]	BOOKER, Thomas J. "Son" (On stone with Shirley Page, mother,		09/25/1957 - 04/16/1967	
[2]	BOOKER, David G. "Son" and Angela Page, sister.)		07/12/1962 - 04/16/1967	
[1]	BORRY, Henry	74-01-23	07/08/1800 - 09/01/1874	
[1]	BORRY, Elizabeth w/o Henry Borry	64-00-08	02/19/1807 - 02/27/1871	
[3]	BORRY, Jacob	66-01-24	02/15/1826 - 04/09/1892	

		NAME	AGE	BORN	DIED
	[3]	BORRY, Lavina	85-00-23	02/07/1828	03/02/1913
(G)	[1]	BARRY, Eli s/o Jacob & Lovena Barry	01-01-21	01/19/1859	03/11/1860
	[2]	BORRY, Susannah W. "Mother"	75-00-21	09/30/1842	10/21/1917
	[2]	BORRY, Hiram W. "Father"	65-01-08	04/04/1842	05/12/1907
	[3]	BORRY, Ezra W.		12/26/1860	06/11/1936
	[3]	BORRY, Amanda S. (See Blossie Dohner)		02/25/1860	03/30/1940
	[3]	BORRY, Levi Homer s/o Ezra & Amanda S. Borry	07-01-22	09/06/1894	10/25/1901
	[3]	BORRY, Urias W.	63-05-02		05/23/1920
	[2]	BORRY, Thomas W.		11/12/1873	07/11/1957
		Annie K., his wife		12/23/1876	03/13/1929
	[1]	BARRY, John s/o John & Lizzie Barry	00-03-26	05/20/1876	09/16/1876
	[2]	BORRY, Joseph W.	75-06-24	03/05/1878	09/29/1953
	[2]	BORRY, James W.		02/02/1882	04/10/1960
		Edna E.		04/17/1894	11/03/1953
	[3]	BORRY, Jacob L.		12/04/1891	02/15/1975
		Lillie M.		12/05/1896	12/29/1973
	[3]	BORRY, Jacob M.		05/10/1914	09/01/1968
		Sallie M.		06/01/1909	
	[2]	BORRY, Ella Mae		Stillborn	03/28/1921
	[2]	BOYD, John H.	65-06-13	06/19/1859	01/02/1925
		Priscilla, his wife	77-03-16	08/04/1861	11/20/1938
	[2]	BOYER, Peter		09/10/1809	02/22/1896
		Hannah Druckenbroad		10/02/1809	09/12/1896
	[5]	BOYER, John P.	68-07-29	01/02/1833	09/01/1901
	[5]	BOYER, Elizabeth w/o John P. Boyer	81-00-12	11/10/1832	11/22/1913
	[1]	BOYER, Cyrus	59-07-09	05/08/1831	12/17/1890
	[1]	BOYER, Mary w/o Cyrus Boyer	51-03-07	01/01/1837	04/08/1888
	[2]	BOYER, Daniel "CO. I 22ND REGT. P.V.I."		03/29/1842	03/17/1924
		Sarah Deemer, his wife		12/07/1845	12/05/1921
	[2]	BOYER, Peter "CO. C. 17TH REFT. P.V.C."		09/06/1844	10/16/1917
		Mary Price, his wife		06/30/1862	04/09/1941
	[2]	BOYER, John D. "CO. B. 190 REG. PA. VOL. CIVIL WAR"		05/14/1846	10/13/1930
	[7]	BOYER, Wayne		1867	1943
		Annie, his wife		1873	1948
		John		1901	1902
		Roy		1911	1911
		Melvin		1914	1914
	[5]	BOYER, Elizabeth		08/08/1872	01/16/1919
	[5]	BOYER, Clinton "Father" (The stones of Annie Boyer Culp		1874	1955
		Carrie M. "Mother" (and Edna M. Snyder are very		1874	1952
		(similar to Clinton & Carrie's.)			
	[3]	BOYER, Jonas		1877	1946
		Ada		1872	1958
	[2]	BOYER, Frank		06/12/1877	10/25/1940
	[2]	BOYER, Allen D. "Father"		1882	1961
		Edna M. "Mother"		1904	1977
	[2]	BOYER, Clayton P. "PVT. HQ. CO 304TH ENG. 79TH DIV. WW I"		1896	1966
		Frederica E.		1896	1979
	[7]	BOYER, Roman		01/09/1896	08/20/1978
		Erna M.		12/29/1899	12/16/1968
	[7]	BOYER, John D.		1901	1934
		Elsie M.		1900	1965
		John W. "In Memory of John W. Boyer, P.F.C.		09/17/1921	02/24/1945
		Died in the service of his country			
		at Lendersdorf Germany."			

		NAME	AGE	BORN	DIED
	[6]	BOYER, Harry N.		07/19/1904	11/26/1982
		Esther M.		04/22/1908	
	[6]	BOYER, Wayne N. "PENNSYLVANIA, TEC 5 CO H, 142 INFANTRY,			
		WORLD WAR II"		07/29/1907	06/11/1962
	[5]	BOYER, Howard M.		05/08/1909	07/16/1982
		Kathryn R.		08/03/1911	09/05/1977
	[3]	BOYER, Mary R.		12/05/1909	02/09/1985
	[2]	BRADLEY, Timothy E.		09/29/1933	09/08/1961
(G)	[1]	BRECHBILL, Abraham	69-01-11	07/19/1789	08/30/1858
	[8]	BRACKBILL, Amanda E.	78-08-19	05/29/1846	02/18/1925
	[8]	BRACKBILL, David A.	48-02-04	04/11/1864	06/15/1912
		Alice A., his wife	46-04-29	01/16/1866	06/15/1912
	[8]	BRACKBILL, Hayden s/o David A. & Alice A. Brackbill	19-01-06	07/01/1892	08/07/1911
	[2]	BRACKBILL, Henry L.	27-07-09	05/13/1872	12/22/1899
	[8]	BRACKBILL, Haydn B.	42-04-09		01/13/1919
	[8]	BRACKBILL (Last name only-funeral home type marker)		1887	1957
(G)	[1]	BRECHT, Johannes	83-06-28	03/31/1764	10/28/1847
(G)	[1]	BRECHT, Barbara NEE Miller	62-11-09	04/23/1777	04/02/1840
(G)	[1]	BRECHT, Georg s/o Johannes & Barbara Brecht	05-07-17	06/04/1798	01/21/1804
	[1]	BRECHT, Margaret	83-11-28	10/10/1800	10/08/1884
	[1]	BRECHT, John	73-06-21	01/18/1803	08/09/1876
	[1]	BRICKER, John	71-07-30	07/13/1772	03/12/1844
	[1]	BRICKER, Barbara w/o John Bricker	80-06-10	06/08/1770	12/18/1850
	[1]	BRICKER, Isaac	61-00-14	03/12/1779	03/26/1860
	[1]	BRICKER, Anna		12/13/1809	10/29/1874
	[1]	BRICKER, William J.	24-06-07	04/20/1831	10/27/1855
	[1]	BRUGGER, Sadie M. (Gravernor Service marker)		1897	1984
	[1]	BRUMBACH, Lawrence E.		1913	1984
		Mary Pippgress		1904	1972
	[2]	BRUMBACH, I. Patrick		02/05/1953	01/12/1954
	[2]	BRUMBACH, Betty J. (Roseboro Funeral Home marker)		1930	1986
	[7]	BRUMBACH, Richard E.		07/03/1932	01/13/1963
	[9]	BUCH, Mary Irene "Ma-Ma"		07/13/1909	11/15/1981
	[6]	BUCH, Frederick		02/08/1931	
		Dawn L.		12/28/1932	07/28/1982
	[9]	BUCH, Shanelle Rene d/o Shaun & Karen Buch			10/05/1979
(G)	[1]	BUCHTER, Jacob	78-03-00	11/11/1777	02/11/1856
	[1]	BUCHTER, Catharine w/o Jacob Buchter	56-10-06	10/11/1784	08/17/1841
(G)	[1]	BUCHTER, Sabea	16-09-04	12/15/1805	09/20/1822
(G)	[1]	BUCHTER, Wilham		10/30/1812	02/02/1842
	[1]	BUCHTER, John W.	68-05-04	01/09/1808	06/13/1876
	[1]	BUCHTER, Hannah w/o John W. Buchter	72 years		08/25/1886
	[1]	BUCHTER, Mary A. Leivig w/o George Buchter	81-11-00	02/19/1812	01/19/1894
(G)	[1]	BUCHTER, Catharina	06-08-01	02/10/1815	10/11/1822
	[5]	BUCHTER, Jacob W.	65-03-08	09/04/1817	12/12/1882
	[5]	BUCHTER, Sarah w/o Jacob Buchter	71-05-26	06/25/1826	12/21/1897
(G)	[1]	BUCHTER, Susanna d/o Jacob & Sarah Buchter (Worn)	01-??-??	09/11/1839	04/13/1841
(G)	[1]	BOFFENMEYER, David	69-09-03	07/27/1766	05/02/1836
(G)	[1]	BAFFENMAYER, Maria Magdalena	63-04-04	09/02/1773	01/06/1837
(G)	[1]	BUFFENMEIER Margaret d/o David & Magdalena	26-02-06	06/02/1802	08/08/1828
		Buffenmeier			
(G)	[1]	BOFFENMEIER, David s/o David & Magdalena	22-05-24	09/12/1803	03/06/1826
		Boffenmeier			
	[1]	BOFFENMEYER, Henry s/o David & Magdalene	72-11-13	12/06/1796	11/19/1869
		Boffenmeyer			

	NAME	AGE	BORN	DIED
[1]	BUFFENMOYER, Samuel	84-11-06	02/18/1795	01/24/1880
[1]	BUFFENMOYER, Catharine w/o Sam'l. Buffenmoyer	74-07-17	05/14/1808	01/01/1883
[1]	BUFFENMOYER, John s/o Peter & Catharine Buffenmoyer	00-00-11	10/22/1865	11/02/1865
[1]	BUFFAMOYER, Berlester		1901	1968
	Elsie B.		1903	1980
[2]	BUFFAMOYER, Monroe		05/30/1922	06/15/1923
[3]	BURGES, Jacob	78-03-17	10/11/1802	06/28/1881
[3]	BURGESS, William	59-01-00	05/07/1825	06/07/1884
[3]	BURGESS, Susan w/o William Burgess	92-05-09	10/15/1817	03/24/1910
[7]	BURKHOLDER, Aaron		04/17/1889	03/24/1981
	Lizzie		07/15/1891	11/29/1952
[1]	BURKHOLDER, Irvin N.		05/12/1900	01/19/1971
	Bertha K.		06/02/1899	
[2]	BURKHOLDER, Clayton N.		1901	1969
	A. Laura		1905	1985
[9]	BURKHOLDER, G.F.		12/25/1909	01/12/1987
	Susan E.		11/29/1917	
	Anna M.		04/17/1910	09/22/1965
[3]	BUSHONG, H. Ray		12/01/1913	
	Anna Mary		01/18/1914	05/07/1975
[8]	BUSSER, Nancy J.	7 mnths.		10/31/1930
[8]	BUSSER, Peggy C.	2 mnths.		03/20/1931
[8]	BUSSER, Joann V.	4 mnths.		08/08/1932
[8]	BUSSER, Patricia F.	10 mnths.		04/29/1934
[2]	BUSSER, Grace W. (On stone with Sarah W. Eckert)		1910	1967
[1]	BUTZER, Earle K.		09/17/1902	09/09/1982
	Dorothy E.		03/02/1913	
[1]	CALLIHAN, Eve	37-08-26	09/14/1788	06/09/1826
[1]	GALEHEN, Herriet	00-04-16	09/11/1835	01/27/1836
[2]	CAPELLO, James L.		04/19/1896	09/30/1959
[7]	CARPENTER, Clayton	53-10-14	03/16/1864	01/30/1918
[7]	CARPENTER, Elmira A. w/o Clayton Carpenter	52-07-22	04/30/1861	12/22/1913
[7]	CARPENTER, Harvey C. s/o C.S. & Elmira Carpenter	02-07-29	05/19/1901	01/18/1904
	(With footstone - H.C.C.)			
[8]	CARPENTER, Morris C.		1884	1969
	Sara L.		1886	1970
	Helen M.		1904	1906
[2]	CARVELL, George W. (Gravenor Service marker)		1910	1983
[2]	CHERNICH, George J.		02/17/1903	06/05/1985
	Clara M.		01/02/1921	
[5]	CHRIST, William "CO. G. 195 REGT. PA. VOL."	61-09-14	No Dates	
[5]	CHRIST, Mary Ann w/o William M. Christ	39-07-23	11/17/1837	07/10/1877
[5]	CHRIST, Emma		02/14/1848	02/24/1928
[5]	CHRIST, Maria d/o Wm. & Emma Christ	05-06-03	11/10/1886	05/13/1892
[2]	CHRIST, Frank F.		03/23/1880	07/06/1919
[5]	CHRIST, Millie		06/17/1881	08/08/1959
(G) [1]	CLAY, Daniel	66-03-06	01/07/1799	04/13/1865
[1]	CLAY, Sarah w/o Daniel Clay	80-00-25	08/26/1803	09/21/1883
[1]	CLAY, Samuel W.	73-09-10	10/31/1835	08/11/1909
[1]	CLAY, Martha d/o Samuel & Sarah Clay	43-08-27	01/01/1838	09/28/1881
(G) [1]	CLAY, Phares s/o Martha Clay	00-06-27	10/02/1865	04/29/1865
	(Dates on above stone are as carved.)			
[2]	CLAY, Esther U.		05/25/1888	08/18/1952

	NAME	AGE	BORN	DIED
[1]	COLEMAN, Stephen Chambers (Box-like tomb)	30th yr.		02/13/1816
[1]	COLEMAN, George s/o Robert & Anne Coleman	31-04-04		11/09/1821
	(Also Box-like tomb)			
[1]	COLLINS, Thomas	50th yr.		05/14/1818
[1]	COLLINS, Elizabeth w/o Thomas Collins	68th yr.		07/25/1825
[2]	CONNELLY Harry E.		1909 -	1958
	Elizabeth		1909 -	1972
[2]	CONNELLY, Dorothy E. d/o Harry & Elizabeth Connelly		06/10/1936 -	10/10/1945
[2]	CONNELLY, Richard E.		1931 -	1972
	Jane S.		1936 -	
[2]	CULP, Simon M.		05/06/1848 -	09/10/1929
	Mary Ann NEE Hartman		03/26/1855 -	01/12/1926
[5]	CULP, Annie Boyer "Mother" (This stone is the same as			
	Edna Snyder's stone and similar to Clinton &			
	Carrie Boyer's stone.)		1895 -	1918
[1]	CULP, Leroy B.		05/19/1913 -	09/30/1970
[1]	CURRY, Harvey W. s/o John & Mary Curry	00-04-22	04/10/1879 -	09/02/1879
[1]	CURRY, Harry J. s/o John D. & Mary Curry	03-04-14	08/25/1881 -	01/08/1885
[1]	DAUB, Henry "Parents"	88-04-29	08/20/1834 -	01/19/1928
	Rebecca	74-06-07	02/18/1836 -	08/25/1910
[1]	DAUB, Sarah A. "Daughters"	93-00-07	01/27/1867 -	02/04/1960
	Katie L.	36-03-29	02/15/1877 -	06/14/1913
[2]	DAUB, Lazarus B.		02/21/1877 -	08/09/1960
	Susan U. NEE Wagner (Next to Francis & Lizzie		05/13/1881 -	07/18/1958
	Ulrich Wagner)			
[2]	DAUB, Willie w/o Lazarus B. & Susan U. Daub		03/07/1904 -	03/30/1905
[8]	DAUB, Peter W.		1905 -	1984
	Gertrude E.		1909 -	1978
	Edith E.		1928 -	1935
[2]	DAVIS, Rev. Robert C.		1907 -	1984
	M. Katherine		1905 -	
[2]	DEEMER, Peter	82-00-01	10/23/1823 -	10/24/1905
[2]	DEEMER, Polly Eckert w/o Peter Deemer	76-11-13	03/27/1824 -	03/10/1901
[2]	DEEMER, Henry E. (This stone is marked "Father" and is		05/13/1849 -	06/23/1916
	the same as the stone for Lizzie Deemer			
	Smith which is marked "Mother")			
[2]	DEEMER, Rosanna Leippi w/o Henry E. Deemer	34-05-17	02/26/1854 -	06/13/1889
[1]	DEAMER, Emma d/o Jacob & Fanny Deamer	04-08-11	03/11/1866 -	11/22/1870
[1]	DEAMER, Lovina d/o Jacob & Fanny Deamer	01-04-16	04/06/1868 -	08/22/1869
[1]	DEEMER, Elizabeth d/o Jacob & Fanny Deemer	03-02-28	`04/04/1875 -	07/02/1878
[5]	DEEMER, William L.		1881 -	1947
[5]	DEEMER, Harry L.		03/25/1883 -	11/28/1955
	Sallie H.		04/02/1889 -	07/19/1963
[5]	DEEMER, Children of Harry & Sallie Deemer			
	Elwood C.		1905 -	1905
	Harry, Jr.		1913 -	1914
	Mary C.		1931 -	1931
[5]	DEEMER, Irvin C.		02/17/1907 -	09/04/1982
	Ada Z. NEE Fry		12/22/1912 -	
[5]	DEEMER, Erla May d/o Irvin C. & Ada Z. Deemer		05/30/1930 -	09/14/1930
[6]	DEEMER, Ralph C.		1918 -	1982
	Ethel E. NEE Bennetch (No Dates)			
[6]	DEEMER, Raymond C. "PVT. 233RD INF. REG. WW II"		1926 -	1977
	Dora S.		1922 -	

NAME	AGE	BORN	DIED
[2] DEIBLER, Hubert		03/14/1914 -	08/11/1977
Ruth B.		12/20/1918 -	
[3] DEMMY, Urias S.	87-07-24	01/20/1838 -	09/14/1925
Mary Ann	79-09-20	12/31/1839 -	10/21/1919
[5] DEMMEY, Amanda Marks		1856 -	1926
[5] DEMMEY, Frank		1865 -	1934
[5] DEMMY, Harvey s/o Franklin & Armanda Demmy	2 days	04/16/1889 -	04/18/1889
[3] DEMMY, Levi W.	52-10-08	09/28/1863 -	08/06/1916
Adaline	83-01-03	12/04/1860 -	01/07/1944
[3] DEMMY, John		04/12/1870 -	06/22/1950
Emma, his wife		02/21/1868 -	12/26/1936
[3] DEMMY, Darius W.		06/01/1876 -	07/04/1947
Emma Palm		08/12/1881 -	12/26/1974
Katie E.		09/30/1910 -	05/05/1911
[3] DEMMY, Paul H. s/o Martin & Susan Demmy	00-06-08	12/29/1897 -	07/07/1898
[3] DEMMY, Stephen Herman "PFC. US ARMY WW II"		03/08/1901 -	04/10/1978
[5] DIEHM, Wendy Sue (Small metal marker.)		07/13/1970 -	02/13/1982
[6] DIIRNER, Jacob F.		03/28/1918 -	
Ida S.		08/17/1921 -	
[2] DILLON, Norman M.		09/25/1903 -	11/23/1983
Florence E.		10/10/1909 -	
[7] DINGER, John M.		07/18/1924 -	
Mildred J. NEE Hacker		12/15/1925 -	09/20/1986
[2] DISSINGER, John	78-08-28	12/08/1856 -	09/06/1935
[2] DISSINGER, Mary C. Enck w/o John Dissinger	44-11-12	08/11/1848 -	07/23/1893
[2] DISSINGER, Philip "Father"		1875 -	1963
Sallie K. "Mother"		1879 -	1948
Leroy "Son"		1905 -	1905
[1] DITZLER, Catharine w/o William Ditzler (Very Worn)		04/01/1809 -	03/01/1862
(G) [1] DITZLER, Maria NEE Fetter	33-01-07	12/12/1816 -	01/19/1850
(G) [1] DITZLER, Edward	37-00-00	10/11/1818 -	08/11/1856
[3] DITZLER, Melchior		02/28/1823 -	03/04/1898
Mary C.		07/03/1853 -	11/30/1934
[1] DIETZLER, Sarah d/o Conrad Engle w/o Melchion Dietzler	45-01-03	12/16/1824 -	01/19/1870
[1] DITZLER, Abraham s/o Melchior & Sarah Ditzler	19-05-05	10/01/1842 -	03/06/1862
"He enlisted in the service of his country in the year 1861 and died at Nashville, Tenn"			
[1] DITZLER, Emeline d/o Melchior & Sarah Ditzler (Worn)		02/??/186? -	04/17/186?
[3] DITZLER, Harrison	49-01-10	02/07/1857 -	03/17/1906
[3] DITZLER, Mary Ann NEE Deemer	57-08-24	10/26/1860 -	07/20/1918
[3] DITZLER, Irvin s/o Harrison & Mary A. Ditzler		05/10/1894 -	12/17/1897
[2] DITZLER, William W.		1860 -	1925
Rebecca C.		1862 -	1933
[2] DITZLER, Albert S. s/o Wm. W. & Rebecca Ditzler	14-01-25	01/09/1884 -	03/04/1898
[2] DITZLER, Charles S. s/o Wm. W. & Rebecca Ditzler	09-02-23	11/21/1888 -	02/14/1898
[8] DITZLER, Francis W.		03/02/1867 -	06/12/1937
Elizabeth, his wife		12/14/1868 -	05/11/1936
[3] DITZLER, Hauly	27-00-15	08/22/1880 -	09/07/1907
[7] DITZLER, Harry S.		1880 -	1960
[7] DITZLER, Emma w/o Harry S. Ditzler		1881 -	1924
[7] DITZLER, Warren s/o Harry & Emma Ditzler		1905 -	1907
[7] DITZLER, H. Irene d/o Harry & Emma Ditzler		1909 -	1923
[7] DITZLER, Harry B. s/o Harry & Emma Ditzler		1914 -	1941

	NAME	AGE	BORN	DIED
[7]	DITZLER, Charles A. s/o Harry & Emma Ditzler		1915 –	1949
[1]	DITZLER, Mary d/o Elizabeth Getz	14-10-10	12/30/1870 –	11/10/1885
[1]	DITZLER, Melvin B.		12/24/1909 –	10/24/1981
	Ella H.		05/14/1909 –	
[6]	DITZLER, Paul L.		1917 –	
	Rachel M.		1922 –	1978
[7]	DITZLER, Arthur H. "WW 1941 – 1945" (Heisey Funeral Home marker)		1919 –	1987
[2]	DOERSON, George J.		08/04/1884 –	03/11/1941
	Alice S.		07/01/1887 –	03/28/1961
[3]	DOHNER, Blossie d/o Amanda S. Scherb	08-05-26	09/19/1879 –	03/15/1888
	(See Amanda S. Borry)			
[1]	DOMMOYER, John	78-05-13	02/01/1823 –	07/14/1901
(G) [1]	DAMMYER, Fanny NEE Ditzler w/o John Dammyer	33-11-05	08/10/1833 –	07/15/1867
(G) [1]	DAMMYER, Fay Anna d/o John & Fanny Dammyer	08-04-28	01/02/1858 –	05/29/1867
[1]	DOMMYER, Catharine	75-05-15	02/16/1832 –	05/31/1908
[2]	DOMMOYER, Henry	86-11-03	10/12/1840 –	09/15/1927
	Mary A.	51-01-02	08/16/1840 –	09/18/1891
[7]	DOMMOYER, Emanuel D.		1864 –	1950
	Lizzie B. NEE Eckert		1867 –	1946
[7]	DOMMOYER, Infant d/o Emanuel & Lizzie Dommoyer		Stillborn	07/09/1891
	(with footstone - D.)			
[7]	DOMMOYER, George E. s/o Emanuel & Lizzie Dommoyer	00-02-23		03/27/1895
	(with footstone - G.E.D.)			
[2]	DOMMOYER, Alice M.	76-09-14	06/16/1868 –	03/30/1945
[2]	DOMMOYER, Annie M.		08/25/1875 –	09/18/1955
	Alta M.		02/27/1900 –	05/02/1986
[2]	DOMMOYER, Edwin E.		03/18/1881 –	03/29/1961
[8]	DOMMOYER, Samuel E.		05/10/1899 –	07/14/1967
	Mary K.		09/15/1901 –	
[1]	DOMMOYER, Harry E.		1910	1972
	Hilda I.		1917 –	
[5]	DORNBACH, William P.		08/17/1846 –	12/03/1913
	Lizzie S., his wife		03/04/1849 –	07/02/1927
	Elizabeth, our daughter		05/06/1886 –	08/10/1926
(G) [1]	DOSTER, Mary NEE Koch w/o Daniel Doster	44-05-09	12/12/1805 –	05/22/1850
[1]	DOSTER, Levi	58-01-10	03/03/1829 –	04/13/1887
[1]	DOSTER, Elias	18-03-20		05/09/1864
[7]	DOSTER, Martin B.		05/20/1867 –	05/17/1935
	Lydia Ann		04/28/1868 –	07/14/1902
[7]	DOSTER, Martin P. "Son"		1892 –	1951
[7]	DOSTER, Clarance s/o Martin & Lydia Doster	00-02-03		12/08/1895
[7]	DOSTER, Lida M. d/o Martin & Lydia Doster	00-03-18		11/24/1897
[7]	DOSTER, Irwin R. s/o Martin & Lydia Doster	00-07-26		09/10/1900
[8]	DOSTER, Herbert P. (See Long-Doster Monument)	77-01-09	09/18/1887 –	10/27/1964
[8]	DOSTER, Lillie R., his wife	83-00-01	04/03/1886 –	04/04/1969
[7]	DOSTER, Roy R.		11/13/1888 –	12/10/1956
	Pauline H.		08/31/1892 –	11/13/1966
[7]	DOSTER, Wayne K.		08/11/1893 –	05/23/1963
[8]	DOSTER, Alvin K.		03/14/1901 –	05/05/1974
	Elsie M.		01/02/1904 –	
[7]	DOSTER, Paul E. s/o Alvin K. & Elsie M. Doster		02/24/1931 –	05/22/1931
[7]	DOSTER, Herbert M. s/o Alvin K. & Elsie M. Doster		09/28/1933 –	03/27/1934
[1]	DOUPLE, Isaac	78-08-09	01/06/1806 –	09/15/1884
[1]	DOUPLE, Elizabeth w/o Isaac Douple	79-05-25	04/13/1810 –	10/08/1889
[5]	DOUBLE, Jacob	91-07-08		05/03/1930
	Elizabeth	68-00-08		12/19/1913

		NAME	AGE	BORN	DIED
	[5]	DOUPLE, Harriet	25-10-04		06/15/1869
	[5]	DOUPLE, Jacob G.		11/04/1880 -	12/25/1946
		Mary A.		04/01/1884 -	03/26/1959
	[5]	DOUPLE, Leroy		06/01/1911 -	09/03/1966
		Myrl A.		07/03/1913 -	02/14/1968
(G)	[1]	DRUCKENBROAD, Lidia d/o Johann & Maria Druckenbroad	02-01-16	05/22/1828 -	07/08/1830
	[1]	DRUCKENBROAD, Peter	64-06-10	07/04/1836 -	01/14/1901
	[1]	DRUCKENBROAD, Annie w/o Peter Druckenbroad	80-09-04	06/18/1851 -	03/22/1932
	[1]	DRUCKENBROAD, Maggie d/o Peter & Anna Druckenbroad	04-10-03	08/30/1871 -	07/03/1878
	[8]	DRYBREAD, Jesse	66-04-28	11/16/1860 -	04/14/1927
	[8]	DRYBREAD, Lizzie Z. w/o Jesse Drybread	55-00-29	03/20/1863 -	04/19/1918
	[1]	DULIBOHNE, Isaac	66-08-09	07/27/1810 -	04/16/1877
	[1]	DULIBOHNE, Elizabeth w/o Isaac Dulibohne	68-08-09	03/17/1807 -	11/26/1875
(G)	[1]	DULLEBON, Andrew s/o Isaac & Elizabeth Dullebon	23-08-13	09/11/1836 -	05/20/1860
(G)	[1]	DULEPAN, Sarah d/o Isaac & Elisabeth Dulepan	21-02-09	02/18/1845 -	04/27/1866
(G)	[1]	DULEPAN, Isaac s/o Isaac & Elisabeth Dulepan	17-11-08	02/15/1848 -	01/23/1866
	[1]	DULLABOHN, Levi "Erected by daughter"	78-00-02	02/06/1827 -	02/08/1905
		Sarah	70-05-13	09/18/1836 -	03/01/1907
	[1]	DULABONE, Adaline d/o Levi & Sarah Dulabone	16-02-07	05/15/1860 -	07/22/1876
	[1]	DULABONE, Jacob s/o Levi & Sarah Dulabone	26-07-06	09/07/1861 -	04/13/1888
	[1]	DULLABOHN, Elias	63-01-22		06/16/1920
		Agnes	69-04-05		11/23/1928
	[1]	DULLABAHN, Mary d/o Elias & Agnes Dullabahn	14-07-20	06/11/1887 -	02/01/1902
	[8]	DULABONE, Adam	55-08-23	08/16/1858 -	05/09/1914
		Martha, his wife	59-04-22	10/01/1861 -	02/23/1921
	[1]	DULABONE, Jacob s/o Adam & Martha M. Dulabone		04/20/1898 -	09/01/1898
	[8]	DULABONE, Harvey		09/22/1873 -	01/09/1948
		Lillie		05/27/1877 -	09/01/1942
	[7]	DULABONE, Floyd P. s/o Paul & Anna Dulabone		1925 -	1925
	[8]	DULL, William C.		1853 -	1937
		Adeline H.		1861 -	1944
	[8]	DULL, Milton H.		1893 -	1981
		Edna E.		1896 -	1973
	[8]	DULL, Betty Jane d/o Milton H. & Edna E. Dull		09/25/1924 -	05/28/1933
	[7]	DULL, Charles L.		06/14/1918 -	01/13/1961
		Lily I. NEE Snyder		05/27/1927 -	
	[7]	DULL, Dolores J.		1939 -	1939
	INITIAL STONES: [1] J.E., [5] M.A.E., [5] A.W.E.				
	[3]	EBERLY, Henry S.		08/06/1830 -	07/03/1899
	[3]	EBERLY, Salinda		11/03/1840 -	09/03/1891
	[5]	EBERLY, Solomon H.	72-08-28	03/08/1843 -	12/06/1915
		Elizabeth O. NEE Elser	72-07-15	03/01/1841 -	10/16/1913
	[8]	EBERLY, Barnhard		02/22/1856 -	01/19/1912
		Annie B.		07/15/1854 -	12/19/1920
	[8]	EBERLY, Annic & Agnes "Daughters"		1915 -	1915
	[3]	EBERLY, Albert H.	31-07-24	06/04/1870 -	01/28/1902
	[3]	EBERLY, Emma F.	32-06-08	01/02/1875 -	07/10/1907
	[7]	EBERLY, Zacharias E.		1871 -	1953
		Mary E.		1875 -	1944
	[8]	EBERLY, Martin E.	60-06-05	01/11/1873 -	07/16/1933
	[1]	EBERLY, William B.		1874 -	1956
		Lizzie B.		1884 -	1966
	[2]	EBERLY, Stella M. Miller w/o Jerome Eberly	27-05-25		06/17/1902

	NAME	AGE	BORN	DIED
[8]	EBERLY, Harry S.		1881 –	1946
	Katie, his wife		1890 –	1958
[8]	EBERLY, Charles		12/13/1889 – 09/29/1956	
[5]	EBERLY, Albert W. s/o D.B. & Sallie D. Eberly	00-08-06	06/05/1892 – 02/11/1893	
[5]	EBERLY, Annie W. d/o D.B. & Sallie D. Eberly	15 days	11/29/1890	
[7]	EBERLY, Emeda d/o D.B. & Sallie D. Eberly	01-01-05	07/28/1899 – 09/03/1900	
[7]	EBERLY, Infant d/o D.B. & Sallie Eberly			10/22/1906
[7]	EBERLY, Ada M. (See Schnerer Monument)		1890 –	1958
[7]	EBERLY, Martin F.		1901 –	1980
[7]	EBERLY, Gussie Irene		08/24/1902 – 07/26/1986	
[7]	EBERLY, Clyde M.		11/04/1904 – 05/24/1986	
	Elizabeth H.		09/20/1904 – 07/04/1936	
	Infant Son		No Dates	
	Elva H.		01/17/1911 –	
[1]	EBERLY, Ivan F.		06/28/1907 –	
	Irene M.		10/28/1912 –	
[7]	EBERLY, Helen w/o Ivan Eberly	28-07-27	1910 –	1939
[1]	EBERLY, Albert W.		11/12/1905 – 12/06/1953	
	Lillian		02/15/1908 –	
[7]	EBY, Jonas M.		1863 –	1963
	Fannie M.		1865 –	1944
[1]	EDY, Mazie W.		05/22/1895 – 02/19/1969	
[5]	ECKERT, George (Stone broken, mended, & broken again.)		??/??/???? – 09/08/1887	
[5]	ECKERT, Maria w/o George Eckert	84-01-26	01/02/1813 – 02/28/1887	
[5]	ECKERT, Samuel	78-00-18	01/10/1836 – 01/28/1914	
[7]	ECKERT, Jacob	49-08-03	10/20/1847 – 06/23/1897	
[7]	ECKERT, Mary Borry	85-04-20	04/30/1849 – 09/20/1934	
[2]	ECKERT, Levi		1849 –	1926
	Sarah		1849 –	1928
[7]	ECKERT, Mary	64-08-27	07/15/1855 – 04/12/1920	
[7]	ECKERT, John D.	87-07-13	05/18/1858 – 01/01/1946	
[3]	ECKERT, Moses		1860 –	1940
	Annie F., his wife		1864 –	1947
[5]	ECKERT, Hiram	37-11-24	01/19/1868 – 01/13/1906	
[2]	ECKERT, Benjamin F.		1870 –	1947
	Catharine E.		1872 –	1916
[6]	ECKERT, John H. "Father"		1875 –	1950
	Amanda W. "Mother"		1882 –	1965
[6]	ECKERT, Russell H. "Son"		1916 –	1972
[8]	ECKERT, Morris G.		10/01/1881 – 12/01/1951	
	Alice I.		08/25/1885 – 09/26/1946	
	Henry M.^{c} "Son"		06/26/1910 –	
	Charles M.^{c} "Son"		05/26/1914 – 03/07/1972	
[7]	ECKERT, William W.		1882 –	1953
[3]	ECKERT, Emma U. w/o William W. Eckert	51-06-08	08/07/1882 – 02/15/1934	
[2]	ECKERT, Peter S.		06/15/1883 – 03/06/1974	
	Lizzie M.		09/15/1886 – 11/06/1955	
[2]	ECKERT, Irvin W.		09/17/1890 – 11/20/1952	
	Alice M. NEE Williams		02/02/1893 – 09/05/1938	
[3]	ECKERT, Paul W.		1895 –	1963
	Clara D.		1897 –	1938
[2]	ECKERT, Sarah W.		1907 –	1924
	Grace W. Busser		1910 –	1967
[2]	ECKERT, Helen M.		1913 –	1918
[2]	ECKERT, Warren W. "PFC. U.S. ARMY WW II"		08/07/1917 – 11/10/1968	

		NAME	AGE	BORN	DIED
	[5]	ECKERT, Leroy and Flora		05/08/1918 –	07/17/ 07/19/ 1919
	[7]	ECKERT, Harold W. "WW II"		1922 –	1964
		Irene S.		1923 –	
	[7]	ECKMAN, Chester H. (Spacht Funeral Home Marker)		1914 –	1985
	[2]	EDWARDS, John E.		11/22/1841 –	09/23/1910
		Caroline Miller, his wife		07/27/1846 –	03/01/1933
	[1]	EDWARDS, Emma d/o John & Caroline Edwards	05-01-20	03/15/1869 –	05/05/1874
	[1]	EDWARDS, Milten s/o John & Caroline Edwards	00-04-17	01/31/1870 –	06/16/1870
	[1]	EDWARDS, Harvey s/o John & Caroline Edwards	06-06-20	09/01/1872 –	03/21/1879
	[1]	EDWARDS, Jerome s/o John & Caroline Edwards	00-05-12	11/06/1873 –	04/18/1874
	[7]	EDWARDS, Lavalan E.	58-11-19		09/06/1907
	[2]	EDWARDS, Frank M. "Father"		1875 –	1962
		Katie E. "Mother"		1891 –	1969
		Roy H. "Son"		1910 –	
		Earl H. "In Loving Memory of Our Son"		04/03/1919 –	11/19/1944
		"CORP. CO. C. 15TH TANK BATTALION"			
		"Died in France"			
	[7]	EDWARDS, Katie Ziss "Daughter"		1880 –	1952
	[2]	EDWARDS, John M.		03/30/1888 –	10/18/1959
	[2]	EDWARDS, Minnie NEE Weidman "Mother"		1888 –	1931
	[7]	EDWARDS, Stephen D.		1891 –	1960
		Katie E.		1897 –	
(G)	[1]	EICHELBERGER(IN), Christina	49-10-29	07/13/1729 –	06/17/1779
		(Stone reset. Age and death date from F.E. Schnerer's List.)			
(G)	[1]	EICHELBERGER, Georg Michael	55 y-3 m 3 w-1 d	09/29/1733 –	01/22/1789
(G)	[1]	EICHELBERGER, Georg	74-09-08	10/19/1773 –	07/27/1848
(G)	[1]	EICHELBERGER, Anna w/o Georg Eichelberger	88-07-06	11/23/1776 –	06/29/1865
(G)	[1]	EICHELBERGER, Catharine d/o Georg & Anna Eichelberger	31-00-03	06/06/1817 –	06/09/1848
(G)	[1]	EICHELBERGER, Hannah NEE Schober	29-04-08	02/16/1814 –	06/24/1843
(G)	[1]	EICHELBERGER, Jeremias s/o Gabriel & Elisabeth Eichelberger	03-03-25	10/12/1835 –	02/06/1839
(G)	[1]	EICHELBERGER, Anna d/o Gabriel & Elisabeth Eichelberger	04-10-04	03/05/1838 –	01/09/1843
(G)	[1]	EICHELBERGER, Urias s/o Gabriel & Elizabeth Eichelberger	06-01-02	04/05/1842 –	07/07/1848
	[1]	EICHELBERGER, Fianna NEE Miller	71-00-26	01/18/1846 –	02/14/1917
		(This stone on same base with Harriet Miller)			
	[1]	EICHELBERGER, Infant s/o M. & S. Eichelberger			10/11/1850
	[1]	EICHELBERGER, Infant twin children of M. & S. Eichelberger			12/13/1853
	[3]	ICEMAN, Barbara w/o Jacob Iceman	?1-11-07		10/17/1870
	[3]	EISEMAN, Emma d/o John & Catharine Eiseman	11-01-13	03/05/1870 –	04/18/1883
(G)	[1]	ELSER, Peter s/o Peter & Anna Maria Elser	78-07-16	02/02/1767 –	10/08/1845
		"The baptismal sponsors were George M. and Christina Eichelberger."			
(G)	[1]	ELSER(IN), Catharina	25 y-10 m 3 w-4 d	07/21/1767 –	06/15/1793
(G)	[3]	ELSER, Johann s/o Peter & Catharine Elser	79-07-09	02/18/1791 –	09/27/1870
(G)	[3]	ELSER, Esther NEE Kimmel w/o Johann Elser	52-00-05	12/20/1799 –	12/25/1851
(G)	[1]	ELSER, Elisabeth NEE Wächter	60-00-02	01/09/1768 –	01/11/1828
(G)	[5]	ELSER, Elizabeth d/o Peter & Elizabeth Elser	71-00-07	11/17/1803 –	11/27/1874
	[5]	ELSER, Sarah d/o Peter S. & Elizabeth Elser	91-02-01	01/08/1806 –	03/09/1897

		NAME	AGE	BORN	DIED
(G)	[1]	ELSER, Georg	61-00-06	12/22/1787 - 12/28/1848	
(G)	[1]	ELSER, Catharin w/o Georg Elser	68 years less 4 d	11/22/1783 - 11/18/1852	
(G)	[1]	ELSER, Matilda d/o George & Catharina Elser	13-02-09	01/03/1821 - 03/12/1834	
	[2]	ELSER, Peter	73-09-17	04/22/1813 - 02/09/1887	
	[2]	ELSER, Elizabeth w/o Peter Elser	66-02-25	03/19/1816 - 06/14/1882	
(G)	[2]	ELSER, Elizabeth d/o Peter & Elizabeth Elser	10-09-18	04/23/1851 - 02/11/1862	
	[3]	ELSER, Samuel	71-02-03	02/28/1808 - 05/01/1879	
(G)	[3]	ELSER, Catharina d/o Johannes & Susanna Oberlin w/o Samuel Elser	52-07-17	06/05/1811 - 01/22/1864	
(G)	[1]	ELSER, Maria Anna d/o Saml. & Catharina Elser	15-02-27	09/23/1836 - 12/20/1851	
(G)	[1]	ELSER, Edelein d/o Samuel & Catharine Elser	01-08-16	05/14/1858 - 01/31/1860	
	[5]	ELSER, John	71-11-20	11/11/1815 - 11/01/1887	
	[5]	ELSER, George	63-08-26	03/16/1818 - 12/12/1881	
	[5]	ELSER, Catharine d/o John Wolf w/o George Elser	51-09-12	01/25/1824 - 11/07/1875	
	[3]	ELSER, Susanna	76-05-25	08/01/1821 - 01/26/1898	
	[2]	ELSER, Jacob	76-05-19	01/06/1821 - 06/25/1900	
	[2]	ELSER, Sallie w/o Jacob Elser	81-10-24	05/02/1827 - 03/26/1909	
	[3]	ELSER, Edwin	75-03-09	06/22/1828 - 10/01/1902	
	[3]	ELSER, Mary Ann d/o Jacob & Elizabeth Miller w/o Edwin Elser	49-10-22	04/08/1826 - 02/29/1876	
	[3]	ELSER, Harrison s/o John & Esther Elser	75-03-19	03/14/1819 - 07/03/1894	
	[2]	ELSER, John L. (John L. and Rebecca stones are	71-07-16	10/23/1906	
	[2]	ELSER, Rebecca identical.)		Nothing Carved	
	[3]	ELSER, Susan O.	51-03-06	07/28/1843 - 11/04/1894	
	[7]	ELSER, Peter O.	81-01-04	03/18/1851 - 04/22/1932	
		Margaret	57-02-03	12/22/1847 - 02/25/1905	
	[2]	ELSER, Catharine w/o Peter O. Elser	31-02-26	12/30/1857 - 03/26/1889	
	[3]	ELSER, Sarah H. d/o Willm & Anna Elser	00-09-25	10/16/1847 - 08/11/1848	
	[3]	ELSER, John O.		1853 - 1932	
		Lydia		1855 - 1938	
		Sarah H.		1880 - 1881	
	[2]	ELSER, Hiram h/o Susan Elser	27-10-08	12/05/1853 - 10/13/1881	
	[2]	ELSER, John K.	67-10-21	03/23/1859 - 02/14/1927	
		Malinda	67-08-10	04/09/1854 - 12/19/1921	
	[2]	ELSER, James s/o George L. & Catharine Elser	01-00-03	08/15/1875 - 08/18/1876	
	[7]	ELSER, Wayne R.		1883 - 1974	
		Minnie M.		1884 - 1959	
		Mary M.		1909 - 1909	
	[7]	ELSER, Samuel W.		05/25/1883 - 08/01/1963	
		Lizzie		04/21/1889 - 07/08/1962	
	[7]	ELSER, John H.		09/26/1907 - 12/03/1976	
		Bertha E.		08/12/1907 - 05/30/1982	
	[8]	ELSER, Harry H.		03/20/1910 -	
		Dorothy M.		05/05/1911 -	
		Helen A.		03/01/1926 -	
		George H. "776 TNK DESTROYER BTN" "PFC WW 2"		11/16/1924 -	
	[8]	ELSER, Earl H. "Killed in Italy"		08/18/1915 - 09/17/1944	
	[6]	ELSER, S. Earl "WW 1941-1943" (Gravenor Service Marker)		1914 - 1986	
	[8]	EMBER, Janice Clair		07/08/1934 - 05/10/1936	
		Marchmont Lee		09/12/1935 - 01/04/1936	
	[5]	EMERICH, Ralph E.		02/29/1896 - 01/27/1952	

NAME	AGE	BORN	DIED
[5] EMERICK, Chester L.		1900 –	1976
Susan D.		1903 –	1982
(G) [1] ENCK, John	76-03-30	05/10/1789 – 09/09/1865	
(G) [1] ENCK, Salome NEE Wolf w/o John Enck	76-03-27	12/03/1787 – 03/30/1864	
[1] ENCK, William	71-05-18	06/21/1796 – 12/10/1867	
[1] ENCK, Catharine NEE Slabach	77-03-16	07/27/1806 – 11/11/1881	
(G) [1] ENCK, Elizabeth d/o William & Catharine Enck	31-11-18	01/22/1836 – 01/10/1868	
(G) [1] ENCK, Samuel	49-06-17	09/27/1799 – 04/14/1849	
(G) [1] ENK, Rebecca NEE Stober w/o Samuel Enk	36-01-13	10/01/1797 – 11/13/1833	
(G) [1] ENCK, Rebecca d/o Samuel & Sara Enck	08-05-21	10/23/1841 – 04/14/1850	
[5] ENCK, Elias	83-10-28	04/19/1813 – 03/17/1897	
[5] ENCK, Mary Ann w/o Elias Enck	61-10-00	06/27/1829 – 04/27/1891	
(G) [1] ENCK, Maria d/o Elias & Mary Ann Enck	00-05-04	07/21/1843 – 12/25/1845	
[5] ENCK, Catharine d/o Elias & Maryann Enck	07-00-01	03/30/1865 – 04/01/1872	
(G) [1] ENCK, Lea w/o Levi Enck	37-01-02	02/09/1823 – 03/11/1860	
(G) [1] ENCK, George s/o Levi & Lea Enck	11-10-27	02/18/1850 – 01/15/1862	
(G) [1] ENCK, Ann Mary d/o Levi & Lea Enck	01-00-28	09/22/1853 – 10/20/1854	
(G) [1] ENCK, Lea Elisabeth d/o Levi & Lea Enck	01-01-13	04/27/1858 – 09/10/1859	
[5] ENCK, Henry K.		01/05/1848 – 11/08/1925	
Amanda G., his wife		09/05/1851 – 09/21/1919	
[5] ENCK, Ezra s/o Henry & Anna Enck (Worn)	00-04-18	09/26/187? – 02/14/187?	
[5] ENCK, Levi s/o Henry & Anna Enck	15 Days	10/24/1879 – 11/09/1879	
[7] ENCK, Thomas K.		07/06/1850 – 05/01/1939	
Sarah Ann, his wife		10/24/1850 – 08/22/1929	
(G) [1] ENCK, Elizabeth d/o John & Elizabeth Enck	00-09-25	06/19/1853 – 04/14/1854	
[5] ENCK, George K.	57-08-17	05/13/1853 – 01/30/1911	
[5] ENCK, Elizabeth NEE Reed w/o George Enck	43-01-00	05/21/1855 – 06/21/1898	
[5] ENCK, Franklin s/o George & Elizabeth Enck	00-07-24	12/10/1874 – 08/03/1875	
[5] ENCK, Katy d/o George & Elizabeth Enck	00-05-07	08/08/1876 – 01/15/1877	
[5] ENCK, Elizabeth d/o George & Elizabeth Enck		07/17/1884 – 09/06/1887	
(G) [1] ENCK, Margaret d/o Samuel & Susanna	00-02-14	05/31/1855 – 08/14/1855	
[1] ENCK, Mary Ann d/o Samuel & Susanna Enck	00-01-22	07/17/1856 – 05/26/1856	
(G) [1] ENCK, Rebecca d/o Samuel & Susanna Enck	01-02-29	01/30/1864 – 04/28/1865	
(G) [1] ENCK, Jacob s/o Samuel & Susanna Enck	00-03-28	04/03/1868 – 07/31/1868	
[5] ENCK, Samuel K.		12/07/1858 – 11/04/1921	
Catherine W.		09/07/1863 – 07/10/1920	
[5] ENCK, Harvey E. s/o S.K. & Catharine Enck	07-04-13	03/27/1884 – 07/10/1891	
[5] ENCK, Francies d/o S.K. & Catharine Enck	16-02-10	09/11/1882 – 11/21/1898	
[5] ENCK, Katie May "Daughter"		01/22/1896 – 12/10/1910	
[5] ENCK, William		1872 –	1948
Lizzie Eberly, his wife		1876 –	1935
ENCK, Eddie E. s/o Wm. & Lizzie W. Enck			12/29/1896
[7] ENCK, Charles G.		05/01/1879 – 09/30/1962	
Jennie G.		11/26/1884 – 06/01/1984	
[7] ENCK, James G.		03/15/1882 – 11/11/1958	
Amanda D.		06/20/1884 – 01/01/1966	
[5] ENCK, George R.		1870 –	1956
Emma S.		1886 –	1968
[5] ENCK, Edwin R.		1889 –	1959
[7] ENCK, Albert E.		09/08/1891 – 09/27/1973	
[7] ENCK, Lillian May w/o Albert E. Enck		04/04/1892 – 01/08/1927	
[5] ENCK, Adam E.		1895 –	1967
Mary R.		1896 –	1972
[7] ENCK, Ralph T.		10/07/1905 –	
Alice G.		11/30/1904 –	

		NAME	AGE	BORN	DIED
	[7]	ENCK, Ella Mae		10/09/1906 -	
	[5]	ENCK, Gilbert Z.		1919 -	1984
		Florence E.		1920 -	
	[3]	ENCK, Dorothy A.		10/25/1922 -	
	[5]	ENCK, James Z. s/o Adam E. & Mary R. Enck		1940 -	1941
	[7]	ENGER, Harry S.		1881 -	1951
		Emma E.		1881 -	1952
(G)	[1]	ENGEL, Conrad	69-02-06	10/01/1778 -	12/06/1847
(G)	[1]	ENGLE, Elisabeth w/o Conrad Engle	81-06-29	06/22/1784 -	02/21/1866
	[2]	ENGEL, John s/o George & Mary M. Engel	71-04-28	11/28/1800 -	04/25/1872
	[1]	ENGLE, James	72-01-17	08/20/1809 -	10/07/1881
(G)	[1]	ENGLE, Catharine d/o Peter & Catharine Herzog w/o James Engle	68-01-18	09/28/1809 -	11/16/1877
	[1]	ENGLE, Samuel	65-03-09	12/21/1816 -	04/03/1882
(G)	[1]	ENGLE, Rebecca NEE Ditzler w/o Samuel Engle	61-05-18	11/20/1814 -	05/08/1876
(G)	[1]	ENGEL, Peter s/o Samuel & Rebecca Engel	11-02-23	03/18/1842 -	06/06/1853
(G)	[1]	ENGEL, Henry s/o Samuel & Rebecca Engel	05-06-10	08/11/1853 -	02/21/1859
(G)	[1]	ENGEL, Joseph s/o Samuel & Rebecca Engel	00-03-00	11/03/1858 -	02/03/1859
(G)	[1]	ENGEL, Peter	17-11-19	04/08/1819 -	03/27/1837
	[2]	ENGLE, Adam	79-02-04	04/04/1817 -	06/08/1896
		Mary	77-07-18	05/13/1821 -	12/31/1898
	[1]	ENGEL, Jacob	40-08-08	06/01/1829 -	02/09/1870
	[1]	ENGLE, Fianna NEE Keener w/o Jacob Engle	77-09-21	10/27/1826 -	08/18/1904
	[1]	ENGLE, Peter	57-11-05	08/19/1833 -	07/24/1890
	[1]	ENGLE, Susan w/o Peter Engle	??-09-18	06/18/18?? -	04/06/18??
		(Susan's stone was broken, mended, and very worn.)			
	[1]	ENGLE, Rolandus s/o Peter & Susanna Engle	02-07-20	01/03/1863 -	08/23/1865
	[1]	ENGLE, Mary d/o Peter & Susan Engle	22-08-04	10/25/1877 -	06/29/1900
	[1]	ENGLE, John	71-04-28	02/09/1841 -	07/07/1912
	[1]	ENGLE, Polly w/o John Engle	65-02-15	02/19/1844 -	05/04/1909
	[1]	ENGLE, Rebecca d/o John & Mary Engle	11-04-08	06/10/1863 -	10/18/1874
	[1]	ENGLE, Edwin s/o John & Polly Engle	01-02-19		06/21/1873
	[1]	ENGLE, William	54-09-21	09/24/1856 -	07/15/1911
	[1]	ENGLE, Kittyann K.	58-10-02	10/04/1857 -	08/06/1916
	[1]	ENGLE, Jeremiah		12/06/1866 -	01/02/1937
	[1]	ENGLE, Cyrus		11/10/1867 -	02/07/1869
	[2]	ENGLE, Simon K.		10/11/1880 -	01/21/1952
		Susan M.		12/25/1886 -	08/23/1965
	[8]	ENGLE, Bertha	60-07-29	07/04/1885 -	03/03/1944
	[8]	ENGLE, Tilman "Son"		11/29/1911 -	09/27/1974
	[1]	ENGLE, Clarence A., Sr.		11/16/1912 -	02/14/1985
		Elleanore B.		08/31/1917 -	07/31/1978
	[1]	ERB, Anna Maria NEE Zerfass w/o Isaac Erb	87-08-28	09/10/1797 -	06/08/1885
		(Anna's Stone was broken, mended, and very worn. Only readable portion was 87 years, 28 days, and September 10. The rest of the inscription was taken from F.E. Schnerer's List.)			
	[1]	ERB, Wilfred B.		05/21/1902 -	08/27/1979
		Beatrice W.		01/02/1915 -	07/10/1978
	[5]	ERWIN, Lloyd P.		1899 -	1967
		Mamie W.		1896 -	1981
	[6]	ESHLEMAN, Sylvan G.		09/28/1923 -	
		Elma F.		12/12/1927 -	
	[2]	ESPENSCHIED, Amanda		08/28/1858 -	01/14/1941

	NAME	AGE	BORN	DIED
[2]	EVANS, Henry Lot	70-06-25		02/17/1928
[2]	EVANS, E. Sadie w/o H. Lot Evans	?2-05-29		12/30/1918
[2]	EVANS, George L. "Father"		1882 -	1963
	Elizabeth M. "Mother"		1880 -	1950
	Mary M. "Daughter"		1905 -	1905
[2]	EVANS, Howard W.		1914 -	1940

INITIAL STONES: F.F., W.F.

	NAME	AGE	BORN	DIED
(G) [1]	FABER, Christina d/o Leonhard & Margareta Miller	56-06-05	02/02/1766 - 08/07/1822	
[5]	FARRINGTON, Horatio H.		1895 -	1973
	Edith R.		1893 -	1977
[2]	FASNACHT, Harvey G.		1863 -	1909
	Susan B. Enck		1859 -	1944
[2]	FASNACHT, Milton "Father"		01/12/1882 - 11/01/1934	
	Margaret "Mother"		01/28/1884 - 08/12/1953	
[8]	FASNACHT, Henry H.		07/14/1885 - 09/12/1949	
	Mabel A.		09/16/1885 - 03/24/1959	
[8]	FASNACHT, Vera K. "Daughter"		1910 -	1910
[2]	FASNACHT, Frank H., brother of Elsie H. Kissinger		1887 -	1952
	(Frank shares stone with Levi O. & Elsie H. Kissinger.)			
[7]	FASNACHT, Roy		07/11/1903 - 03/22/1977	
	Elsie		06/13/1904 -	
[8]	FASNACHT, Harvey E.		1905 -	
	Florence H.		1907 -	
[1]	FAUSSET, William, Sr.	84-08-26	10/17/1777 - 06/13/1862	
[1]	FAUSSET, Elisabeth w/o William Fausset	88-08-20	06/15/1776 - 03/05/1865	
[1]	FAUSSET, Peggy	58-05-14	09/19/1801 - 03/05/1860	
[1]	FAUSSET, Charles	42-11-22	05/28/1803 - 05/16/1846	
[1]	FAUSSET, William	72-11-07	02/17/1808 - 01/24/1881	
[1]	FAUSSET, Mary Ann	69-04-28	05/05/1811 - 10/03/1880	
[1]	FAUSSET, John	69-05-15	06/16/1825 - 12/01/1894	
(G) [1]	FEIRSTONE, Susanna NEE Illig(in)			
	w/o George Feirstein	41-05-19		08/22/1824
(G) [1]	FIERSTEIN, Daniel s/o George & Margaretha Fierstein	01-02-05	06/01/1828 - 08/05/1829	
[1]	FELLER, Clementine d/o Cornelius & Polly Feller	00-01-19		08/09/1867
(G) [1]	FEDER, Georg	62-10-11	08/10/1785 - 06/21/1848	
(G) [1]	FETTER, Susanna d/o Henrich Weit w/o Georg Fetter	69-01-07	03/05/1783 - 04/12/1852	
[1]	FETTER, George (Also carved in German)	48-08-01	09/12/1812 - 05/16/1861	
[1]	FETTER, Sarah Stober w/o George Fetter	77-05-18	04/05/1819 - 09/23/1896	
	(Also carved in German)			
(G) [1]	FETTER, Sutata d/o Henry & Sarah Fetter	06-09-09	08/07/1850 - 05/16/1857	
(G) [1]	FEDER, Henrich	35-10-24	03/31/1820 - 02/20/1856	
(G) [1]	FETTER, Infant s/o George & Sarah Fetter			1842
[5]	FETTER, Moses (With Footstone: M.F.)	60-09-26	02/15/1811 - 12/11/1871	
[5]	FETTER, Elizabeth Mellinger w/o Moses Fetter	71-01-18	10/09/1809 - 11/27/1880	
[5]	FETTER, George M. "CO. F. 1/9 REGT. PA. I"	75-11-27	01/24/1838 - 01/21/1914	
[5]	FETTER, Lydia Stohler w/o George M. Fetter	65-03-25	04/13/1847 - 08/08/1912	
[1]	FETTER, John S.	63-05-27	08/30/1850 - 02/27/1914	
[8]	FETTER, Jeremiah	74-06-21	09/19/1855 - 04/10/1930	
	Arabella, his wife	62-04-15	10/01/1855 - 02/16/1918	
[5]	FETTER, Cyrus N.		1879 -	1957
	Susan M.		1883 -	1968
[8]	FETTER, Harry S.		05/01/1881 - 07/19/1970	
	Amanda A.		11/05/1882 - 09/28/1960	

		NAME	AGE	BORN	DIED
	[5]	FETTER, Harvey I.		1881 –	1965
		Lizzie W.		1884 –	1974
	[5]	FETTER, Howard M. "Sparky" "Son"		03/19/1906 –	04/02/1979
	[8]	FETTER, Esther M. "Mother"		12/10/1905 –	
		Richard F. "Son"		08/08/1929 –	08/28/1950
	[8]	FETTER, Huber P.		03/28/1908 –	12/24/1968
		Helen H. NEE Keller		10/26/1910 –	04/27/1976
	[8]	FETTER, Elvin H. "PVT. CO. D. 103RD INF. 43RD. DIV. WW II"		06/15/1915 –	05/01/1970
		A. Elizabeth "Married June 15, 1941"		10/28/1917 –	
(G)	[1]	FIDLER, George s/o Peter & Margareta Fidler	02-11-12	06/09/1834 –	05/21/1837
	[7]	FIDLER, Raymond		1898 –	1974
		Edith		1913 –	
	[7]	FIDLER, Edna W. w/o Raymond Fidler	39-01-08	1897 –	1937
	[7]	FORRY, Zacharias H. "Father"	85-03-20	12/07/1848 –	03/27/1934
	[7]	FORRY, Fannie O. NEE Elser "Mother"	62-02-17	12/07/1848 –	02/24/1911
	[7]	FORRY, Samuel E.		01/27/1873 –	08/23/1957
	[5]	FOX, John Allen		07/18/1906 –	03/21/1937
	[2]	FRABLE, Alvin H.		07/31/1890 –	11/06/1969
		Roma M.		05/28/1910 –	
	[5]	FRANKFORD, Harry		1887 –	19__
		Mary E.		1907 –	1946
(G)	[1]	FREY, Sarah d/o Christoph & Anna Maria Frey	00-04-20		10/20/1840
	[3]	FRY, Hiram	69-01-00		11/04/1916
		Margaret	76-02-21		06/05/1919
	[3]	FRY, Phares M.		11/20/1867 –	10/10/1953
		Alice H.		08/30/1868 –	11/01/1956
		Alvin P.		07/29/1898 –	04/05/1957
	[3]	FRY, Samuel s/o Phares & Alice Fry		Born & Died	03/23/1888
	[2]	FRY, Harry H.		05/31/1889 –	03/12/1969
		Silva H.		07/15/1894 –	10/18/1967
	[3]	FRY, David Z.	01-09-12		02/09/1916
	[3]	FRY, Charles	1 day		03/07/1921
(G)	[1]	FRIEDERICH, J. Christian	75-02-19	06/02/1787 –	08/21/1862
	[1]	FREDERICK, Elizabeth NEE Buchter w/o Christian	81-09-10	02/07/1795 –	11/17/1876
	[8]	FRYMYER, Calvin K.		05/08/1892 –	05/01/1976
		Mamie H.		10/29/1894 –	
	[8]	FRYMYER, Chester		1915 –	
		Mabel		1904 –	
	[4]	FULIR, Lynda L. NEE Donmoyer w/o William G. Fulir, Jr.		05/23/1944 –	02/27/1985
	[1]	FUNSTON, Issabel w/o Isaac Funston	37 yrs.		05/04/1815
	[2]	FURLOW, Vester		01/03/1860 –	07/17/1950
		Ida		10/23/1867 –	03/29/1906
		Minerva		09/29/1883 –	06/29/1932
	[2]	FURLOW, Henry s/o Andrew & Malinda Furlow	01-07-21	05/26/1869 –	01/16/1871
	[2]	FURLOW, Carrie V. w/o D. Furlow		1872 –	1919
	[2]	FURLOW, Infant d/o D.E. & Carrie V. Furlow		12/20/1907	
		(Carrie and Infant Daughter are on Dr. J.K. Hertz Stone.)			
	[3]	GALL, Erica L. (Funeral Home Type Market with no I.D.)		1977 –	1986
	[3]	GANTZ, Jacob	56-01-24	03/26/1825 –	05/20/1881
	[3]	GANTZ, Sarah Ann d/o John & Margaret Kline w/o Jacob Gantz	77-07-01	10/05/1824 –	05/06/1902
	[2]	GANTZ, John H.	73-07-28	07/30/1850 –	03/28/1924
		Mary L.	84-00-27	08/17/1845 –	09/13/1930
	[2]	GANTZ, Cora E. d/o John H. & Mary Gantz	24-05-20	02/12/1873 –	08/02/1897

	NAME	AGE	BORN	DIED
[3]	GANTZ, Franklin J.	71-05-02	05/24/1860 - 10/26/1931	
	Mary M., his wife	63-08-17	10/04/1861 - 06/21/1925	
[5]	GANTZ, Amelia S., d/o F.J. & Mary Gantz		09/10/1896	
[2]	GANTZ, Wilson		1875 - 1970	
	Sarah		1877 - 1952	
[2]	GANTZ, Wayne A.		1879 - 1939	
	Gertrude		1882 - 1964	
[3]	GANTZ, Jacob D.	32-08-13	01/11/1893 - 07/24/1926	
(G) [1]	GERMAN, Johann	80-09-17	06/08/1789 - 03/25/1865	
[1]	GARMAN, Mary w/o John Garman	92-10-26	05/27/1786 - 04/22/1879	
[8]	GAUS, Joseph Y.		1863 - 1937	
	Lizzie B., his wife		1867 - 1954	
[8]	GAUS, Henry H.		11/03/1888 - 02/05/1912	
	Sadie S.		06/10/1890 - 06/06/1955	
[5]	GAUS, Frances F. (Rohland Service - marker)		1896 - 1969	
[7]	GELNETT, Samuel R.		06/02/1880 - 04/10/1981	
	Nora		03/29/1880 - 08/31/1958	
[7]	GERHART, J. William		1867 - 1943	
	Lily W.		1873 - 1936	
[1]	GERHART, Geo. M.	67-02-10	09/15/1877 - 11/25/1944	
[1]	GERHARD, Nancy NEE Heinsey	38-00-21	10/18/1878 - 11/09/1916	
[8]	GERHART, Rev. H.A.		06/23/1896 - 01/16/1971	
	M. Miriam		11/09/1899 - 09/23/1968	
[3]	GERHART, Joseph E.		1903 - 1978	
	Mabel M.		1908 - 1962	
[7]	GERHART, Elser		No Dates	
	Edith		1905 - 1978	
[7]	GERHART, Margareta	19-01-01	10/28/1910 - 11/29/1929	
[5]	GETZ, John	78-04-06	12/13/1819 - 04/19/1898	
[5]	GETZ, Fanny NEE Engle w/o John Getz	63-09-24	08/09/1815 - 06/03/1870	
[5]	GETZ, John H.	37-05-19	01/30/1847 - 07/19/1884	
[5]	GETZ, George		03/20/1849 - 01/27/1914	
	Emma Ruth, his wife		07/16/1854 - 05/03/1927	
[8]	GETZ, John H. (Shares Monument with John & Annie Souders)		1871 - 1934	
	Katie E., his wife		1880 - 1964	
[7]	GINDER, Carl Elser		08/06/1948 - 08/08/1948	
(G) [1]	GIVLER, Anna NEE Boffenmeyer w/o Johnnes Givler	28-06-16	05/29/1805 - 12/15/1833	
[5]	GOCKLEY, Edwin		1871 - 1959	
	Cora		1874 - 1947	
[2]	GOOD, Carl Lee		1953 - 1982	
[1]	GOSHERT, John	55-00-08	08/12/1802 - 08/20/1857	
[1]	GOSHERT, Elizabeth d/o Peter & Elizabeth Eckert			
	w/o John Goshert	49-00-11	04/06/1806 - 04/17/1855	
[1]	GOSHERT, Cyrus h/o Hanna Goshert	50-02-12	05/10/1830 - 07/22/1880	
[1]	GOSHERT, Hanna w/o Cyrus Goshert	79-10-15	08/27/1830 - 07/12/1910	
(G) [1]	GOSHERT, John Henry s/o Cyrus & Hanna Goshert	01-07-04	10/12/1860 - 03/16/1862	
(G) [1]	GOSHERT, Elisabeth d/o Cyrus & Hanna Goshert	01-01-00	06/07/1866 - 0?/0?/1867	
[1]	GOSHERT, Jacob		09/12/1832 - 03/17/1882	
	Lusetta, his wife		01/24/1828 - 07/19/1910	
[1]	GOSHERT, Rebecca L. d/o John & Jane Goshert	17-08-24	08/21/1856 - 05/15/1874	
[2]	GRAUL, William F. "Father"		1885 - 1969	
	Nora H. "Mother"		1885 - 1967	
[2]	GRAUL, Daniel D. "Son"		1906 - 1906	
	Marguerite E. "Daughter"		1908 - 1912	
	Marion E. "Daughter"		1912 - 1912	

NAME	AGE	BORN	DIED
[2] GRAUL, Donald W. "Father" "CORP. 4TH DIV U.S.M.C. WW II"		1919 -	1948
Alta L. Kreiner "Mother"		1924 -	
[8] GRISWOLD, Rex		05/18/1878 -	01/04/1959
May		10/10/1880 -	05/02/1951
[5] GROVE, Henry M.		1910 -	
Kathryn		1915 -	
[5] GROVE, Warren E.	17 days		1935
[5] GRUBE, David B.	58-03-27	12/27/1867 -	04/24/1926
[5] GRUBE, Emma E.	54-09-13	05/02/1874 -	02/15/1929
[5] GRUBE, David M.		1901 -	19__
Elva		1908 -	1935
[1] GRUBE, Christian O.		12/01/1903 -	08/22/1978
Dorothy E.		10/12/1917 -	

INITIAL STONES: [5] A.H., [5] J.A.H., [2] M.H.

NAME	AGE	BORN	DIED
[2] HABECKER, Augustus	76-07-23	01/04/1840 -	09/07/1916
[2] HABECKER, Elizabeth w/o Augustus Habecker	70-02-12	06/19/1842 -	10/01/1912
[1] HABECKER, Hiram K.	67-05-20	08/27/1846 -	02/17/1914
[1] HABECKER, Caroline NEE Miller	89-03-26	09/28/1846 -	01/23/1936
[1] HABECKER, Franklin s/o Hiram & Caroline Habecker	02-05-14	04/17/1871 -	08/31/1873
[1] HABECKER, Amos s/o Hiram & Caroline Habecker	07-03-26	09/11/1875 -	01/07/1883
[2] HABECKER, William	65-11-11	09/15/1867 -	08/26/1933
[5] HABECKER, Moses S.		1876 -	1943
[2] HABECKER, Ralph H. "WW I 80 DIV"		1895 -	1963
Gertrude U.		1899 -	1976
[1] HABECKER, David M. "Father" (David & Mildred are		1921 -	
Mildred M. "Mother" on front of stone.)		1923 -	
Stanley D. (Stanley, Marlene, and		1949 -	
Marlene M. Brian are on back of stone.)		1944 -	
Brian K. "Infant Son"		1972 -	1972
(G) [1] HACKER, Friederich	56-00-09	01/17/1756 -	01/26/1812
(G) [1] HACKER(IN), Catharina w/o Friederich Hacker	49-06-14	09/23/1756 -	04/06/1806
(G) [1] HACKER, Georg	79-11-03	10/09/1766 -	09/12/1846
(G) [1] HACKER, Jacob	55-08-05	05/23/1791 -	02/01/1847
(G) [1] HACKER, Catharina NEE Steiner(n)	24-00-09	03/27/1799 -	04/05/1823
[1] HACKER, Samuel	56-03-10	07/24/1799 -	11/04/1855
[1] HACKER, Susanna w/o Samuel Hacker	85-02-18	02/05/1806 -	04/23/1891
(G) [1] HACKER, William s/o Samuel & Susannah Hacker	15-02-03	01/10/1832 -	03/13/1847
[1] HACKER, Levi C. s/o Samuel & Susanna Hacker	20-03-29	12/02/1836 -	04/01/1857
[1] HACKER, Amanda d/o Samuel & Susanna Hacker	17-02-14	01/29/1840 -	04/12/1857
(G) [1] HACKER, Jeremias s/o Samuel & Susanna Hacker	02-02-16	05/22/1845 -	08/07/1847
[2] HACKER, Jacob	69-09-28	09/28/1803 -	07/26/1873
[2] HACKER, Mary	78-07-17	08/15/1819 -	03/22/1898
[1] HACKER, Emma d/o Joseph & Susan Hacker (Very Worn)		10/25/1815 -	03/??/1817
[3] HACKER, Benjamin C.	84-02-12	01/03/1842 -	03/15/1926
[2] HACKER, Martin K.	56-09-21	01/25/1850 -	11/16/1906
[2] HACKER, Annie w/o Martin K. Hacker	30-09-08	06/27/1863 -	04/15/1894
[2] HACKER, May Bell d/o Martin K. & Annie Hacker	(Buried)		11/09/1890
[7] HACKER, Benjamin H.		1856 -	1938
Annie H., his wife		1861 -	1939
[2] HACKER, William E. s/o __?__ & Lydia Hacker	05-02-15	11/31/1871 -	02/15/1877
[2] HACKER, Infant d/o Martin & Lydia Hacker			04/07/1875
[2] HACKER, Cora Addie d/o E_____ & Isabella Hacker	04-00-12	11/08/1872 -	12/20/1876

(Dates and age as they are carved on stone.)

		NAME	AGE	BORN	DIED
	[2]	HACKER, J. Blaine & J. Logan, Sons of H.K. & Kate Hacker		Born & Died	09/09/1885
	[7]	HACKER, William H.		01/04/1881 -	02/04/1959
	[7]	HACKER, Alice Z. w/o William H. Hacker	31-00-03	06/06/1886 -	06/09/1917
	[7]	HACKER, Mayme F.		06/27/1891 -	
		Anna M.		05/17/1919 -	11/01/1946
	[7]	HACKER, Victor L. s/o Wm. & Mayme Hacker	01-02-24		11/02/1931
	[2]	HACKMAN, Jacob	83-04-18	10/09/1805 -	02/27/1889
		Rebecca	81-03-07	05/22/1813 -	08/29/1894
(G)	[1]	HACKMAN, Fianna d/o David & Sarah Hackman	21-03-24	07/16/1820 -	11/10/1841
	[1]	HACKMAN, Eliza w/o John Hackman	21-08-00		02/13/1850
	[2]	HACKMAN, Chas. D. "PRIV. CO. F. 9 PA. V.V. CAV."	88-03-15	01/29/1843 -	05/14/1931
		Lucy A.	74-08-15	10/20/1842 -	07/05/1917
	[2]	HACKMAN, John A. s/o Charles & Lucy Hackman	25-11-27	07/08/1866 -	07/05/1892
	[2]	HACKMAN, Mary Elizabeth d/o C.D. & Lucy Hackman	01-08-23	12/09/1880 -	09/02/1882
	[2]	HACKMAN, John T. "Father"	69-06-13	02/11/1849 -	08/24/1918
	[2]	HACKMAN, Sarah NEE Neisinger "Mother"	73-03-02	11/30/1847 -	03/02/1921
	[3]	HACKMAN, Albert D.		01/14/1867 -	07/06/1944
	[3]	HACKMAN, Emma S.		07/05/1880 -	03/28/1965
	[8]	HACKMAN, Aaron S.		1874 -	1916
		Alice Flory		1877 -	1971
	[4]	HACKMAN, Arlington F.		06/03/1896 -	
		Grace Good		10/04/1899 -	09/07/1980
	[8]	HACKMAN, Floyd		07/02/1899 -	
		Charlotte Bachman		03/05/1901 -	04/04/1972
	[4]	HACKMAN - CARROLL "Sweethearts"			
		Lloyd W.		09/26/1899 -	01/23/1973
		Mabel G.		05/11/1911 -	01/01/1975
	[1]	HACKMAN, Raymond I.		1910 -	1975
		Mabel M.		1914 -	1977
	[2]	HACKMAN, Henry	00-03-07		03/07/1915
	[2]	HACKMAN, Mabel G.	00-07-09		12/27/1918
(G)	[1]	HAGY, Susanna w/o Isaac Hagy	22-05-06	09/28/1819 -	03/05/1842
	[2]	HAINES, Joseph J.		12/15/1900 -	12/07/1956
		Della M.		12/01/1893 -	12/18/1980
(G)	[1]	HALDEMAN, Matilda El. H. d/o John & Priscilla	02-07-23	08/17/1858 -	04/07/1861
	[7]	HALDEMAN, Monroe		1875 -	1958
		Emma Landis, his wife		1883 -	1916
	[3]	HALDEMAN, Harvey J.		08/30/1877 -	04/03/1930
		Anna M.		10/27/1882 -	04/14/1957
	[3]	HALDEMAN, Tobias J.		1879 -	1944
		Amanda E. Palm, his wife		1884 -	1964
	[3]	HALDEMAN, Earl E.		1905 -	1980
		Ella Mae		1907 -	1960
	[7]	HALDEMAN, John E. "TEC 4 US ARMY WORLD WAR II"		01/19/1908 -	01/26/1985
	[3]	HALDEMAN, Howard P.		1904 -	1962
		Carrie E.		1906 -	1972
	[2]	HALDEMAN, John E.		1932 -	
		Florence M.		1932 -	1964
	[6]	HALL, Pauline		1919 -	1979
(G)	[1]	HAMMER(IN), Anna Maria	41-10-00	03/09/1762 -	01/09/1804
	[1]	HAMMER, George s/o Henry & Elisabeth Hammer	51-06-28	01/05/1816 -	08/03/1867
	[1]	HAMMER, Mary w/o Geo. F. Hammer	77-00-10	01/01/1817 -	01/11/1894
	[1]	HAMMER, George K. s/o George & Mary Hammer	47-04-04	02/02/1839 -	06/06/1886
	[1]	HAMMER, a daughter of Geo. & M.A. Hammer		Born & Died	03/29/1844
	[1]	HAMMER, a daughter of G. & M. Hammer	6 days	12/06/1849	
		a son of G. & M. Hammer	3 hours	12/06/1849	

	NAME	AGE	BORN	DIED
[1]	HAMMER, David	01-06-20	01/24/1843	
[1]	HAMMER, Harry A.		10/20/1888 - 05/20/1959	
[7]	HAMMER, Ned S. (Shares stone with Curtis &		1918 -	
	Clara A. Stella Withers)		1911 -	1982
[1]	HARNER, Clara E. d/o Abraham & Caroline Harner	01-09-12	01/27/1858 - 11/08/1859	
[1]	HERNER, William L. s/o Abraham & Caroline Herner	06-04-02	12/13/1861 - 05/03/1868	
[1]	HARNER, Geo. Morris s/o Abrm. & Caroline Harner	10-05-14	05/03/1868 - 10/17/1878	
[1]	HARRELL, Lela E.		04/09/1871 - 06/02/1936	
[6]	HARRINGTON, Garfield F. "WW II"		06/16/1914 - 11/09/1978	
	Anna Ruhl		01/29/1921 -	
[8]	HARTMAN, Israel		1858 -	1927
	Amanda		1865 -	1942
[7]	HARTMAN, Thomas I.		1888 -	1959
(G) [1]	HARTRANFT, Hannah NEE Wolfe w/o John Hartranft	84-03-07	10/29/1780 - 02/05/1865	
(G) [1]	HARTRANFT, Joseph	55-00-29	05/21/1802 - 06/22/1857	
(G) [1]	HERDRANFT, Sarah w/o Joseph Herdranft	58-00-16	12/01/1802 - 12/17/1860	
(G) [1]	HARTRANFT, Joseph s/o Joseph & Sara Hartranft	00-08-10	10/28/1845	
(G) [1]	HERDRANFT, infant d/o Joseph & Sarah Herdranft		Born & Died 09/10/1846	
[7]	HARTRANFT, Mary	74-04-18	10/26/1823 - 03/14/1898	
[8]	HARTRANFT, John F. (The stones of Martin B. &	82-04-11	09/04/1834 - 01/15/1917	
	Susanna K. Sallie P. Hartranft, Samuel	74-10-22	10/14/1836 - 09/06/1911	
[8]	HARTRANFT, Martin B. L. & Alice B. Schilling,	85-11-11	04/27/1872 - 04/07/1958	
	Sallie P. and John F. & Susanna K.	59-11-07	10/28/1880 - 10/05/1940	
	Hartranft are all the same.)			
[8]	HARTRANFT, Sallie B.		1875 -	1963
[1]	HARTZ, Eliza w/o John K. Hartz, formerly widow of			
	John Lupold, d/o Samuel & Susanna Hacker	28-06-24	09/13/1830 - 04/07/1859	
(G) [1]	HAACK, Eva Margaretha	07-09-11	08/08/1794 - 05/19/1802	
[2]	HAUCK, Lydia w/o Henry Hauck, d/o Geo. & Susan Scharb		04/01/1812 - 12/24/1875	
(G) [1]	HAUER, Johannes	01-02-28	03/13/1798 - 06/10/1799	
(G) [1]	HAUER, Isaac	04-03-24	03/17/1799 - 07/11/1803	
(G) [1]	HAUER, Anna Maria	01-07-20	11/18/1801 - 07/08/1803	
(G) [1]	HAUSZHALTER, Lorenz	78-04-21	08/13/1727 - 01/03/1805	
	"Born in Ruszheim in the Province of the Border Count			
	Durlach in Europe."			
(G) [1]	HAUSZHALTER(IN), Margaretha NEE Hacker(in)	76-03-19	12/24/1730 - 04/12/1807	
	"Born in Ruszheim in the Province of the Border Count			
	Durlach in Europe."			
(G) [1]	HAUSHALTER, Jacob	52-06-13	09/30/1761 - 04/12/1814	
(G) [1]	HAUSZHALTER, Gottlieb	05-01-04	07/26/1770 - 08/30/1775	
[1]	HAWKINS, Richard I. s/o James & Mary Hawkins	30-00-03	03/17/1844	
[2]	HEHNLY, Martin H.		1874 -	1949
	Emma D.		1871 -	1950
[2]	HEHNLY, Lizzie d/o M.H. & Emma Hehnly	8 days	09/12/1902 - 09/20/1902	
[7]	HEHNLY, Anna Mae	17-00-17	08/18/1927 - 09/05/1944	
(G) [1]	HEIL(IN), Elisabeth	68-10-24	02/01/1762 - 12/24/1831	
[3]	HEILAND, Henry A. (Zartman is carved on the back		01/19/1879 - 03/19/1951	
	Frances L. of this stone.)		04/10/1884 - 08/16/1950	
[1]	HEINSEY, Jacob	58-00-29	08/08/1836 - 09/07/1894	
[1]	HEINSEY, Nancy NEE Miller s/o Jacob Heinsey	72-09-22	11/24/1843 - 09/16/1916	
[1]	HINSEY, Henry s/o Jacob & Nancy Hinsey	5 days	10/31/1868 - 11/05/1868	
[1]	HINSEY, Elizzie d/o Jacob & Nancy Hinsey	13-05-07	12/23/1871 - 05/31/1885	
[1]	HINSEY, Daniel s/o Jacob & Nancy Hinsey		01/18/1875 - 04/27/1875	
[1]	HINSEY, Catharina d/o Jacob & Nancy Hinsey	29 days	09/18/1881 - 10/17/1881	

	NAME	AGE	BORN	DIED
[1]	HEINSEY, John M.	83-02-16	11/15/1865 - 02/01/1949	
[1]	HEINSEY, Abr. M.	47-11-12	12/17/1869 - 11/29/1917	
[7]	HEISEY, B. Almenara		10/12/1904 -	
[7]	HEISEY, Elwood G. s/o Rufus & Almenara Heisey		10/19/1928 - 09/30/1947	
(G) [1]	HEISSEN, Maria w/o Fridrich Heissar	about 45		
	"Had with him 4 sons and 2 daughters"	years	1786 - 01/19/1831	
[2]	HEISER, Owen B.	62-05-29	11/16/1850 - 05/15/1919	
[2]	HEISER, Annie H. w/o Owen B. Heiser	68-08-12	05/29/1840 - 02/11/1909	
[2]	HEISER, John S.	39-02-03		01/31/1920
	Minnie H.	82-03-25		02/15/1966
[2]	HEISER, Bertha May d/o John S. & Minnie H. Heiser	02-00-02		09/10/1906
[2]	HEISER, Infant s/o Mr. & Mrs. J.S. Heiser			10/31/1915
[2]	HELMAN, John M. "Husband"		1857 -	1943
	Emma E. "Wife"		1858 -	1905
	Ida M. "Wife"		1861 -	1942
[3]	HELMAN, David M.		1866 -	1948
	Elizabeth Z.		1869 -	1939
[2]	HELMAN, Preston H.		1887 -	1966
	Jennie A.		1890 -	1939
[3]	HELMAN, Ernest B.		1899 -	1982
	Ella M.		1900 -	1974
[2]	HELMAN, Carl E. "S/SGT 212 AGF BAND WW II"		07/28/1913 - 04/23/1979	
[3]	HERCHELROTH, Christian	43-01-25	08/11/1823 - 10/05/1866	
[3]	HERCHELROTH, Catharine Hacker		05/03/1828 - 01/07/1918	
(G) [3]	HERCHELROTH, Susanna Barbara d/o Christian &			
	Catharine Herchelroth	02-06-22	06/22/1846 - 06/14/1849	
(G) [3]	HERCHELROTH, Samuel D. s/o Christ^{n} & Catha^{r}			
	Herchelroth	01-06-11	02/17/1853 - 08/28/1854	
[3]	HERCHELROTH, Emma Naela d/o Christian & Catharine			
	Herchelroth	06-02-22	01/10/1857 - 04/02/1863	
[1]	HAIR, Jane (Stone reset-death year from earlier			
	record.)	46-09-14	01/07/1737 - 10/22/1783	
[3]	HERR, Lester K. (Roseboro Funeral Home marker)		1905 -	1982
[3]	HERR, Grace D.		03/26/1906 - 10/25/1976	
[8]	HERR-WITMER			
	Harold W.		07/07/1911 - 02/23/1970	
	Agnes Mae		05/01/1901 - 06/03/1961	
[3]	HERR, Rhoda Mae	8 days	05/17/1929	
[3]	HERR, Mary Louise	17 days	10/30/1931	
[2]	HERTZ, Mathias K.	46-07-29	05/15/1830 - 01/11/1877	
[2]	HERTZ, John Krick, M.D. "Physician at Lexington for			
	for 50 years."	78-09-07	No Dates	
	Sallie w/o Dr. J.K. Hertz	66-03-23	12/20/1838 - 04/13/1905	
[2]	HERTZ, Romanus s/o Dr. John K. & Sallie Hertz	22 days	02/28/1863 - 03/21/1863	
[2]	HERTZ, Kate Elizabeth d/o Dr. John K. & Sallie			
	Hertz	03-10-17	12/25/1866 - 11/12/1870	
[2]	HERTZ, Clara Alda d/o Dr. J.K. & Sallie Hertz	19-10-10		06/22/1890
	(Carrie w/o D. Furlow and Infant daughter			
	are also on Hertz stone.)			
[5]	HERTZOG, Jerome	76-05-26	06/22/1874 - 12/18/1950	
[5]	HERTZOG, Katie E. Eberly w/o Jerome K. Hertzog	41-02-08	09/13/1875 - 11/21/1916	
[5]	HERTZOG, Katie		03/21/1898 - 12/03/1966	
[6]	HERTZOG - WADE (Last names not paired with first names.)			
	Roy		04/08/1900 - 11/28/1980	
	Raymond L.		10/24/1901 -	
	Emma		05/01/1902 - 04/28/1980	

	NAME	AGE	BORN	DIED
[2]	HERTZOG, Walter M.		1904 –	1966
	Lillie L.		1907 –	
[2]	HESS, Franklin S.		1855 –	1943
	Clara M., his wife		1859 –	1933
	Victor K.		1894 –	1922
	Flora K.		1884 –	1953
[8]	HETRICH, Oliver M.		06/06/1884 –	01/20/1965
	Estella Eckert		09/12/1911 –	
[1]	HEVERLING, Minnie E.	59 y.–5 m.		
		1 dy.	12/31/1891 –	06/02/1951
[2]	HEBERLING, Paul C.		11/11/1902 –	
	Florence S.		03/22/1912 –	03/10/1949
[2]	HEBERLING, Harvey (Robert W. Reider is also on		1906 –	1965
	Alice this stone.)		1911 –	19
	Elva		1927 –	1927
[2]	HICKMAN, William Earle		08/16/1894 –	01/18/1970
	Winifred Maurer		11/03/1894 –	07/09/1971
[6]	HILTON, Roy T.		12/18/1911 –	12/28/1985
	Estella K.		08/08/1916 –	
[1]	HIMMELBERGER, Reuben s/o Jacob & Adaline	6 wks.		02/03/1890
[5]	HIRNEISEN, Cora w/o Samuel E.	17-10-04	07/01/1885 –	05/05/1903
[7]	HIRNEISEN, Henry M.		03/19/1873 –	03/11/1942
	Cora D.		08/19/1879 –	06/27/1967
	Ella W.		10/16/1902 –	03/08/1903
[7]	HIRNEISEN, Raymond W.		09/29/1897 –	03/08/1980
	Elsie B.		06/11/1902 –	
[7]	HOFFER, Benjamin K.		1875 –	1945
	Mattie I.		1877 –	1966
[7]	HOFFER, Viola M. d/o Benjamin & Mattie Hoffer		04/19/1901 –	11/08/1902
[7]	HOFFER, Emanuel B. s/o Benjamin & Mattie Hoffer		01/17/1919 –	10/16/1919
[3]	HOFFER, Thelma J. d/o Elam S. & Esta Hoffer		1946 –	1946
[8]	HOFFMAN, John		01/06/1879 –	08/09/1959
	Katie		11/21/1887 –	11/10/1973
	Floyd, our son		No Dates	
[8]	HOFFMAN, Floyd J. "Son"		07/31/1915 –	08/01/1960
[8]	HOFFMAN, Robert		No Dates	
(G) [1]	HOLL, Margaretha NEE Wechter w/o Isaac Holl	35-10-03	05/30/1804 –	04/03/1840
(G) [1]	HOLLINGER, Barbara w/o Jacob Hollinger	48-06-25	05/17/1783 –	12/12/1831
[1]	HOLLINGER, Benjamin	78-06-11	11/06/1815 –	05/17/1894
[1]	HOLLINGER, Harriet w/o Benjamin Hollinger	79-03-02	01/26/1808 –	04/28/1887
[1]	HOLLINGER, Priscilla E. d/o Benj. & Harriet			
	Hollinger	54-01-25	06/02/1851 –	07/27/1905
(G) [1]	HOLLINGER, Sarah E. d/o Benjamin & Harriet			
	Hollinger	2 days		11/27/1857
[3]	HOLLINGER, Christian D.		11/15/1901 –	12/06/1979
	Pauline P.		07/31/1903 –	05/26/1970
[7]	HOLLINGER, Jacob G.		1908 –	1964
	Elsie M. (See Elsie M. Sprecher)		1902 –	1967
[8]	HOLLINGER, Infant s/o Jacob & Elsie Hollinger			1932
[7]	HOLLINGER, Martin W. (Shares stone with Levi &		1901 –	1972
	Helen W. Ella Zellers.)		1909 –	
	Infant daughter			1929
[3]	HOLSINGER, Jacob E.			
	Ethel J.		05/06/1925 –	12/19/1985

	NAME	AGE	BORN	DIED
[5]	HOOVER, Harry K.		1889 –	1950
	Anna Mary		1889 –	1953
[5]	HOOVER, Ella Nora "Daughter"		06/28/1911 –	07/27/1979
[1]	HORNBERGER, Elizabeth d/o John & Mary Ann			
	Hornberger	01-01-20	01/01/1845 –	02/20/1846
[3]	HORNBERGER, Lottie G. "Mother"		03/10/1930 –	06/22/1972
	Wanda J. "Daughter"		02/02/1961 –	06/22/1972
[1]	HORNING, Jacob	81-04-30	09/05/1762 –	01/04/1844
[1]	HORNING, Magdalene	81-02-08	09/17/1772 –	11/25/1853
[1]	HORNN, Wendel (Stone very worn.)	??-??-??	10/?5/17?9 –	09/04/17?5
	(Earlier listing gives age as 48-11-11, and			
	dates as 10/15/1729-9/4/1775.)			
[1]	HOUSER, William G.		1922 –	
	Mary E.		1925 –	
(G) [1]	HOWARDER, Henrich	About 25 years	11/--/1793 –	11/10/1818
[2]	HUBER, John	66-06-04	12/29/1837 –	07/03/1904
[2]	HUBER, Eliza	89-09-25	05/15/1837 –	03/10/1927
[3]	HUBER, John		1868 –	1925
[2]	HUBER, J. Irwin		10/29/1876 –	10/14/1937
[3]	HUBER, Samuel S.		10/16/1905 –	
	Edith M.	39-06-05	10/14/1900 –	04/19/1940
[3]	HUBER, Carl s/o Samuel & Edith M. Huber		Stillborn	02/07/1931
[3]	HUBER, Catharine d/o Samuel & Edith M. Huber			09/23/1931
[7]	HULL, Effenger M.		1872 –	1935
	Isabella D. Enck, his wife		1878 –	1937
[7]	HULL, Howard s/o E.M. & Bella Hull	00-01-16	08/07/1900 –	09/23/1900
[8]	HUMMER, Edward F.		12/28/1892 –	10/22/1926
	Ella H.		07/23/1884 –	10/27/1966
[1]	HUSSON, Lloyd S.		03/01/1895 –	09/11/1978
	Sarah E.		02/12/1896 –	
(G) [1]	ILLIG, Georg	59-07-26	04/22/1744 –	12/18/1803
(G) [1]	ILLIG, Margaretha	53-05-05	12/19/1747 –	05/24/1801
(G) [1]	ILLIG, Georg	58-07-08	09/20/1771 –	04/28/1830
(G) [1]	ILLIG, Anna Maria w/o George Illig d/o Jacob & Elisabeth Weisser	70-01-05	05/17/1778 –	07/22/1848
(G) [1]	ILLIG, Georg s/o Georg & Maria Illig	28-10-01	12/30/1808 –	11/01/1837
(G) [1]	ILLIG, Wilhelm s/o Georg & Maria Illig	6 mnths.	09/10/1812 –	03/10/1813
(G) [1]	ILLIG, Leonhard	02-02-11	03/08/1773 –	05/19/1775
[1]	ILLIG, Samuel, M.D.	52-08-05	09/15/1802 –	05/20/1855
[1]	ILLIG, Mary Ann d/o Samuel & Anna Illig*	00-03-04	05/22/1845 –	08/26/1845
[1]	ILLIG, Susan H. w/o Jacob Illig*	41-11-00	02/10/1817 –	01/10/1859
[1]	ILLIG, Margaret Ann d/o Jacob & Susanna Illig*	04-08-04	01/13/1843 –	10/09/1847
(G) [1]	ILLIG, Amanda Louisa d/o Jacob & Susanna Illig*	02-04-02	06/11/1848 –	10/16/1850
(C) [1]	ILLIG, Samuel Yeager s/o Jacob & Susanna Illig*	00-07-23	08/30/1850 –	04/23/1851
[1]	ILLIG, William Lemon s/o Jacob & Susanna Illig*	00-08-06	07/25/1852 –	04/18/1853
[1]	ILLIG, Daughters of Jacob & Susan H. Illig*			
	Fatima Cecilia	00-07-19	04/28/1854 –	02/17/1854
	Clara Ottilia	00-01-19	06/10/1856 –	07/29/1856
	* These are all above ground box-like tombstones.			
[1]	ILLIG, Louisa Fisher d/o Edward & Sarah Illig	01-02-27	03/16/1837 –	06/13/1838
[5]	IPINZA, Luella F. NEE Fasnacht		04/13/1922 –	10/21/1985
[1]	JACK, James			05/17/1824

	NAME	AGE	BORN	DIED
[2]	JACOBY, Jesse	68-11-29	08/30/1817 - 08/29/1886	
[2]	JACOBY, Fianna w/o Jessie Jacoby d/o Samuel & Hannah Miller	67-01-10	No Dates	
[2]	JACOBY, John M. s/o Jesse & Fianna Jacoby	34-11-16	12/05/1841 - 11/21/1876	
[2]	JACOBY, Daniel	62-08-08	03/24/1840 - 12/02/1902	
[2]	JACOBY, Samuel M.	65-11-29	10/30/1916	
[2]	JACOBY, Emma F.	71-01-11	03/09/1925	
[2]	JACOBY, Sarah Fianna d/o Samuel M & Mary Jacoby	00-04-08	08/07/1876	
[2]	JEFFRIES, Matthew Scott (Funeral Home type marker-no name.)		07/21/1982	
[1]	JONES, Elizabeth	25 yrs.	05/09/1746 - 10/12/1771	
[1]	JONES, Elizabeth d/o J^{no} & Elizabeth Bar	53-11-22	02/26/1752 - 02/04/1806	

Initial Stones: [2] W.K., [5] K.

	NAME	AGE	BORN	DIED
(G) [1]	KARL, Elisabeth d/o Jacob & Maria Karl	00-04-09	04/06/1836	
[2]	KAUFFMAN, Henrietta M.		1834 - 1905	
[2]	KAUFFMAN, Daniel S.		1836 - 1892	
[5]	KAUFFMAN, Emanuel B.	84-08-05	08/29/1861 - 05/04/1946	
	Ida Corry w/o Emanuel B. Kauffman d/o Joseph & Mary Ulrich	65-01-20	06/24/1865 - 08/14/1930	
[5]	KAUFFMAN, Reuben K.		1903 - 1948	
	Elsie B.		1902 - 1983	
[1]	KEATH, Michael "Father"	94-08-08	03/09/1799 - 11/17/1893	
[1]	KEATH, Elizabeth "Mother"	79-09-16	09/17/1811 - 07/03/1891	
[3]	KEATH, Samuel		09/07/1854 - 03/09/1923	
	Sallie, his wife		07/11/1854 - 04/06/1931	
[3]	KEATH, John C. s/o Samuel & Sallie Keath	10 mnths.	09/09/1875	
[3]	KEATH, Willis Z.		1876 - 1913	
	Susan M.		1870 - 1947	
	Ruth C.		1901 -	
	Ellwood D.		1901 - 1954	
[8]	KEEBLER, Benjamin F.		03/01/1909 - 02/14/1948	
	Martha		No Dates	
[8]	KEEBLER, Benjamin C. s/o Benj. F. & Martha M. Keebler	00-07-15	1936	
[9]	KEENEN, Jay Russell		12/20/1906 -	
	Lydia Irene		12/15/1903 -	
[5]	KEENER, Sarah S. NEE Tschudy w/o John G. Keener	63-07-25	09/10/1850 - 05/05/1914	
[8]	KELLER, Samuel K. (Shares stone with Moses &		09/05/1886 - 03/11/1956	
	Elsie M. NEE Hehnly Grace Zook)		03/31/1887 - 07/30/1965	
[2]	KELLER, William K.		1891 - 1957	
	Mary W.		1893 - 1973	
[5]	KELLER, Elmer G.		03/05/1892 - 10/27/1970	
	Sadie M.		11/28/1889 - 07/05/1964	
[3]	KELLER, Lester K.		12/09/1892 - 07/11/1984	
	Helen W.		01/07/1899 - 04/03/1977	
[3]	KELLER, Infant s/o David & Alice Keller	6 days	05/20/1894	
[3]	KELLER, W. Glenn		08/23/1926 - 04/27/1927	
	Erma J.		01/14/1936 - 01/15/1936	
[2]	KELLER, C. Lynn "Conservation Pledge" carved on stone.		1940 - 1978	

"I give my pledge as an American to save and
faithfully to defend from waste the natural
resources of my country - its air, soil, and
minerals, its forests, waters, and wildlife."

	NAME	AGE	BORN	DIED
[8]	KETNER, Frank G.		11/26/1880 - 03/28/1937	
[8]	KETNER, Lizzie E.		03/01/1879 - 11/01/1951	

		NAME	AGE	BORN	DIED
	[7]	KEYTON-BLECKER (Sundial on square base on pedestal with three smaller stones. Inscribed on sundial is "I count none but the sunny hours.")			
		Albert W. Keyton		1889 –	1934
		Ida Blecker Keyton		1877 –	1950
		Wilbert Blecker on this stone also.			
	[1]	KILE, Peter	31-07-06	01/10/1841 – 08/16/1872
	[1]	KEIL, Lydia w/o Peter Keil, Sr., d/o Jacob & Harriet Weaver	25-09-04	07/19/1841 – 04/23/1867
(G)	[1]	KISSINGER, Phillip	58-11-00	11/01/1746 – 10/30/1806
(G)	[1]	KESSINGER, Jacob		08/16/1749 – 11/27/1801
(G)	[1]	KESSINGER(N), Susanna (Stone reset and rest of information is buried. Death date from earlier list. Back of stone has Susan Kegern.)			03/17/1873
	[1]	KISSINGER, Frank P. s/o Joseph & Anna Kissinger	19-10-26		10/26/1872
	[2]	KISSINGER, Levi O.		1892 –	1957
		Elsie H. "Sister of Frank H. Fasnacht"		1890 –	1976
(G)	[1]	KLEIN, Daniel	86-00-09	04/27/1762 – 05/06/1848
(G)	[1]	KLEIN, Margaretha w/o Daniel Klein	59 y. 4 m. and some days	1777 – 06/07/1836
(G)	[1]	KLEIN, Michael	77-09-21	11/29/1764 – 09/16/1842
(G)	[1]	KLEIN, Catharina NEE Eichelberger w/o Michael Klein	83-08-10	12/23/1767 – 09/02/1851
(G)	[1]	KLEIN, Michael*	79-02-27		08/26/1847
(G)	[1]	KLEIN, Susanna*	60-02-23		06/20/1853
	[1]	KLINE, Lydia, d/o Meichel, Esqr. & Susanna Kline ('Meichel' as carved on stone. Stone marked- I. Erb No. 102)	26-01-25	03/30/1810 – 05/25/1836
(G)	[1]	KLEIN, Catharine*	30-04-08		03/08/1849
	[1]	KLINE, Esren s/o Michael, Esq. & Susanna Kline (Stone marked-I. Erb No. 100)	13 days	01/29/1833 – 02/11/1833
	[1]	KLINE, Eliza d/o Michael, Esq. & Susanna Kline (Stone marked - I. Erb No. 107)	01-03-01	11/21/1828 – 02/22/1830
	[1]	KLINE, Sarahann d/o Michael, Esq. & Susanna Kline (Stone marked - I. Erb No. 101)	02-11-24	07/14/1831 – 07/08/1834
(G)	[1]	KLEIN, Adeline*	17-00-23		07/20/1860
(G)	[1]	KLEIN, Johannes (Surface peeling in areas.)	33-11-08	11/23/1792 – 11/01/1826
(G)	[1]	KLEIN, Margaret NEE Elser(n) w/o Johannes Klein	64-04-11	10/02/1797 – 02/13/1862
	[3]	KLINE, George	80-09-27	03/08/1786 – 01/04/1867
	[3]	KLINE, Mary NEE Scheaffer w/o George Kline	84-08-20	02/13/1786 – 11/04/1870
(G)	[1]	KLEIN, Daniel	30-03-23	04/05/1798 – 07/28/1828
	[3]	KLINE, William, Sr.	91-09-06	11/04/1799 – 08/10/1891
	[3]	KLINE, Anna NEE S__nger w/o William Kline	75-11-05	05/13/1802 – 04/18/1878
(G)	[1]	KLEIN, Sarah w/o Henrich Klein	17-09-02	05/16/1806 – 02/18/1824
(G)	[1]	KLEIN, Sarah d/o Henrich & Sarah Klein	00-11-10		01/24/1825
	[3]	KLINE, Joseph (Shares stone with Jacob L & Lydia Sadie H. Snyder.)	78-11-14	01/29/1805 – 01/13/1884
		Lydia	57-09-20	12/28/1805 – 10/10/1863
(G)	[1]	KLEIN, Johañes	6 days	04/16/1812 – 04/22/1812
(G)	[1]	KLEIN, Infant s/o Henry & Catharine Klein (Stone reset and most of dates are buried.)		03/05/????
	[2]	KLINE, Allen	80-09-22	10/24/1813 – 08/16/1894
	[2]	KLINE, Mary w/o Allen Kline	72-00-19	06/06/1816 – 06/25/1888
	[3]	KLINE, Cyrus	82-02-15	02/12/1816 – 04/27/1898
	[3]	KLINE, Matilda w/o Cyrus Kline	37-04-22	07/03/1834 – 11/25/1871

* These four stones are all alike.

NAME	AGE	BORN	DIED
[3] KLINE, Reuben	66-09-02	04/29/1828 - 02/01/1895
[3] KLINE, Hiram	55-03-03	09/23/1829 - 12/26/1884
[3] KLINE, Barbara w/o Hiram Kline	87-03-29	11/17/1831 - 03/16/1919
[3] KLINE, Monroe B. s/o Hiram & Barbara Kline	00-03-13	10/20/1867 - 02/02/1868
[3] KLINE, William	76-10-20	01/02/1832 - 11/22/1908
[3] KLINE, Susan w/o William Kline	75-05-02	11/01/1838 - 04/03/1914
[7] KLINE, Rufus		03/22/1839 - 07/26/1912
Mary Fry, his wife		01/19/1840 - 01/13/1920
[3] KLINE, Infant s/o Rufus & Mary Kline		01/12/1861
[3] KLINE, Infant s/o Rufus & Mary Kline		11/27/1877
[3] KLINE, Aaron "Father"		01/22/1900
Fianna H. "Mother"		03/01/1911
Laura "Daughter"	76-06-22	06/14/1861 - 01/06/1938
Martin H. "Son"	21-03-08	09/19/1862 - 02/18/1883
[7] KLINE, C. Franklin	75-03-10	05/30/1853 - 09/10/1928
Susanna Koehler, his wife	70-07-22	04/25/1851 - 12/17/1921
[7] KLINE, Grace M. (These three Kline children	00-01-11	12/18/1914
[7] KLINE, George F. stones are located behind	01-02-09	02/08/1917
[7] KLINE, Charles R. C. Frankline & Susanna Kline.)	1 day	03/08/1921
[7] KLINE, Ezra S.		10/10/1859 - 02/23/1951
Lizzie B.		05/31/1861 - 10/16/1934
[3] KLINE, William E.	65-04-21	01/07/1865 - 05/28/1930
[3] KLINE, Hiram P.		11/03/1861 - 05/12/1919
Flora I.		10/04/1868 - 09/18/1956
[7] KLINE, Phares C.		05/24/1862 - 10/14/1936
Rosa V. Biemesderfer, his wife		02/25/1867 - 11/14/1913
[7] KLINE, Wayne J.		01/30/1875 - 01/06/1952
Annie B.		09/15/1875 - 11/09/1957
[7] KLINE, Harvey K.		06/01/1877 - 08/23/1949
Stella A.		07/27/1885 - 12/22/1970
[7] KLINE, E. Samuel		04/23/1895 - 04/08/1968
Ada M.		03/09/1897 - 08/14/1982
[3] KLINE, Howard F.		01/25/1899 -
Margie E.		07/05/1896 - 03/28/1980
[7] KLINE, Rufus S.		10/30/1902 - 02/23/1964
Dora M.		08/08/1906 - 01/08/1984
[2] KLINE, Ray Marcus		01/02/1909 - 02/07/1909
[2] KLOPP, Merle E.		1904 - 1965
Ida M.		1910 -
[8] KOPP, Edward		1876 - 1961
Ida G.		1879 - 1946
Harry		1910 - 1910
[3] KOPP, Elam P.		09/21/1899 - 04/23/1981
Elizabeth M.		09/01/1902 -
[3] KOPP, Adam P.		11/02/1912 - 05/27/1970
Mary E.		10/17/1917 -
[3] KOPP, Gloria Fay d/o Adam & Mary Kopp		12/02/1936 - 03/05/1943
[8] KOPP, Samuel "TEC 5 US ARMY WW 2"		07/10/1915 - 06/09/1974
[7] KREINER, Edward M.		1911 - 1946
Bessie W.		1910 - 19
[6] KREINER, Robert P.		01/28/1919 - 06/10/1952
[5] KREISER, John	63-07-26	05/25/1850 - 01/21/1914
[5] KREISER, Sallie E.	45-09-19	01/16/1874 - 11/05/1919
(G) [1] KREK, Edward	19-00-12	08/05/1835 - 08/17/1854
[4] KROECK, Gladys A.		1930 - 1963

	NAME	AGE	BORN	DIED
[3]	LABER, George	74-01-19	04/03/1773 - 05/22/1847
(G) [3]	LABER, Eva Catharina w/o Georg Laber			
	d/o Leonhard & Dorothea Illig	64 y.10 m.		
		less 3 d.	01/22/1774 - 11/19/1838
(G) [3]	LABER, Catharina d/o Georg & Catharina Laber	18-04-14	11/10/1806 - 03/24/1825
[3]	LABER, Jonas	77-04-13	02/02/1811 - 06/15/1888
[3]	LABER, Sarah w/o Jonas Laber d/o Daniel & Sarah			
	Baumen	33-03-17	02/14/1814 - 06/02/1847
[3]	LABER, Sarah d/o Jonas & Sarah Laber	81-08-26	03/06/1840 - 12/02/1921
(G) [3]	LABER, Martin	85-00-13	08/20/1738 - 09/02/1823
(G) [3]	LABER, Catharina NEE Enck(in)	75-08-02	01/21/1738 - 09/23/1813

        All the above are large ostentatious stones and are
        enclosed by a high iron fence with a four foot wide
        gate on the one side.

	NAME	AGE	BORN	DIED
(G) [1]	LAD(IN), Marya	23 years	1752 - 06/08/1775
[7]	LANDIS, John S.	73-07-10	06/14/1856 - 01/24/1930
	Elizabeth E. w.o John S. Landis	55-07-20	09/08/1858 - 05/28/1914
[7]	LANDIS, Edmund W. s/o John & Elizabeth Landis	27-11-08	04/08/1891 - 03/16/1919
[7]	LANDIS, Elsie W. d/o John S. & Elizabeth Landis	00-08-26	05/23/1897 - 02/17/1898
[7]	LANDIS, Samuel W.		08/15/1888 - 10/22/1955
	Ida L.		03/26/1889 - 03/23/1947
[7]	LANDIS, Roy C. s/o Samuel & Ida Landis	2 days	03/10/1909
[7]	LANDIS, Lester C.	3 days	10/13/1924
[5]	LANDIS, Amos W.		05/20/1885 - 12/09/1971
	Mabel M.H.		04/22/1900 - 07/11/1970
	Infant son, Ralph		No Dates
[7]	LANDIS, Katharine W.		1886 - 1963
[3]	LANDIS, John W.		1893 - 1964
	Mary H.		1889 - 1961
[8]	LAWLER, Michael F. (Charles F. Snyder Funeral-marker)		1941 - 1986
[3]	LAWRENCE, Melvin G.		06/28/1917 -
	Edna O.		01/24/1920 -
[1]	LEAMAN, Isaac L. (Mason Symbol on stone)		1892 - 1979
	Anetta Erb (Eastern Star Symbol on stone)		1897 - 1973
[8]	LEED, Arthur N.		1913 - 1970
	Esther M.		1913 - 1974
[2]	LEEKING, Monroe Z.		11/22/1888 - 10/23/1968
[2]	LEEKING, Sadie H. NEE Steiner	26-08-05	01/27/1892 - 10/02/1918
[2]	LEEKING, Luther S. s/o Monroe & Sadie Leeking	14 days	01/08/1917
[2]	LEH, Carl E. "PFC TROOP D. 11TH CAV. WW II"		1897 - 1957
	Grace F.		1904 - 19
[1]	LEHN, John V.		11/27/1914 - 09/15/1968
	Mary Rose		06/26/1909 - 10/27/1983
[7]	LEIDICH, Rev. Otis O.		03/08/1870 - 02/11/1951
[7]	LEIDICH, Fannie B. Minnich w/o Otis O. Liedich		08/21/1871 - 01/15/1936
[7]	LEIDICH, David R.		01/25/1913 - 03/07/1956
[8]	LEIPHART, Katie		04/02/1092 - 03/03/1985
[8]	LEIPHART, Pvt. Samuel W. "CO. H. 2ND 7TH MARINES"		1923 - 1942
[5]	LEIPPI, Gottleib F.		10/11/1817 - 07/03/1904
[5]	LEIPPI, Kate E.		12/18/1833 - 06/08/1917
[5]	LEIPPI, William F.		11/04/1856 - 03/01/1947
[5]	LEISEY, William M.		1872 - 1946
	Sallie		1874 - 1968
[2]	LEITNER, Alice P. Boyer w/o Harry Leitner		04/03/1880 - 03/14/1928
[2]	LENHERT, Urias	89-09-21	02/08/1830 - 11/29/1919

		NAME	AGE	BORN	DIED
(G)	[1]	LENHERT, Sarah NEE Zartman w/o Urias Lenhert	30-04-16	08/14/1832 -	12/30/1862
(G)	[1]	LENHERT, Ementa d/o Urias & Sarah Lenhert	06-00-01	08/30/1854 -	09/01/1860
(G)	[1]	LENHERT, Issabella d/o Urias & Sarah Lenhert	01-07-16	01/07/1859 -	08/23/1860
(G)	[1]	LENHERT, Infant s/o Urias & Sarah Lenhert	10 days	11/28/1861 -	12/07/1861
	[2]	LENHERT, Rachel	78-00-11	08/08/1839 -	08/19/1917
	[6]	LESHER, Clarence E.		03/19/1899 -	05/28/1961
		Irene M.		03/07/1898 -	06/21/1982
	[6]	LESHER, Clarence E., Jr. "Clem" "			
		"CHIEF WARRANT OFFICER US ARMY AIR CORPS WW II"		10/06/1918 -	08/25/1978
	[1]	LEVERS, Alice	02-10-06	04/27/1868 -	03/03/1871
	[8]	LICHTY, Paul C.		03/18/1901 -	05/05/1986
		Jennie K.		04/20/1900 -	06/28/1983
	[1]	LINGLE, Charley Abner s/o Edward L. & Susan Lingle	24 days	01/02/1893 -	01/26/1893
	[7]	LIPPART, Edward F.		05/01/1905 -	12/16/1960
		Lydia A.		09/22/1920 -	
	[2]	LIVERINGHOUSE, William	56-09-07	01/24/1845 -	10/31/1901
	[2]	LIVERINGHOUSE, Rebecca w/o William Liveringhouse	57-04-27	08/11/1843 -	01/08/1901
	[8]	LONG-DOSTER Large monument with five smaller lettered stones.			
		Includes Herbert & Lillie Doster, Rosa Zentmyer, and			
		Howard & Alice Long.			
	[8]	LONG, Howard A., M.D.	60-11-01	10/15/1872 -	09/14/1933
	[8]	LONG, Alice M., his wife	50-00-17	03/25/1881 -	04/12/1931
	[7]	LONG, James B.		1925 -	
		Edna		1924 -	1975
		James A.		1952 -	1961
	[7]	LOOSE, Alvin E.		07/28/1892 -	06/04/1965
		Ada		06/04/1900 -	
		Marcella E.		01/12/1918 -	
		Marguerite S.		01/16/1919 -	04/17/1939
		Marvin R.		10/17/1942 -	
	[7]	LOOSE, Raymond G.		1907 -	1981
		Irene M.		1907 -	1982
	[7]	LOOSE, Russell E. "Korea 1950-1955" (Spacht Funeral Home-marker)		1936 -	1986
	[5]	LORAH, Miriam M. d/o Charles W. Rettew (On same stone.)		09/29/1919 -	
(G)	[1]	LOWRY, Sarah NEE Illig w/o John Lowry	74-06-04	06/26/1794 -	02/01/1869
(G)	[1]	LORRY, Georg s/o John & Sarah Lorry	19-10-18	10/19/1820 -	09/08/1840
		(Surface of above stone peeling in layers.)			
(G)	[1]	LAURE, Maria NEE Becker(n) w/o John Laure	41-10-10	12/11/1819 -	10/21/1861
(G)	[1]	LAURE, Sarah Amanda d/o John & Mary Laure	03-06-24	07/31/1843 -	02/24/1847
	[2]	LOWRY, George s/o John & Mary Lowry	27- -19	11/11/1845 -	07/30/1873
		(Age as carved on stone. No months!)			
	[1]	LOWRY, Jonathan H.	74-06-14	04/18/1852 -	11/02/1926
		Elizabeth	93-09-24	10/06/1855 -	07/30/1949
	[1]	LOTT, Hannah	23-06-21	04/10/1776 -	10/31/1799
	[6]	LUDWIG, Richard G.		10/26/1910 -	11/26/1979
		Martha M.		08/25/1909 -	03/04/1979
	[1]	LUPOLD, John	61-02-09	11/21/1781 -	01/30/1843
(G)	[1]	LUPOL, Elisab^H (Dates & Age as carved on stone.)	06-11-04	10/08/1817 -	09/12/1828
(G)	[1]	LUPOL, Catarina	02-05-00	07/02/1820 -	12/--/1822
(G)	[1]	LUPOLD, Rahel	01-09-26	09/05/1827 -	07/01/1829
	[1]	LUPOL?, Hannah (Large chip out of stone)	02-02-28	11/??/1828 -	02/11/1831
	[1]	LUPOLD, John (See Eliza Hartz)	29-11-10	02/03/1823 -	01/13/1853
	[1]	LUPOLD, John Samuel s/o John & Eliza Lupold	04-04-17	08/27/1853 -	01/13/1858
	[7]	LUTZ, Mary Alice "Mother" (Dommoyer on back of		1906 -	1978
		Roberta Lorraine "Daughter" this stone.)		1924 -	1927

NAME	AGE	BORN	DIED
[7] LUTZ, Roberta Lorraine d/o Robert & Mary Lutz	02-10-14	1924 –	1927
(This is a small stone)			
[1] LUX, Susanna	46-00-27	04/07/1836 – 05/04/1882	
[1] LUX, Helen	20-01-02	07/06/1873 – 08/08/1893	
[6] LYNN, Daniel L.		12/05/1960 – 12/16/1979	
[1] McCAUSLAND, James (with footstone – J M^{C}C)	63-03-08	10/15/1799 – 01/23/1862	
(G) [1] McCLAUGHLIN, Sarah w/o Henry McClaughlin			
d/o Daniel & Elizabeth Ressler		07/18/1833 –	?
(The above stone was reset and the rest of the			
inscription was buried. Next to Sarah's stone			
is a small stone that is very similar to Sarah's			
stone. On it is "a son born and died 9/9/1860.)			
[1] McCLOUD, Christian with footstone C.M.	about 64 years	No Dates	
(G) [1] McCLURE, Amos		09/19/1815 – 04/22/1820	
[1] McDONNEL, Eliza d/o John & Mary McDonnel	17-03-20		11/19/1826
[1] McTONALD, Peter	15-08-19		07/19/1831
[1] McDANEL, Mary	09-07-19	1818 –	1829
[2] McQUATE, John R. "Father		10/28/1887 – 08/26/1950	
[2] McQUATE, Goldie V. "Daughter"		06/11/1916 – 07/27/1936	
[2] McQUATE, Rodger M. "Son"		01/15/1922 – 02/17/1978	
[2] McQUATE, Richard C. "Son"		02/26/1924 – 09/10/1981	
(The above four stones are in a group.)			
[2] McQUATE, Katie W. "Mother"		1898 –	1963
[2] McQUATE, Fern Arlene d/o Katie McQuate		11/11/1930 – 04/11/1931	
[2] McQUATE, Grace L. d/o Katie McQuate		10/14/1933 – 04/25/1936	
(The above three stones are in a group.)			
Initial Stones: [1] J.M., [1] S.M.			
[8] MACE, Samuel	29-10-03	07/09/1877 – 05/12/1907	
[2] MACE, Martin		1902 –	1955
Alice M. NEE Smith		1908 –	1960
[2] MACE, Martin, Jr.		06/15/1940 – 03/01/1986	
Audrey A.		06/05/1942 –	
Debra K.		12/29/1959 – 09/21/1981	
[2] MADLEM, Paul L.		12/13/1897 – 01/14/1980	
Emma L.		05/20/1900 – 01/09/1981	
[1] MARKS, John	88-04-25	01/01/1800 – 05/26/1888	
[1] MARKS, Anna	68-09-08	02/28/1801 – 12/06/1869	
[5] MARKS, Alfred	67-11-07	10/14/1832 – 09/21/1900	
[5] MARKS, Maria w/o Alfred Marks	75-06-11	06/26/1835 – 02/16/1911	
[5] MARKS, Harriet d/o Alfred & Maria Marks	23-08-19	03/17/1854 – 12/06/1877	
[5] MARKS, Nathaniel s/o Alfred & Maria Marks	12-09-16	07/03/1857 – 04/19/1870	
[5] MARKS, John	74-07-24	12/13/1833 – 08/07/1908	
[5] MARKS, Sarah	76-03-26	06/24/1837 – 10/20/1913	
[1] MARKS, Isabella d/o John & Sarah Marks	01-02-23	07/22/1860 – 10/17/1861	
[5] MARKS, William N.	79-02-23	10/07/1839 – 12/30/1918	
[5] MARKS, Mary N. w/o William N. Marks	63-09-16	06/03/1841 – 03/19/1905	
[5] MARKS, John Galbreath s/o William & Mary Marks	01-09-00	12/05/1875 – 09/05/1877	
[5] MARKS, Charles G.		1862 –	1948
Emma Z.		1863 –	1932
[5] MARKS, John G.	67-00-07	05/28/1875 – 06/04/1942	
Sarah M.	80-08-07	08/26/1869 – 05/03/1950	

		NAME	AGE	BORN	DIED
	[2]	MARKS, Howard		1902 –	1973
		Mamie E.		1890 –	1936
	[5]	MARTZALL, Infant d/o _____ & Mar__			01/28/1889
(G)	[1]	MATTHEWS, Sarah d/o Joseph & Anna Matthews	68-08-02	04/08/1796 –	12/10/1864
	[2]	MATTHEWS, John D.		1838 –	1911
		Lydia Douple, his wife		1839 –	1936
(G)	[1]	MATTHEWS, Jerome s/o John & Lydia L. Matthews	00-07-25	08/08/1860 –	04/02/1861
	[2]	MATTHEWS, William I.		10/20/1869 –	05/23/1959
		Frances R., his wife		04/03/1876 –	09/15/1953
	[1]	MATTHEWS, Walter s/o W.I. & Frances B. Matthews	4 days		12/08/1892
	[1]	MATTHEWS, Elsie E. d/o W.I. & Frances Matthews	02-06-25	04/29/1901 –	11/24/1903
	[2]	MATTHEWS, Charles D.		07/02/1877 –	07/01/1960
	[1]	MAYBERRY, Gane (spelling as on stone)	25-01-16	02/03/1765 –	03/19/1790
(G)	[1]	MUCKE, Mathias s/o Christian & Catharine Mücke	13-02-22		12/23/1832
	[2]	MECK, Samuel B. "Father"	76-04-13	07/18/1840 –	12/01/1916
	[1]	MECK, Susanna NEE Miller "Mother"	75-05-08	10/23/1837 –	03/31/1913
(G)	[1]	MECK, Jacob	09-10-18	11/21/1837 –	10/18/1846
	[3]	MECK, Annie L. (On Steinmetz monument)	74-02-11		08/19/1912
	[2]	MECK, Samuel M.	58-10-17	1874 –	1933
	[2]	MECK, Ezra M.	63-07-28	1877 –	1940
	[2]	MECK, John Ezra	00-06-03		09/06/1913
(G)	[1]	MEILI(N), Biena "Born in Warwick"	30 y.8 m.		
		(This stone is mended and very worn.)	3 w.3 d.	11/08/1756 –	08/01/1787
(G)	[1]	MEILY, Jacob	70-04-00	10/--/1773 –	02/03/1844
(G)	[1]	MEILE, Matthäus	83 yrs.	1783 –	10/23/1866
(G)	[1]	MEILE, Maria Sophia NEE Armbrister w/o Matthäus			
		Meile	79-03-06	11/20/1784 –	03/06/1864
(G)	[1]	MAILE, Eilsabeth d/o M. Maile & wife M.	22-03-20	10/01/1812 –	01/21/1835
	[5]	MEILEY, Mathias A.		1820 –	1908
	[5]	MEILEY, Anna w/o Mathias Meiley	41 yrs.	05/21/1829 –	05/21/1870
	[1]	MEILEY, Faras G. s/o Mathias & Anna Meiley	05-00-20	12/26/1854 –	01/16/1860
	[1]	MEILEY, Hariet d/o Mathias & Anna Meiley	03-04-16	11/01/1859 –	03/20/1863
	[1]	MEILEY, Levantine C. d/o Mathias & Anna Meiley	06-07-22	06/02/1857 –	01/24/1864
	[5]	MEILEY, Ezra M. s/o Mathias & Anna Meiley	13-11-14	05/17/1862 –	04/04/1876
	[5]	MEILEY, Lizzie d/o Mathias & Anna Meiley	00-09-23		02/03/1871
	[1]	MEILE, Catharine		05/22/1847 –	05/14/1849
	[8]	MILEY, Mary	75 yrs.	06/06/1847 –	06/06/1922
	[1]	MEILEY, Uriah		06/19/1849 –	07/19/1849
	[1]	MEILEY, Peter		10/24/1850 –	01/27/1852
	[7]	MEILEY, George Z.		03/02/1878 –	06/03/1925
		Katie B.		11/14/1884 –	05/29/1956
	[1]	MILEY, John Z.		1889 –	1956
		Laura F.		1892 –	1967
	[2]	MEILEY, Infant s/o Addison M. & Lizzie K. Meiley		Born & Died	11/01/1892
	[1]	MEISKY, Franklin s/o David & Mary Meisky	01-05-00	03/17/1855 –	08/16/1856
	[1]	MEASKY, Harriet R. w/o Henry S. Measky	22-03-02	01/25/1856 –	04/27/1878
	[7]	MEISKEY, Abraham S. "Father"	79-11-18	1858 –	1938
	[7]	MEISKEY, Catharine H. "Mother"	68-03-12	1862 –	1930
	[7]	MEISKEY, Harry W. "Son"	77-10-28	1880 –	1958
	[7]	MEISKEY, Arthur W. "Son"	94-01-20	1882 –	1977
	[7]	MEISKEY, Charles W. "Son"	70-01-25	1886 –	1956
	[5]	MELLINGER, Henry	43-03-02	04/13/1844 –	07/15/1887
	[5]	MELLINGER, Hannah O.	87-01-08	01/02/1846 –	02/10/1933
	[5]	MELLINGER, Susan E. d/o Henry & Hannah O. Mellinger	16-07-08	01/25/1873 –	09/03/1889
	[5]	MELLINGER, Maggie E. d/o Henry & Hannah O.	22-04-03	05/20/1883 –	09/23/1905

		NAME	AGE	BORN	DIED
	[7]	MELLINGER, Rolandus	47-10-26	06/04/1875 - 04/30/1923	
		Katie M.		02/01/1885 -	No Date
	[8]	MELLINGER, Anna Kopp "Mother"		02/19/1905 - 08/14/1965	
(G)	[1]	MENGEL, Maria	57-04-21	12/29/1784 - 05/19/1842	
(G)	[1]	MENTZER, Sara NEE Scherb	24-04-07	08/02/1811 - 12/10/1835	
	[9]	MENTZER, Alverta Z. (Shares stone with Anna Zeller)		1908 -	
	[1]	MESSNER, Maria w/o Joel Messner (Stone very worn)		02/12/18?? - 08/31/18??	
(G)	[1]	MESSNER, Catharina d/o Joel & Maria Messner		03/02/1840	
(G)	[1]	MESSNER, Maria d/o Joel & Maria Messner	05-03-10		03/24/1850
	[2]	MESSNER, Charles (C. Stanley Eckenroth, Funeral Director, Terre Hill, PA Funeral home marker-no stone)	75-11-24		10/29/1985
	[2]	MESSNER, Dorothy I.		1915 -	1964
		Charles, Jr.		1935 -	1935
	[3]	METZLER, Abram H.		06/11/1875 - 07/17/1949	
		Clara K. NEE Zartman		06/12/1879 - 10/27/1974	
	[5]	METZLER, Clyde Z.		04/07/1907 -	
		Dorothy M.		05/11/1907 -	
(G)	[1]	MILLER, Jacob	70 y.10 m. 2 wks.	01/12/1733 - 11/26/1803	
(G)	[1]	MILLER, Leonhard	68-09-00	12/--/1738 - 09/11/1807	
(G)	[1]	MILLER, Margaretha NEE Stober w/o Leonhard Miller	82-06-02	03/20/1748 - 09/22/1830	
(G)	[1]	MILLER, Christoph	71-02-29	07/16/1744 - 10/14/1815	
(G)	[1]	MILLER, Barbara w/o Christoph Miller (Age & dates as carved on stone)	52 y.2 w. 6 days.	09/28/1752 - 10/18/1805	
(G)	[1]	MÜLLER, _athar. NEE Stober (Stone very eroded)	25-04-??	07/26/1750 - 12/09/1774	
(G)	[1]	MILLER(N), Barbara	25 y.1 m. 2 w.1 d.	07/20/1770 - 09/04/1795	
(G)	[1]	MILLER, Jacob	71-02-01	02/18/1771 - 04/19/1842	
(G)	[1]	MILLER, Leonhard	22-07-01	02/03/1772 - 09/04/1794	
(G)	[1]	MILLER, Johannes	69-08-10	06/24/1774 - 03/04/1844	
(G)	[1]	MILLER(IN), Susana	20 y.6 m. 3 w.2 d.	04/23/1774 - 11/16/1794	
(G)	[1]	MILLER, Georg	16 days	12/08/1777 - 12/24/1777	
	[1]	MILLER, Christiana	80-09-28	01/01/1778 - 10/29/1858	
(G)	[1]	MILLER, Susanna	47-02-03	03/12/1779 - 05/15/1826	
(G)	[1]	MILLER, Leonhard	73-04-02	05/16/1780 - 09/18/1853	
(G)	[1]	MILLER, Eve Catharina w/o Leonhard Miller	81-07-20	03/01/1780 - 10/21/1861	
(G)	[1]	MILLER, Daniel s/o Leonhard & Eva Miller	15-03-01		07/28/1826
(G)	[1]	MILLER, Elias s/o Leonhard & Eva Miller	01-06-28		08/31/1816
(G)	[1]	MILLER, Leonhard s/o Leonhard & Eva Miller	01-06-08		05/27/1820
(G)	[1]	MILLER, Susanna d/o Leonhard & Eva Miller	08-00-18		10/12/1829
(G)	[1]	MILLER, Infant d/o Leonhard & Eva Miller		Born & Died	02/03/1822
(G)	[1]	MILLER, Georg	33-04-23	06/26/1783 - 11/18/1816	
(G)	[1]	MILLER, Catharine w/o George Miller	77-03-28	08/20/1779 - 12/18/1856	
(G)	[1]	MILLER, Georg s/o Georg & Catarina Miller	01-02-01	04/10/1816 - 06/11/1817	
(G)	[1]	MILLER, Anna	42 y. less 7 days	11/08/1783 - 11/01/1825	
(G)	[1]	MILLER, Christoph	80-04-04	07/26/1786 - 11/30/1866	
(G)	[1]	MILLER, Anna NEE Wolf w/o Christopher Miller	60-01-10	02/02/1790 - 03/12/1850	
	[1]	MILLER, Anna d/o Christopher & Anna Miller	63-00-14	08/23/1819 - 09/07/1882	
(G)	[1]	MILLER, Salome d/o Christop & Anna Miller	51-01-01	07/28/1813 - 08/29/1861	
	[3]	MILLER, Jacob s/o Jacob & Christina Miller		11/29/1789 - 12/22/1879	
		Elizabeth w/o Jacob Miller d/o James & Susannah Huston	46-05-27	08/02/1791 - 01/29/1838	

		NAME	AGE	BORN	DIED
	[3]	MILLER, Caroline H. d/o Jacob S. & Elizabeth Miller	20-01-08	08/12/1829	09/20/1849
(G)	[1]	MILLER, Samuel	46-08-26	07/14/1791	04/09/1838
(G)	[1]	MILLER, Hannah w/o Samuel Miller (She was married a second time to George Scherb.)	66-10-??	07/17/1795	05/23/1862
(G)	[1]	MILLER, Ladia d/o Samuel & Hanna Miller	01-01-13	05/25/1821	07/08/1822
(G)	[1]	MILLER, Henrich	25-02-14	01/29/1792	04/16/1817
(G)	[1]	MILLER, George	62-10-29	03/03/1803	02/01/1866
	[1]	MILLER, Barbara NEE Houser w/o George Miller	76-01-09	11/18/1799	12/27/1875
(G)	[1]	MILLER, George s/o George & Barbara Miller	18-10-12	09/05/1839	07/07/1858
(G)	[1]	MILLER, Catharina	14-10-23	05/11/1799	03/06/1814
	[3]	MILLER, Samuel	77-11-08	10/23/1803	10/01/1881
		Margaret NEE Weachter w/o Samuel Miller	80-03-18	06/15/1801	10/03/1881
	[1]	MILLER, John (Stone very worn)	77-07-25	03/16/1805	??/??/1833
(G)	[1]	MILLER, Susanna w/o John Miller	??-06-17	10/11/1805	04/28/1861
(G)	[1]	MILLER, John B. s/o John & Susanna Miller	25-05-26	09/13/1841	05/09/1867
		(Age and dates as carved on stone.)			
(G)	[1]	MILLER, Elisabeth	02-06-01	02/21/1809	08/22/1811
	[1]	MILLER, Leah	83-00-26	01/24/1810	02/20/1893
	[1]	MILLER, Mary	82-07-26	10/27/1811	06/23/1894
(G)	[1]	MILLER, Edward	00-02-01	01/13/1812	03/14/1812
	[3]	MILLER, Samuel H.	61-05-26	05/28/1813	11/24/1874
	[3]	MILLER, Harriet w/o Samuel H. Miller	23-00-12	11/11/1826	11/23/1849
		Albert W. s/o S.H. & Harriet Miller	00-02-19		08/23/1849
	[3]	MILLER, Anna	89-00-07		02/10/1914
	[3]	MILLER, Amanda E. d/o Samuel H. & Anna Miller	04-11-25	06/12/1857	06/07/1862
	[1]	MILLER, Moses	88-08-16	07/19/1816	04/05/1905
	[1]	MILLER, Margaret w/o Moses Miller	85-08-28	10/26/1816	07/24/1902
(G)	[1]	MILLER, Emma d/o Moses & Margaret Miller	11-04-21	07/09/1851	11/30/1862
	[1]	MILLER, David	81-01-07	04/04/1817	05/11/1898
	[1]	MILLER, Maria w/o David Miller	69-03-26	10/17/1817	02/13/1887
(G)	[1]	MILLER, George s/o David & Maria Miller	02-00-26	07/30/1854	08/25/1856
(G)	[1]	MILLER, Peter s/o David & Maris Miller	00-04-27	04/11/1856	09/07/1856
(G)	[1]	MILLER, Harrison s/o David & Maria Miller	01-03-01	12/10/1858	03/11/1860
(G)	[1]	MILLER, Anna "Died in the year 1817"			1817
(G)	[1]	MILLER, Salome	00-01-11	11/28/1818	01/08/1819
(G)	[1]	MILLER, Lea "Died in the year 1820"			1820
	[1]	MILLER, Rebecca d/o Samuel & Christina Weidman w/o Jonas Miller	26-02-12		05/29/1849
(G)	[1]	MILLER(IN), Maria Anna	02-09-13	10/16/1824	07/30/1826
(G)	[1]	MILLER, Infant d/o Peter Miller "Died in the year 1825"			1825
	[1]	MILLER, Samuel W.	72-09-10	05/12/1825	02/22/1898
	[1]	MILLER, Elizabeth Eberly w/o Samuel W. Miller	73-08-26	12/14/1825	09/10/1899
	[3]	MILLER, John W.	82-06-00	02/28/1828	08/28/1910
	[3]	MILLER, Mary B. w/o John W. Miller	82-02-17	06/22/1817	09/10/1899
	[1]	MILLER, Lydia	73-00-25	10/14/1828	11/09/1901
	[1]	MILLER, Isaac	52-05-06	10/21/1826	03/27/1889
	[3]	MILLER, Curtis	79-03-09		04/15/1915
	[3]	MILLER, Cassandra	82-10-25		08/22/1921
	[3]	MILLER, Edwin R. s/o Curtis & Cassandra Miller	23-08-03	08/17/1858	04/20/1882
	[3]	MILLER, Ann Mary d/o Curtis & Cassandra Miller			08/11/1868
(G)	[1]	MILLER, Mary E. d/o Peter C. & Sophea Miller	??-08-19	12/13/1844	09/02/1852
(G)	[1]	MILLER, Catharina d/o Peter & Sophia Miller	??-??-??	04/21/1847	09/02/1848
	[2]	MILLER, Israel E.	84-11-29	09/02/1847	09/01/1932
	[2]	MILLER, Caroline B. NEE Mellinger	62-03-07	06/18/1852	09/25/1914
	[2]	MILLER, Lizzie Diora d/o Israel E. & Caroline B. Miller	15-03-07	05/10/1873	08/17/1888

		NAME	AGE	BORN	DIED
	[1]	MILLER, Susanna	68-08-02	11/03/1848 - 07/05/1917	
(G)	[1]	MILLER, Elisabeth C. d/o Johann & Maria Miller	02-06-03		09/21/1853
	[3]	MILLER, Samuel E.		08/15/1853 - 10/30/1927	
		Emma A., his wife		01/21/1858 - 02/23/1932	
	[1]	MILLER, Harriet (Same base as Fianna Eichelberger)	63-07-03	07/19/1853 - 02/22/1917	
(G)	[1]	MILLER, Licy Ann d/o Isaac & Herriet Miller	1 day	12/27/1866 - 12/28/1866	
(G)	[1]	MILLER, John H. s/o Isaac & Herriet Miller	3 days	12/27/1866 - 12/30/1866	
	[1]	MILLER, Earas s/o Isaac & Kate Miller	20 days	11/25/1868 - 12/15/1868	
	[3]	MILLER, Bertha D.	22-01-16		01/08/1904
	[8]	MILLER, William E.		1885 - 1957	
		Lillian G.		1897 - 1959	
		Jay D. "1ST SGT. US ARMY 1941-1945"		1917 - 1982	
		O. Eileen		1926 -	
	[3]	MILLER, Margaret Kline		04/19/1890 - 11/03/1966	
	[8]	MILLER, Charles K.		04/05/1891 - 05/02/1980	
		Minnie M.		02/02/1894 - 05/14/1965	
	[7]	MILLER, Ida		1894 - 1965	
	[5]	MILLER, Charlie W.		1901 - 1962	
	[1]	MILLER, Mae (Clausen Funeral Home marker)		1910 - 1981	
	[7]	MILLER, Carolyn (Shares stone with Howard Palm)		07/08/1921 -	
	[1]	MILLER, William C. (Clausen Funeral Home marker)		1927 - 1986	
	[1]	MILLER, Howard J.		07/09/1931 - 09/15/1978	
	[8]	MILLER, Robert C., Jr. "Pennsylvania, MM 1 US NAVY"		04/26/1938 - 12/17/1965	
	[5]	MILLER, Ralph J. (Clausen Funeral Home marker that is coming apart.)		1959 - 1967	
	[8]	MILLHOUSE, Roy W.		12/02/1911 -	
		Esta B.		11/18/1915 - 09/15/1971	
	[7]	MISHLER, John W.		1855 - 1923	
		Amelia D.		1866 - 1939	
	[9]	MOHLER, R. Donald		1932 - 1975	
		Erla J.		1933 -	
	[9]	MOHLER, Darbi M. (Spacht Funeral Home marker)		1981 - 1981	
	[1]	MOYER, Jacob	79-03-06	11/22/1804 - 02/28/1884	
	[5]	MOYER, John E.		1829 - 1898	
		Elizabeth M.		1841 - 1929	
	[5]	MOYER, Magdalena w/o Theadore Moyer	78-01-18	02/18/1830 - 04/06/1908	
	[1]	MOYER, William s/o Lydia Nixon "Born in Tulpehocken Berks County"	25-06-25	11/02/1826 - 06/19/1852	
	[2]	MOYER, Jacob E.		11/21/1844 - 01/23/1920	
		Mary McCloud, his wife		07/18/1845 - 04/18/1923	
	[8]	MOYER, Samuel E.		02/04/1848 - 04/20/1926	
	[8]	MOYER, Hettie C. w/o Samuel E. Moyer	57-07-04	06/02/1848 - 01/06/1906	
	[2]	MOYER, Allen		09/20/1859 - 11/16/1944	
	[2]	MOYER, Joanna		09/20/1861 - 11/12/1963	
	[5]	MOYER, Thomas M.		1870 - 1918	
		Elizabeth		1874 - 1949	
	[3]	MOYER, Samuel		1877 - 1942	
	[3]	MOYER, John		1880 - 1959	
	[3]	MOYER, Harry C.		10/23/1885 - 01/27/1940	
	[8]	MOYER, Lizzie Dulabone		1899 - 1945	
	[1]	MOYER, Elmer		03/01/1900 - 06/09/1975	
		Jessie M.		03/23/1909 - 10/19/1983	
	[5]	MOYER, Clarence C. "PVT. CO. K 1ST CWS TRNG REGT. WW II"		11/04/1902 - 06/19/1959	
		Louella S.		09/13/1903 - 10/02/1981	
	[1]	MOYER, Frank		01/02/1908 - 05/08/1986	

	NAME	AGE	BORN	DIED
[4]	MOYER, Pauline M. (Buch Funeral Home marker)		1913 –	1986
(G) [1]	MÜKSCH, Elisabeth d/o William & M___ (Very worn)	??-??-??	12/16/1830 – 07/26/1831	
[3]	MYER, Eliza Kline	83-11-25	04/21/1833 – 04/16/1917	
[1]	NAGEL, Marks	74 years	1738 – 10/06/1812	
[1]	NAUGEL, Henry	34 y.3 w.		
		2 d.	01/03/1776 – 01/25/1804	
[3]	NAGEL, Elizabeth NEE Gephard (Stone reset-death			
	from earlier record.)		09/23/1776 – 11/30/1794	
[1]	NEIL, Margaret (Very small stone)	72 years		10/__/1860
[7]	NESSINGER, Clara	51-04-11		05/04/1923
[1]	NESSINGER, Jennie		1904 –	1983
[7]	NETZLEY, Henry U.		02/17/1881 – 11/14/1936	
	Emma		11/01/1875 – 07/24/1959	
[7]	NETZLEY, Charles		06/13/1893 – 08/21/1948	
	Fannie		11/16/1892 – 04/08/1978	
[7]	NETZLEY, Isaac	No Age		03/31/1913
[7]	NETZLEY, Elsie d/o Charles & Fannie Netzley		02/17/1925 – 04/29/1925	
[2]	NEWCOMER, Ralph D.		1899 –	1983
	Margareta M.		1901 –	1966
[2]	NISSLY, Christian H.		1903 –	1955
	Frances R.		1904 –	
[4]	NISSLEY, Rufus H.		1911 –	
	Mabel C.		1911 –	1985
[7]	NIXDORF, Edward S.		1880 –	1960
	Elva G.		1896 –	1983
[1]	NIXON, Joseph	71-09-20	01/23/1792 – 11/12/1863	
[1]	NIXON, Lydia w/o Joseph Nixon	76-00-16	08/06/1807 – 08/22/1883	
[5]	NIXON, Robert	75-03-28	10/10/1804 – 02/08/1880	
[5]	NIXON, Catharine w/o Robert Nixon	83-09-26	04/28/1817 – 02/24/1901	
[8]	NOLT, Harry E.	34-05-23	06/12/1884 – 12/05/1918	
	Alice P. NEE Ditzler		06/30/1887 – 01/24/1970	
[8]	NOLT, Helen E. d/o Harry & Alice Nolt	00-04-13		09/11/1909
[8]	NOLT, Doris G.		08/10/1918 – 04/21/1935	
[5]	OBER, Harvey P.		09/27/1904 – 09/13/1981	
	Elsie S.		12/24/1901 –	
[7]	OBER, Lloyd, B. "Father"		1905 –	1970
	Edna F. "Mother"		1901 –	
[7]	OBER, L. Carl "Son"		1944 –	
[2]	OBER, David R.		1905 –	1972
	Mildred I.		1908 –	1969
[1]	OLD, James		10/16/1773 – 05/10/1777	
[2]	PAGE, Shirley R. NEE Ober "Mother"		07/08/1932 – 04/16/1967	
[2]	PAGE, Angela M. "Daughter"		05/07/1964 – 04/16/1967	
[2]	BOOKER, Thomas J. "Son"		09/25/1957 – 04/16/1967	
[2]	BOOKER, David G. "Son"		07/12/1962 – 04/16/1967	
	(The above four are all on one stone. They all died			
	in a house fire in the Midwest and were returned here			
	for burial.)			
[5]	PAINTER, John R.	46-00-19	05/10/1857 – 05/29/1903	
[5]	PAINTER, Catherine	77-03-04	04/10/1858 – 07/14/1935	
[5]	PAINTER, Edgar s/o John & Kate Painter	02-09-22	06/11/1880 – 04/03/1883	
[3]	PALM, William R.	67-04-17	09/10/1837 – 01/27/1905	
[3]	PALM, Elizabeth w/o William R. Palm	54-09-22	01/16/1840 – 11/08/1894	
[3]	PALM, William H.	36-03-12	11/01/1866 – 02/13/1903	
	Ada Alice NEE Fetter	84-05-04	09/23/1870 – 02/27/1955	

NAME	AGE	BORN	DIED
[3] PALM, Ralph Z. s/o Wm. & Alice Palm	00-02-08		06/22/1892
[3] PALM, Mary Ann	00-11-07	10/07/1900 -	09/14/1901
(Ralph and Mary Ann are beside each other.)			
[3] PALM, Jacob C.	75-05-05	03/21/1871 -	08/26/1947
Clara J.	52-08-06	01/31/1871 -	10/07/1923
[3] PALM, Elam B. s/o Jacob C. & Clara Palm			
"PVT. CO. I. 4TH INF., 3RD. DIV."	22-01-12	05/16/1896 -	06/28/1918
[7] PALM, Edwill F.		01/08/1893 -	08/03/1978
Maybelle W.		09/04/1899 -	
[7] PALM, William H. s/o Edwill & Maybell Palm		09/20/1915 -	05/22/1925
[2] PALM, Harry W. "CPL. CO. E 316 INF. A.E.F."		01/03/1896 -	04/03/1932
Mary		09/18/1900 -	
[3] PALM, Harry B.		04/29/1899 -	02/21/1970
Ella Mae		09/12/1898 -	08/23/1986
[7] PALM, Howard (Shares stone with Carolyn Miller)		07/26/1916 -	12/27/1978
[1] PARKE, John	27 years		03/07/1799

[1] PARKE, John   "Reader whom pious Curiosity
        has led to view the Sacred
        record of the Silent grave
        Stay not the soft tribute
        of a tear o're this Stone."
        Rais'd to the Memory
        of John Park
        who died March 7,
        1799.
(Stone has been reset and no age shows. F.E. Schnerer

NAME	AGE	BORN	DIED
[5] PARSON, Elsie E. Eberly w/o Wm. E. Parson	34-09-06	12/30/1881 -	10/06/1916
[8] PARSON, William F.		04/02/1914 -	12/07/1986
Ellen E.		05/30/1915 -	05/14/1966
[1] PETERS, Jacob	59-08-04	02/22/1789 -	11/26/1848
[1] PETER, Barbara w/o Jacob Peter	84-01-14	01/11/1788 -	02/25/1872
[1] PETER, Sarah d/o Willm. & Leah Peter	06-02-26	10/30/1843 -	01/25/1850
[1] PETER, William s/o William & Leah Peter	01-09-01	01/16/1847 -	10/17/1848
[2] PETERS, Frank		12/21/1880 -	12/25/1970
Sadie		05/19/1883 -	12/05/1926
[2] PETERS, Robert	6 mnths.		06/19/1924
[7] PETTICOFFER, Henry B.		01/22/1906 -	07/19/1932
Esther R.		11/01/1911 -	
[2] PHILLIPPI, John H.	70-00-09		06/19/1906
[2] PHILLIPPI, S. Amanda	57-01-21		12/14/1897
[2] PHILLIPPI, Laura d/o John H. & Sarah A. Phillippi	03-11-23	02/03/1864 -	01/26/1868
[9] PHILLIPS, Clifford		1903 -	1987
Grace R.		1903 -	1975
[1] PIET, Eliza d/o Peter H. & Ann Piet	17th yr.		02/03/1825
[7] PIFER, William F.		1855 -	1934
Catharine R.		1859 -	1937
Harvey A.		1881 -	1957
Amanda W.		1882 -	1962
[1] POKE, Elisabeth	17-05-07	03/18/1822 -	08/25/1839
[7] POTTEIGER, Consuela Hoffer w/o David Potteiger		01/30/1896 -	12/09/1918
[7] POTTEIGER, John David s/o David & Consuelo Potteiger		03/25/1918 -	05/25/1918
[7] PREIS, Carrie D. Boyer w/o John C. Preis	40-09-00	02/23/1869 -	11/23/1909
[7] PRITZ, Gerald S. "Father"		1876 -	1930
[1] RANCK, Jacob	67-08-07	07/08/1811 -	03/15/1879
(G) [1] RANCK, Catharina	81-02-13	03/20/1810 -	06/03/1891

		NAME	AGE	BORN	DIED
(G)	[1]	RAUP, Maria	10-05-10	11/01/1818 – 04/10/1829	
	[7]	REBER, Pierce		09/25/1869 – 07/20/1950	
		Emeline NEE Eckert		10/19/1871 – 03/15/1967	
	[7]	REBER, Josephine M.		07/15/1899 – 12/30/1968	
	[2]	REIDER, John Y.	60-10-08	1871 – 1932	
		Lizzie E.	78-02-00	1876 – 1955	
	[2]	REIDER, Virgie H. d/o John & Lizzie Reider	12-09-25	11/17/1905 – 09/12/1918	
	[2]	REIDER, Sylvester "U.S.A. WW II"	70-02-04	01/01/1898 – 03/05/1968	
	[2]	REIDER, Stella w/o Sylvester Reider	23-07-27	02/15/1895 – 10/12/1918	
	[1]	REIDER, Daughters of John L. & Mary E. Reider			
		Sallie Mae		1941 – 1942	
		Mary Joyce		1947 – 1948	
	[1]	REIDER, Robert W. (Shares stone with Harvey, Alice,			
		& Elva Heberling.)		1945 – 1963	
(G)	[1]	REIFSNYDER, Benjamin	75-05-06	10/06/1784 – 03/12/1860	
	[8]	REIFSNYER–Large monument on slight round mound with			
		five smaller lettered stones which include			
		the following::			
		Henry H. Reifsnyder		1863 – 1951	
		Lizzie A. Reifsnyder		1863 – 1918	
		Nathan K. Reifsnyder		1887 – 1912	
		Lottie A. Reifsnyder		1890 – 1904	
		Henry M. Reifsnyder		1895 – 1896	
	[8]	REIFSNYDER–Large monument with three smaller lettered			
		stones which include the following:			
		Harvey K. Reifsnyder		1884 – 1978	
		Agnes Burkholder		1887 – 1949	
		Freemont B. Reifsnyder		1914 –	
	[8]	REIFSNYDER, Phares K.		02/19/1883 – 03/15/1971	
		Anna M.		07/25/1893 – 07/15/1969	
	[8]	REIFSNYDER, Arden P.		10/11/1902 – 08/12/1981	
		Christine K.		05/10/1905 – 02/21/1986	
	[8]	REIFSNYDER, Alton M.		03/28/1906 – 02/25/1978	
		Carrie S.		06/17/1912 –	
	[7]	REIST, Abraham B.		09/20/1851 – 04/06/1919	
	[7]	REIST, Arthur K.		01/09/1878 – 02/28/1962	
		Amanda NEE Kline		04/04/1879 – 02/06/1931	
	[8]	RENNINGER, Wayne W.		1887 – 1973	
		Elizabeth		1892 – 1950	
	[1]	RESSLER, Susanna	79-09-16	04/22/1806 – 02/08/1886	
	[8]	RESSLER, Harry H.		06/26/1885 – 09/23/1972	
		Sadie D.		09/23/1887 – 10/10/1947	
	[3]	RESSLER, Ira B.		05/01/1900 – 04/16/1985	
		Minerva E.		09/08/1903 –	
	[8]	RETTEW, John H.		02/26/1885 – 09/05/1962	
		Mary D.		09/20/1885 – 11/13/1964	
	[5]	RETTEW, Charles W. father of Mirian M. Lorah		02/02/1893 – 05/23/1975	
		(Shares stone with daughter.)			
	[8]	RETTEW, Lester E.		11/10/1908 –	
		Anna Mary		04/08/1910 – 02/13/1983	
	[8]	RETTEW, Dorothy Mae		07/13/1929 – 04/15/1930	
	[1]	RHOADS, Keziah d/o William & Sarah Rhoads	00-11-02	07/31/1848	
	[1]	RHOADS, Henrietta d/o Wm. & Sarah (Stone very worn)		??/??/???? – ??/??/1845	
	[3]	RITTER, Paul B.		1907 – 1982	
		Bertha M.		1904 –	

		NAME	AGE	BORN	DIED
	[1]	ROBESON, Samuel L.	39-06-08		04/28/1836
	[1]	ROBESON, Margaret Coleman d/o Samuel L & Christianna Robeson	8 mnths.		02/21/1833
	[7]	ROCK, Harvey O.		04/17/1880 -	02/26/1948
		Ursula B., his wife		06/12/1878 -	02/12/1964
	[7]	ROCK, Elmer H.		01/16/1902 -	11/12/1978
		Anna J.		07/03/1901 -	
	[1]	ROEHRER, Ludwig	76-07-21	05/15/1769 -	01/05/1846
	[1]	ROEHRER, Margaret w/o Ludwig Roehrer	76-08-25	01/05/1780 -	09/30/1856
	[8]	ROHRER, Benjamin L.	58-01-02	11/18/1864 -	12/20/1922
		C. Louisa	61-03-09	09/15/1871 -	12/24/1932
	[8]	ROHRER, Robert Earl	00-09-14		01/03/1919
	[8]	ROHRER, Harold Dale		Born & Died	10/15/1941
	[1]	ROETHER, Daniel	65-05-11	03/15/1797 -	08/26/1862
	[1]	ROETHER, Mary w/o Daniel Roether	71-00-18	03/24/1797 -	04/11/1868
(G)	[1]	ROETHER, William s/o Daniel & Maria Roether	28-02-23	08/04/1821 -	10/27/1840
(G)	[1]	ROMIG, Henrich	67-09-07	03/21/1776 -	12/27/1843
(G)	[1]	ROMIG, Catharine w/o Henry Romig	86-04-18	03/20/1774 -	08/08/1860
(G)	[1]	ROMIG, Susanna NEE Weidman w/o Henrich Romig	47-06-20	03/05/1798 -	09/25/1845
	[1]	ROMIG, Margaretta w/o Jacob Romig	36 years	08/07/1820 -	08/07/1856
	[1]	ROMIG, Sarah d/o Jacob & Margaretta Romig	01-02-08	05/24/1855 -	08/01/1856
	[5]	ROMIG, William	84-06-14	03/06/1842 -	09/20/1926
		Catharine O. NEE Elser	82-10-23	07/28/1843 -	06/21/1926
	[1]	ROSE, James M. "Son"		1968 -	1969
		Louis M. "Son"		1970 -	1970
	[8]	ROSHORN, George	72-06-03	1860 -	1933
		Amanda	81-02-20	1858 -	1940
	[8]	ROSHORN, David D. s/o Geo. & Amanda Roshorn	29-03-24	07/03/1889 -	10/27/1918
	[1]	ROSSEL, James	27 years	07/02/1804 -	07/02/1831
	[6]	RUHL, Allen R.		10/01/1883 -	09/24/1972
		Marie J.		04/24/1889 -	02/04/1951
	[8]	RUHL, Samuel		1893 -	1957
		Nettie M.		1894 -	1976
	[6]	RUHL, Cloyd W., Sr.		08/28/1915 -	05/14/1982
		Grace R.		07/17/1918 -	
	[6]	RUHL, Raymond H.		1917 -	1984
		Pauline E.		1922 -	
	[6]	RUHL, John W.		10/22/1916 -	03/17/1984
	[6]	RUHL, Allen W.		1918 -	1967
	[9]	RUHL, Robert E.		02/15/1935 -	
		Janet Y.		12/11/1935 -	08/14/1975
	[6]	RUHL, Jay R. (Double stone-other half empty)		09/20/1940 -	07/23/1981
	[8]	RUTH, Miles E.		1906 -	
		S. Alvera		1914 -	
	[7]	RUTH, children of Miles & Alverta S. Ruth			
		Aaron G.		08/04/1939 -	01/02/1940
		Stillborn Son		08/08/1936	

INITIAL STONES: [1] M.S., [2] S.S., [2] S.A.S.

		NAME	AGE	BORN	DIED
(G)	[1]	SAHM, David	65-10-25	11/04/1799 -	09/29/1865
	[1]	ZAHM, Eve w/o David Zahm	74-02-27	12/25/1800 -	03/10/1875
(G)	[1]	SAHM, Catharina d/o David & Eva Sahm	33-04-20	03/07/1827 -	07/27/1861
(G)	[1]	SAHM, George s/o David & Eva Sahm	21-04-12	04/30/1828 -	04/12/1850
	[6]	SATHMARY, Rev. Julius (Shares stone with Rev.		1908 -	
		Helen B. Lawrence & Helen S. Tropp.)		1913 -	

		NAME	AGE	BORN	DIED
(G)	[1]	SAUER, Adam "Born in Grosherzogthum Hessen			
		Darmstadt Europa"	18-09-20		02/25/1843
	[1]	SAYLOR, John	88-01-21	02/25/1800 -	04/16/1888
	[1]	SAYLOR, Catharine w/o John Saylor	67-05-27	04/20/1806 -	10/17/1873
	[1]	TAYLOR, Mary d/o John & Catharine (Stone reset)	10-01-??		10/29/1829
	[1]	SAYLOR, Michael	64-04-19	09/12/1805 -	01/31/1870
	[1]	SAYLOR, Elizabeth w/o Michael Saylor	64-10-23	03/23/1805 -	02/16/1870
	[3]	SAYLOR, Charlotte D.		1898 -	19
(G)	[1]	SCHOEFFER, Anna Maria (Stone reset)		08/15/1763 -	04/21/1797
	[3]	SCHAEFFER, Morris H.		01/25/1879 -	10/09/1957
		Lizzie M.		03/31/1878 -	05/27/1970
	[2]	SCHAEFFER, Warren G.		03/09/1904 -	
		Elsie H.		07/26/1905 -	
(G)	[1]	SCHIFFLER, Johannes	80 years		
			less 6 d.	12/20/1769 -	12/14/1849
(G)	[1]	SCHIFFLER, Barbara NEE Schmidt w/o Johannes Schiffler			
			67-08-10	09/16/1769 -	05/26/1837
(G)	[1]	SCHIFFLER, Catharina NEE Miller w/o Johannes Schiffler			
		(Age and dates as on stone.)	61-08-00	07/24/1770 -	03/23/1832
(G)	[1]	SCHLEBAC(IN), Elisabet	84-05-17	04/03/1761 -	09/20/1845
(G)	[1]	SCHNIERER, Johannes	42-11-17	05/17/1786 -	05/03/1829
	[2]	SCHNERER, Catharine w/o John Schnerer	80-09-27	08/22/1795 -	06/19/1876
(G)	[1]	SCHNIERER, Peter s/o Johannes & Catharina Schnierer	05-02-00	11/10/1822 -	08/10/1828
(G)	[1]	SCHNIERER, Georg	30-09-02	08/15/1817 -	05/17/1848
	[2]	SCHNERER, Samuel	65-05-02	09/20/1825 -	02/22/1891
	[2]	SCHNERER, Sarah Ann	75-09-13	10/03/1826 -	07/16/1902
	[2]	SCHNERER, Edward	69-04-05	12/11/1828 -	04/16/1898
	[1]	SCHNERER, Elizabeth w/o Edward Schnerer	22-07-00	11/22/1834 -	06/22/1857
	[1]	SCHNERER, Madison M. s/o Edward & Elizabeth Schnerer			
			01-02-03	03/23/1852 -	05/26/1856
	[1]	SCHNERER, Sarah E. d/o Edward & Elizabeth Schnerer	00-04-20	10/26/1856 -	03/16/1857
	[2]	SCHNERER, Rebecca O. w/o Edward Schnerer			
		d/o Samuel & Catharina Elser	46-04-25	07/25/1838 -	12/20/1884
	[5]	SCHNERER, John "Died near Strasburg, Va. while in			
		the service of his country. Member			
		of CO. G. 195 REGT. P.V."	40-10-16	09/21/1824 -	07/27/1865
	[5]	SCHNERER, Sarah w/o John Schnerer			
		"Died at Reading, Pa."	57-10-15	01/15/1827 -	11/30/1884
	[7]	SCHNERER-Large monument with four smaller lettered			
		stones which include the following:			
		Lizzie G. Scnherer		1863 -	1908
		Frank E. Schnerer		1866-	1923
		Ellen C. Schnerer		1865 -	1946
		Ada M. Eberly		1890 -	1958
	[3]	SCHWARTZ, Andrew, Sr.		1884 -	1956
		Agnes J.		1882 -	1972
	[3]	SCHWARTZ, Harry J.		10/11/1913 -	01/04/1965
	[3]	SCHWARTZ, Louise F. (Schwartz-Mifflinburg marker)		1917 -	1986
	[2]	SCOTT, Melissa Keith		10/12/1832 -	03/30/1923
	[2]	SCOTT, Samuel M.		02/14/1870 -	01/27/1955
		Amelia P. Boyer		12/06/1878 -	02/17/1971
	[2]	SCOTT, Alice E.		08/27/1909 -	09/28/1971
	[2]	SCOTT, Gladys C.		12/25/1917 -	11/10/1925
	[5]	SECHRIST, Elizabeth w/o Adam Sechrist	64-05-08	10/13/1850 -	03/21/1915
		(See Jonathan Strickler)			

	NAME	AGE	BORN	DIED
[5]	SECHRIST, Adam Z. s/o Adam & Elizabeth Sechrist	05-06-12	07/27/1879 - 02/09/1885
[5]	SECRHIST, Allen Z. s/o Adam & Elizabeth Sechrist	04-05-24	04/18/1887 - 10/12/1891
[3]	SEIBERT, Maria w/o John Seibert		
	d/o Michael & Catharine Kline	68-03-23	08/04/1803 - 11/27/1871
(G) [1]	SEIBERT, William s/o John & Maria Seibert	28-11-15	12/23/1831 - 12/07/1860
[3]	SEIBERT, Edward K.	64-04-04	03/25/1830 - 07/29/1894
[3]	SEIBERT, Caroline w/o Edward K. Seibert	68-09-21	04/23/1832 - 02/14/1901
[2]	SEIBERT, John F.	57-04-03	01/09/1859 - 05/12/1916
	Amanda NEE Ziegler	89-00-08	07/30/1856 - 08/08/1945
[2]	SEIBERT, Edward K. "Son"	57-01-03	10/02/1889 - 11/05/1946
	Alice Z. "Daughter"	78-08-14	08/31/1896 - 05/15/1975
[3]	SEIBERT, Infant d/o John F. & Amanda K. Seibert		Stillborn 07/23/1891
[1]	SEIBERT, Miles s/o William S. & Sarah Seibert	07-09-23	09/05/1858 - 07/27/1866
[1]	SEIBERT, Levi F.		11/18/1887 - 01/01/1981
	Anna E.		09/23/1892 -
[2]	SEIBERT, Landis E.	31-08-14	02/02/1887 - 10/16/1918
	Lavina P. NEE Mease	82-04-29	01/15/1890 - 06/14/1972
[2]	SEIBERT, William C.	79-11-17	11/14/1861 - 11/01/1941
	Anna M. NEE Landis	87-02-26	07/31/1861 - 10/26/1948
[2]	SEIBERT, W. Weidler		09/07/1890 - 01/01/1980
	Lizzie J.		10/04/1891 -
[2]	SEIBERT, John Z. "Married February 16, 1918"		03/11/1894 - 05/01/1966
	Lillie S.		02/17/1892 - 10/30/1978
	Paul E.		04/06/1931 - 02/24/1934
[5]	SEIBERT, William H.		11/17/1916 - 05/16/1965
	Miriam E.		10/31/1918 -

		NAME	AGE	BORN	DIED
	[6]	SEIVERLING, Harry		1870 -	1956
		Ella		1875 -	1959
	[8]	SEIVERLING, James		09/15/1894 -	
		Naoma		03/12/1894 -	
	[6]	SEIVERLING, Harry		03/18/1910 -	10/31/1979
		Amanda		05/18/1912 -	
	[3]	SEPPI, Philip W.		06/16/1900 -	
		Helen M.		12/06/1901 -	
		Ruth S.		1926 -	1926
	[2]	SEPPI, James Lee	22-00-23	01/15/1959 -	02/07/1981
		Jeffrey Allen		03/13/1970 -	
	[1]	SESSEMAN, Anna w/o Alfred Sesseman	49-07-01	07/10/1825 -	02/11/1875
	[1]	SESSEMAN, Samuel s/o Alfred & Anna Sesseman	00-05-01		02/21/1851
	[1]	SESSEMAN, Benj. Franklin s/o Alfred & Anna Sesseman	04-05-00	07/20/1857 -	02/20/1862
	[7]	SHAAK, Samuel J.		1891 -	1968
		Savannah M.		1897 -	1985
(G)	[1]	SCHERB, Susanna NEE Haushalter	69-07-03	09/14/1774 -	04/17/1844
(G)	[1]	SCHERB, Georg	62-09-00	02/24/1788 -	11/24/1850
(G)	[1]	SCHERB, Johann	79-08-22	04/12/1785 -	01/04/1865
(G)	[1]	SCHERB, Susanna NEE Appel w/o Johannes Scherb	73-03-01	02/26/1785 -	05/27/1858
(G)	[1]	SCHERB, Jacob	74-03-08	06/08/1786 -	09/16/1860
(G)	[1]	SCHERB, Sarah w/o Jacob Scherb	76-10-14	09/16/1794 -	08/01/1871
(G)	[1]	SCHERB, Samuel s/o Adam & Barbara Scherb	59-08-10	01/30/1795 -	10/10/1854
(G)	[1]	SCHERB, Elisabeth	24-05-16	04/30/1809 -	10/16/1833
(G)	[1]	SCHERB, Emanuel s/o Adam & Catharina Scherb	24-11-11	06/09/1812 -	05/10/1837
	[3]	SHARP, Adam	76-01-12	10/20/1816 -	12/02/1892
	[3]	SHARP, Rachel w/o Adam Sharp	90-03-11	12/16/1817 -	03/27/1908
	[1]	SHARP, Adam s/o Adam & Rachel Sharp	39-02-21	05/16/1842 -	08/06/1881
	[3]	SHARP, Samuel W. s/o Adam & Rachel Sharp	34-00-16	10/11/1851 -	10/27/1885
	[3]	SCHERB, Levi	81-01-00	08/06/1825 -	09/16/1906
	[3]	SCHERB, Sophia Nagle w/o Levi Scherb	73-10-24	11/01/1822 -	09/25/1896
	[2]	SHARP, Isaac M.		11/05/1835 -	11/28/1907
	[2]	SHARP, Fianna S.		11/26/1836 -	05/25/1909
	[2]	SHARP, Phares s/o Isaac & Fianna Sharp	23-09-06	09/18/1858 -	06/24/1882
(G)	[1]	SCHERB, Salmi d/o Noa & Maria Scherb	00-09-01	05/22/1843 -	02/23/1844
	[2]	SHARP, Barton "Brother"		04/04/1862 -	09/23/1933
	[5]	SHARP, Infant s/o John M. & Fianna Sharp		Stillborn	04/21/1878
	[5]	SHARP, Katie d/o John & Fianna Sharp	5 days		02/16/1881
	[2]	SHARP, Ella P. Bergman w/o Isaac Sharp	30-10-11	02/26/1881 -	01/06/1912
	[5]	SHARP, Fanny d/o Evan & Agnes Sharp	01-04-22	01/31/1882 -	06/24/1883
	[2]	SHARP, Infant s/o Isaac S. & Ella Sharp			08/26/1904
	[6]	SCHERPF, Milton J.		05/05/1909 -	03/01/1974
		Lillian J.		09/27/1907 -	
	[6]	SCHERPF, Cynthia Leah d/o Milton J. & Lillian J. Scherpf		09/25/1948 -	03/27/1960
	[9]	SHAUB, Willis J.		1886 -	1980
		Gertrude K.		1893 -	1981
	[1]	SHEALER, Lawrence V.		12/10/1904 -	01/25/1985
	[3]	SHELLY, Elam D.		10/28/1902 -	12/17/1974
		Elva Z.		08/07/1902 -	08/29/1986
	[2]	SHELLY, Ammon F.		1907 -	1979
		Annie M.		1908 -	
	[3]	SHELLY, PFC. Kenneth M. "CO. F 8232D A.V. ENGRS."		05/11/1927 -	03/06/1955

		NAME	AGE	BORN	DIED
	[2]	SHELLY, Carl H.		1940 –	1967
		Jeffrey L.		1961 –	1961
(G)	[1]	SCHENCK, Johannes	21-00-13	03/02/1821 –	03/15/1842
	[7]	SHENK, Mary Ann "Mother"	68-10-16		06/15/1924
	[8]	SHENK, Morris W.	88-01-21	06/20/1866 –	08/10/1954
		Lizzie M.	58-06-05	06/28/1867 –	01/03/1926
	[2]	SHENK, Mary Ann d/o M.W. & Lizzie	00-03-08	02/18/1904 –	05/26/1904
	[8]	SHENK, Ada D.		01/23/1889 –	03/11/1965
	[8]	SHENK, Henry D.		10/22/1893 –	03/20/1958
		Carrie M. NEE Ulrich		12/08/1898 –	
	[8]	SHENK, Howard M. "US ARMY WW I"		1897 –	1974
		Anna E.		1901 –	
	[9]	SHENK, Henry G.		1904 –	1972
		Mae S.		1901 –	
	[6]	SHANK, Anthony Lamar s/o Abram & Arlene Shank	5 days		Nov. 1960
	[3]	SHERMAN, Reuben G.		12/05/1827 –	07/08/1886
		Sarah A. Bentz, his wife		01/07/1830 –	09/17/1904
	[3]	SHARMAN, John Jacob s/o Ruben & Sarah A. Sharman	06-06-12	06/10/1853 –	12/22/1859
	[3]	SHARMAN, Alice Eliza d/o Ruben & Sarah Sharman	03-08-27	04/03/1856 –	12/30/1859
	[8]	SHILLING, Samuel L.	72-05-17	05/09/1867 –	10/26/1939
		Alice B.	69-05-00	09/23/1865 –	02/23/1935
	[1]	SHIMP, Harry G.		10/08/1882 –	12/14/1966
		Laura E.		05/27/1883 –	06/15/1955
	[1]	SHIMP, Mary E. w/o Harry G. Shimp		11/17/1882 –	02/16/1960
	[1]	SHIRK, Sophia NEE Kline w/o John S. Shirk	20-05-02	11/30/1816 –	05/02/1837
	[1]	SHIRK, Susanna w/o Jacob Shirk d/o Michael Kline,			
		Esqr. & wife Susanna	24-07-16	07/10/1822 –	02/26/1847
	[7]	SHIRK, Richard L. "WW II"		1906 –	1966
	[9]	SHIRK, Joseph K.		1910 –	1981
		Mary S.		1909 –	
	[7]	SHIRK, Robert C.		10/06/1914 –	05/11/1984
		Ruth I.		02/02/1921 –	
	[9]	SHIRK, Sharon K. "Beloved Daughter, Sister & Aunt"		1956 –	1982
	[8]	SHOEMAKER, Titus P.		1893 –	1949
		Ellen H. (Part of death date underlined was		1887 –	1970
		written in pencil on the stone.)			
	[8]	SHOEMAKER, Minerva S. d/o Titus & Ellen Shoemaker		11/04/1921 –	07/24/1923
	[9]	SHOLLY, Clarence I.		1894 –	1974
	[8]	SHOLLY, Sivilia M.		1900 –	1938
(G)	[1]	SHOUER, Catharina w/o John Shouer	82-09-19	08/21/1782 –	06/09/1865
	[4]	SHREINER, Victor M.		1912 –	1965
		Louella M.		1917 –	
	[2]	SHREINER, Charles	28 days		1923
	[7]	SHUE, Alvin		1883 –	1970
		Linnie		1891 –	1966
		Ursula		1907 –	1911
(G)	[1]	SIELER, Henrich	19-08-04	12/19/1804 –	08/23/1823
	[3]	SIELING, A.M., M.D.		08/19/1860 –	11/12/1927
	[3]	SIELING, Lillie P.		11/01/1866 –	04/30/1939
	[3]	SINGER, Paul		1889 –	1959
		Elsie		1887 –	1986
		Rena		1917 –	1919
		Charlotte		1914 –	1914
		Luther		1915 –	1915
		Nevin		1928 –	1928

		NAME	AGE	BORN	DIED
	[7]	SINGER, Earl D.		1898 –	1983
		Ida H.		1907 –	1956
	[5]	SMITH, Susanna	76-01-25	03/18/1824 –	05/13/1900
	[2]	SMITH, Lizzie Deemer "Mother"	79-01-26	11/15/1869 –	11/11/1949
		(This stone is the same as Henry E. Deemer's stone which is marked Father)			
	[1]	SMITH, Mary E. d/o George W. & Ellenora M. Smith	02-01-09	12/14/1870 –	01/23/1871
	[2]	SMITH, Charles E.		1897 –	1953
		Katie H.		1898 –	19
	[5]	SMITH, Albert C.		1905 –	1960
		Rena F.		1913 –	
	[5]	SMITH, Albert C.		01/08/1934 –	07/29/1951
	[5]	SMITH, James S. s/o Albert & Rena Smith	01-03-23		03/07/1944
	[4]	SNADER, Joseph W. "CP. US ARMY WW II"		1907 –	1980
	[4]	SNADER, Clarence R.		09/27/1914 –	07/18/1978
		Anna K.		06/26/1912 –	12/15/1977
	[5]	SNOWDEN, Allen R.		04/02/1954 –	07/16/1980
(G)	[1]	SNYDER, Ann Mary d/o Isaac & Elizabeth Snyder	01-11-04	09/24/1859 –	08/29/1861
	[2]	SNYDER, Hiram L.	88-09-05	03/06/1862 –	12/11/1950
		Miranda M.	58-08-19	05/12/1870 –	01/31/1929
	[2]	SNYDER, Chester s/o Hiram & Miranda Snyder		01/24/1894	
	[2]	SNYDER, Joseph L.	60-02-15	12/12/1860 –	02/27/1921
	[3]	SNYDER, Jacob L. (Shares stone with Joseph &		01/04/1872 –	08/16/1949
		Sadie H. Lydia Kline)		03/13/1871 –	01/26/1952
	[5]	SNYDER, John s/o John W. & Susanna Snyder	03-08-23	08/08/1878 –	05/01/1882
	[5]	SNYDER, Callie d/o John W. & Susanna Snyder	00-03-01	08/22/1870 –	11/23/1870
	[5]	SNYDER, Edna M. (This stone and Annie Boyer Culp's stone are very similer to Clinton & Carrie Boyer's stone.)		1931 –	1944
	[8]	SOUDERS, John A. (Shares stone with John H.		1851 –	1938
		Annie B., his wife & Katie Getz.)		1853 –	1926
		Monroe E.		1874 –	1877
		Elsie E. Children of John A. & Annie B. Souders		1889 –	1910
	[1]	SPANGLER, Angeline E.		06/16/1834 –	04/16/1855
	[1]	SPANGLER, H.D. "CO. H. 203RD. PA. INF."			1896
	[1]	SPANGLER, Clyde G. "Father"		1918 –	1985
		Ruth C. "Mother"		1928 –	
		Carl R. "Son"		1959 –	
	[2]	SPAYD-Large monument with five smaller lettered stones as follows:			
		Oscar Spayd	76-03-18	01/02/1882 –	04/20/1958
		Katie R. Spayd NEE Meck	68-09-26		08/08/1951
		Elmer M. Spayd	59-02-18	02/03/1904 –	04/21/1963
		Margaret B. Spayd NEE Antes	30-11-10		09/17/1937
		Margaret Virginia Spayd	08-09-03	08/02/1926 –	05/05/1935
	[8]	SPAYD, Harry W.		1899 –	1973
		Olive E.		1902 –	
	[4]	SPADE, Samuel B.		1910 –	1962
		Alverta E.		1914 –	1972
	[7]	SPADE, William B.		1912 –	1964
		Alverta L.		1918 –	
(G)	[1]	SPICKLER(IN), Sara	2 y.2 w. 5 d.	05/15/1797 –	06/04/1799
	[7]	SPRECHER, Franklin T.		04/10/1903 –	04/18/1926
		Elsie M., his wife (See Elsie M. Hollinger)		09/13/1902 –	
	[8]	SPRECHER, Robert F. s/o F.T. & Elsie M. Sprecher		Born & Died	04/12/1924

		NAME	AGE	BORN	DIED
	[2]	STAMM, Laura E. (This stone is the same as the stone			
		of Zackarias T. Wike)		1877 –	1961
	[4]	STEELY, Earl E.		1916 –	1968
		Minnie C.		1895 –	1972
	[1]	STEELY, Henry M.		03/29/1928 –	06/29/1972
	[1]	STEFFE, Daniel	71-11-02	10/27/1800 –	09/29/1872
(G)	[1]	STEFFE, Susanna w/o Daniel Steffe	64-00-02	11/13/1799 –	11/15/1863
	[1]	STEFFY, Richard	51-00-18	03/11/1827 –	03/29/1879
	[1]	STEFFY, Maria Goshard w/o Richard Steffy	75-03-16	05/24/1826 –	09/10/1901
(G)	[1]	STEFFY, Ellen s/o Richard & Mary Steffy	11-02-28	02/03/1849 –	05/02/1860
		(s/o is carved on stone)			
(G)	[1]	STEFFY, James Wallis s/o Richard & Maria Steffy	00-10-19	09/07/1860 –	06/26/1861
	[1]	STEFFY, Monroe s/o Richard & Mary Steffy	01-05-11	10/07/1868 –	05/18/1870
	[1]	STEFFEE, Priscilla (Age & dates as carved)	00-11-04	10/06/1852 –	09/20/1853
	[2]	STEFFY, Edwin husband of Ada Alice Fetter	83-04-03	10/24/1861 –	02/27/1945
	[2]	STEFFY, Amanda Moyer w/o Edwin Steffy	39-09-15	01/21/1865 –	11/06/1904
	[3]	STEFFY, Paris s/o John H. Steffy & Mary Ulrich	18-04-10	01/27/1872 –	06/06/1890
	[5]	STEFFY, Harvey S.		02/02/1877 –	08/06/1954
		Fannie G.		03/12/1879 –	07/31/1942
	[2]	STEFFY, Edwin F.		08/01/1912 –	10/30/1979
		June E.		06/21/1907 –	08/07/1967
		Linda L.		09/15/1945 –	06/14/1963
	[4]	STEFFY, Lester S. "USA WW II"		07/05/1924 –	07/05/1969
		Mabel I.		05/09/1924 –	
	[2]	STEFFY, Edwin F.		1939 –	1939
		Mabel F.		1941 –	1949
		Allen L.		1944 –	1944
	[2]	STEFFY, Rick L.		05/03/1953 –	03/02/1978
	[1]	STEIGER, George J.	66-05-20	08/27/1819 –	02/17/1886
(G)	[1]	STEIGER, Elisabeth NEE Friederich w/o Georg Steiger	40-07-14	07/03/1827 –	01/17/1868
	[5]	STEIGER, Geo. F.	52-01-20	08/24/1849 –	10/14/1901
	[5]	STEIGER, Lydia Ann w/o George Steiger	33-04-13	01/12/1854 –	05/25/1887
	[5]	STEIGER, Herman F.		1875 –	1942
		Maria Z., his wife		1873 –	1975
(G)	[1]	STEINER, Henrich	61-07-10	10/27/1766 –	06/06/1828
(G)	[1]	STEINER, Christina NEE Weber (Age & dates as carved)	47-02-10	08/21/1774 –	11/01/1823
	[1]	STEINER, John	77-09-03	12/27/1796 –	09/30/1874
(G)	[1]	STEINER, Magdalena NEE Zartman w/o Johann Steiner	56-10-06	03/03/1791 –	01/09/1848
(G)	[1]	STEINER, Heinrich s/o Johanes & Magdalena Steiner	04-01-18	01/09/1822 –	02/27/1826
(G)	[1]	STEINER, Enrietta d/o Johannes & Magdalena	01-10-15	05/31/1828 –	04/15/1830
(G)	[5]	STEINER, Elizabeth NEE Fehly w/o Joseph Steiner	72-01-26	12/22/1797 –	02/18/1870
(G)	[1]	STEINER, Anna d/o George & Anna Eichelberger	21-08-05	09/04/1812 –	05/09/1834
	[3]	STEINER, Levi	79-01-00	03/03/1819 –	04/03/1878
	[3]	STEINER, Ann Mary w/o Levi Steiner	71-11-02	11/14/1815 –	10/16/1887
(G)	[3]	STEINER, Agnes Amanda d/o Levi & Anna Maria Steiner	03-07-13	07/26/1859 –	03/08/1863
(G)	[1]	STEINER, Sarah NFF Williams w/o William Steiner	42-02-17	02/29/1820 –	05/16/1862
(G)	[1]	STEINER, Anna Maria d/o Will. & Sarah Steiner	00-01-00		05/08/1841
	[5]	STEINER, Elizabeth	80-05-29	12/18/1829 –	06/17/1910
		Jefferson Jacoby	71-06-00	09/01/1849 –	03/01/1921
	[3]	STEINER, John H.	58-02-21	12/03/1849 –	02/24/1908
	[3]	STEINER, Caroline NEE Yocum	83-03-01	08/14/1854 –	11/15/1937
	[3]	STEINER, Ida May d/o John H. & Caroline Steiner	18-07-08	07/01/1876 –	02/09/1895
		"Our Only Daughter"			
	[2]	STEINER, Calvin F.	73-08-26	04/29/1870 –	01/25/1944
		Lizzie H.	95-07-22	08/17/1871 –	04/09/1967

		NAME	AGE	BORN	DIED
	[3]	STEINER, Harvey Y.	74-06-29	04/09/1873 - 11/08/1947	
	[3]	STEINER, Sallie Keath w/o Harvey Y. Steiner	74-06-29	04/09/1873 - 11/08/1947	
(G)	[1]	STEINMETZ, Susanna NEE Feirstein	45-11-20	04/01/1784 - 03/21/1830	
	[3]	STEINMETZ-Large monument inscribed with the following names:			
		George W. Steinmetz	82-11-13		07/24/1910
		Priscilla Cecilla w/o George W. Steinmetz			
		d/o John & Barbara Erb	48-07-30		06/05/1870
		Annie L. Meck	74-02-11		08/19/1912
		Hiram E. Steinmetz (Carved under his name	63-04-01		02/21/1918
		is: "He was the founder of this cemetery."			
	[2]	STEINMETZ, Isaac M.		02/28/1900 - 11/27/1962	
		Mabel H.		08/28/1900 - 03/18/1979	
	[2]	STEINMETZ, Harry R.		05/28/1918 - 01/22/1983	
	[2]	STEINMETZ, Alice R.		03/03/1925 - 09/30/1931	
	[2]	STEINMETZ, Isaac, Jr.		1922 -	
		Leona E.		1932 -	
(G)	[1]	STEPHAN, J. Gottfried s/o J. Gottfried & Friedricka			
		Stephan	00-08-02	01/26/1860 - 09/28/1860	
	[3]	STEPHAN, Margie		04/02/1891 - 04/15/1958	
	[1]	STEWARD, Robert "born in London Darry Ireland and			
		died in America."	86 years		11/15/1845
	[1]	STEWART, Elizabeth w/o Robert Stewart	about 80 years		02/01/1858
	[1]	STEWARD, John "born in the County Derry Ireland"	53-00-28	12/04/1797 - 08/02/1851	
	[1]	STHEGEL, Elisabet d/o Jacob Huber		03/27/1734 - 02/13/1758	
		"married Henri Guilhelmo Sthegel on November			
		7, 1752. Died at her father's home." This is			
		a box-like tomb. Verse is in German and dates			
		and family information are in Latin.			
	[1]	STIEF, Jonathan	45-01-15		02/05/1851
	[1]	STIEF, Elizabeth w/o Jonathan Stief	76 years	No Dates	
	[1]	STIEF, Henry s/o Jonathan & Elizabeth Stief	14-09-21	04/05/1845 - 01/26/1860	
	[1]	STIEF, Franklin s/o Jonathan & Elizabeth Stief	4 m.3 d.	11/24/1848 - 03/27/1849	
	[1]	STIEF, Jonathan s/o Jonathan & Elizabeth Stief	11-02-12	11/24/1848 - 01/31/1860	
(G)	[1]	STOBER(IN), Eva Elisabeth	60-03-13	09/29/1725 - 01/12/1786	
(G)	[1]	STOBER, Johan Georg	60-07-28	06/27/1767 - 02/25/1828	
(G)	[1]	STOBER, Catharina NEE Haushalter w/o George Stover	68-02-17	02/17/1766 - 05/05/1834	
(G)	[1]	STOBER, Johannes s/o Georg & Catharina Stober	60-04-23	11/27/1801 - 01/20/1862	
(G)	[1]	STOBER, Jacob	40-02-14	01/05/1790 - 03/19/1830	
(G)	[1]	STOBER, Mary w/o Jacob Stover	75-10-15	03/20/1787 - 02/05/1862	
(G)	[1]	STOBER, Juliana	10-07-26	01/09/1813 - 09/04/1823	
(G)	[1]	STOBER, Peter	01-00-26	10/23/1814 - 11/18/1815	
(G)	[1]	STOBER, Chatarina	00-05-30	03/26/1818 - 09/25/1818	
(G)	[1]	STOBER, Cyrus John s/o Elias & Sarah Stober	00-05-28		04/23/1845
(G)	[1]	STOBER, Isabela Jane d/o Elias & Sarah Stober	00-02-04	10/13/1847 - 12/17/1849	
	[1]	STOBER, Sarah Elizabeth d/o Elias & Sarah Stover	02-02-22	07/03/1849 - 09/25/----	
(G)	[1]	STOBER, Mary Francis d/o Elias & Sarah Stober	02-09-29	10/17/1853 - 08/13/1856	
	[2]	STOHLER, John H.	71-00-04	11/13/1861 - 03/13/1933	
	[2]	STOHLER, Susan M. Moyer w/o John H. Stohler	32-09-08	01/23/1868 - 11/01/1900	
	[2]	STOHLER, George W.		08/04/1863 - 09/26/1953	
		Ida D. NEE Boyer		03/19/1866 - 08/11/1945	
	[2]	STOHLER, George B. "PVT. CO. M. 56TH INF. WW I"		1888 -	1962
	[2]	STOHLER, George M.		08/22/1897 -	
		Edna M. (Fresh burial Spring 1987)		10/10/1899 -	
	[2]	STOHLER, Harvey Boyer "Father"		02/09/1901 - 01/16/1961	
		George Rose "Son"		03/12/1931 - 01/27/1979	

NAME	AGE	BORN	DIED
[6] STOKES, Robert E. "CORP. MED. CORPS. WORLD WAR II"		1901 -	1957
[6] STOKES Esther L. (Good Service marker)		1912 -	1980
[2] STOLL, Ellsworth C. L.		06/01/1903 -	06/24/1984
Erla Peters		12/09/1906 -	
[8] STRAUSS, Harry W.		1884 -	1977
Annie M. NEE Hartman		1886 -	1954
[7] STRAUSS, David S. "Father"		01/16/1896 -	01/02/1966
Mary L. "Mother"		01/29/1897 -	
L. Woodrow "Son"		06/10/1917 -	04/16/1979
Mary K. "Wife"		01/24/1921 -	
Russell A. "Son"		02/27/1922 -	
Mary A. "Wife"		01/30/1927 -	
Thomas R. "Son"		01/03/1950 -	09/18/1971
[7] STRAUSS, Harvey		1898 -	1965
Mazie		1900 -	1938
[9] STRAUSS, George H.		1908 -	1984
Emma E.		1906 -	
[8] STRAUSS, Marvin H. "US AIR FORCE"		11/12/1910 -	08/20/1973
[8] STRAUSS, Warren K. "PFC. CO. C. 851ST ENG. AVIATION BN. WW II"	1922 -	1964
Mary Meck		1919 -	
[2] STRICKLER, Margret w/o John Strickler	43-02-01	05/12/1842 -	07/13/1885
[5] STRICKLER, Johathan s/o Jonathan Strickler &			
Elizabeth Zeller (See Elizabeth			
Sechrist)	27-10-22	02/05/1871 -	12/27/1898
[2] STRICKLER, Robert L. s/o William & Mary Strickler		07/21/1885 -	07/26/1885
(G) [1] STROH, Eva NEE Huber w/o Nicolaus Stroh	94-09-19	11/30/1737 -	09/19/1832
(G) [1] STROH, Johan Nicolaus	73-04-27	02/12/1739 -	07/09/1812
(G) [1] STROH, Elisabeth	25 y.5 m.		
	3 w.1 d.	10/11/1771 -	04/03/1797
[8] STROHM, Irvin W.		1880 -	1962
Alice B.		1885 -	1937
[8] STROHM, Elsie B. d/o Irvin W. & Alice F. Strohm	19-07-18	04/15/1904 -	11/23/1923
[8] STROHM, Claude B. s/o Irvin W. & Alice F. Strohm	14-07-17	03/12/1921 -	10/29/1935
[8] STROHM, Elmer B.		03/21/1907 -	12/13/1976
Mildred K.		09/14/1914	
[9] STROHM, Walter B.		1911 -	1982
Pauline S.		1914 -	
(G) [1] SUMMY, Heinrich	53-06-18	01/20/1792 -	08/07/1845
[1] SUMMY, Elizabeth	84-08-22	12/09/1807 -	07/01/1892
(G) [1] SIES, Emanuel		03/25/1731 -	05/06/1791
(G) [1] SUS(IN), Susanna	65-03-03	07/16/1734 -	10/19/1799
(G) [1] SIES, Leonhart	29 y.2 w.		
	3 d.	09/08/1761 -	09/26/1790
(G) [1] SUES, M. Barbara	68-03-18	03/01/1766 -	06/18/1834
(G) [1] SUS, Jacob	44-03-14	01/02/1768 -	04/16/1812
(G) [1] SUS, Elisabeth w/o Jacob Sus d/o W. Gesell & wife	30-02-15	12/10/1778 -	02/25/1808
(G) [1] SUESZ, Christina	35-11-17	08/28/1770 -	08/14/1806
[1] TAYLOR, Mary d/o John & Catharine (Stone reset)	10-01-??		10/29/1829
(The above stone should be Saylor. See			
John & Catharine Saylor.)			
(G) [1] THIMMER, Georg		01/18/1788 -	03/28/1779
(The above dates are as they are carved on the stone.			
They could be reversed.)			

	NAME	AGE	BORN	DIED
[7]	TODD, John D.		10/05/1878 - 01/31/1961	
	Lillian H.		06/09/1882 - 04/14/1968	
[7]	TODD, J. Theodore s/o John & Lillie Todd	08-01-07	05/12/1912 - 06/19/1920	
[7]	TODD, James Harlan "Son"		07/07/1926 - 06/15/1927	
[5]	TSHUDY, Peter	72-04-09	11/06/1815 - 03/15/1888	
[5]	TSHUDY, Susanna Schiffer w/o Peter T. Tshudy	80-00-09	04/04/1817 - 04/13/1897	
[6]	TROPP, Rev Lawrence (Shares stone with Rev. Julius		1934 -	
	Helen S. & Helen B. Sathmary)		1925 -	
[6]	TROPP, Robert L.		02/10/1963 - 02/26/1963	

INITIAL STONE: [5] J.U.

	NAME	AGE	BORN	DIED
[7]	UHLIG, Ralph F.		1905 -	1974
	Matilda E.		1907 -	
[5]	ULRICH, Henry "CO.G. 195 REGT. PA. VOL."	61-04-16		10/05/1886
[8]	ULRICH, David	70-06-19	03/02/1826 - 09/02/1896	
[8]	ULRICH, Elizabeth w/o David Ulrich	82-01-26	12/16/1826 - 02/12/1909	
[5]	ULRICH, Joseph	56-11-26	01/09/1831 - 01/05/1888	
[5]	ULRICH, Mary Corry w/o Joseph Ulrich	81-02-14	05/03/1833 - 07/17/1914	
[1]	ULRICH, John s/o John & Susanna Ulrich	11-08-24	09/21/1857 - 06/15/1869	
[8]	ULRICH, Levanus		02/16/1856 - 08/13/1921	
	Susan A., his wife		05/26/1864 - No Date	
[8]	ULRICH, Mary A. d/o Levanus & Susan Ulrich	15-04-26	03/26/1882 - 08/22/1897	
[8]	ULRICH, Thomas C.	70-11-15		08/08/1933
	Mary Ann	63-03-05		01/18/1923
[8]	ULRICH, John F. s/o Thomas C. & Mary Ulrich	19-08-28	03/29/1888 - 12/27/1907	
[5]	ULRICH, James		1872 -	1945
	Elizabeth		1871 -	1937
[5]	ULRICH, Harvey		1870 -	1939
	Kate		1876 -	1934
[5]	ULRICH, Frank M. s/o Harvey & Kate Ulrich	33-10-09	1899 -	1932
[5]	ULRICH, John s/o Alfred & Lavina Ulrich	00-07-02	02/21/1882 - 09/29/1882	
[8]	ULRICH, Fred S.		06/24/1884 - 01/05/1968	
[8]	ULRICH, Martin H.		1887 -	1963
	Lillian E.		1891 -	1978
	George A.		1867 -	1940
	Kate B.		1870 -	1962
[5]	ULRICH, Edwin H. s/o Geo. A. & Kate B. Ulrich	04-02-17	01/03/1890 - 03/20/1894	
[3]	ULRICH, Howard M.	64-01-09	01/12/1895 - 02/21/1959	
	Ella S.	73-00-21	09/29/1892 - 10/20/1965	
[8]	ULRICH, William W.		03/22/1899 - 09/17/1975	
	Elsie B.		10/27/1905 - 07/13/1971	
[8]	ULRICH, Leon R.		1922 -	1983
	Hazel H.		1918 -	
[7]	VIA, Susan G. (Spacht Funeral Home marker)		1897 -	1982

INITIAL STONE: [1] P.W. (next to Peter Williams)

	NAME	AGE	BORN	DIED
[6]	WADE [HERTZOG-WADE] (Surnames not paired with given names)			
	Roy		04/08/1900 - 11/28/1980	
	Raymond L.		10/24/1901 -	
	Emma		05/01/1902 - 04/28/1986	
[7]	WAGNER, Susan Heck w/o William Wagner	87-11-24	09/23/1829 - 09/17/1917	
[2]	WAGNER, Francis		12/08/1856 - 08/19/1932	
	Lizzie Ulrich, his wife		08/23/1862 - 01/29/1923	
[8]	WAGNER, William	38-07-02	03/11/1863 - 10/13/1901	

	NAME	AGE	BORN	DIED
[8]	WAGNER, Ida d/o William & Annie Wagner	15-00-07	09/24/1886 -	10/01/1901
[8]	WAGNER, Thomas		1869 -	1948
	Alice, his wife		1869 -	1924
[8]	WAGNER, William		1889 -	1945
[8]	WALTER, Jacob B.		1877 -	1949
	Nora D.		1882 -	1942
	Frank R.	5 days	1912 -	1912
[2]	WALTERS, Thomas B.		1887 -	1963
	Mary U.		1886 -	1954
[2]	WALTERS, Beatrice Marie d/o Thomas & Mary Walters	02-09-17	01/09/1916 -	10/26/1918
[6]	WALTERS, Jacob R.		05/07/1900 -	03/09/1976
	Geraldine M.		04/15/1905 -	
[9]	WALTER, George R.		11/26/1903 -	11/16/1983
	Mildred Foose		01/23/1906 -	
[5]	WALTZ, Anna Manerva	05-08-08	03/11/1871 -	11/19/1876
[1]	WATSON, John	68-05-25	06/12/1820 -	12/07/1888
[1]	WATSON, Louisa w/o John Watson	69-07-04	01/18/1827 -	08/22/1896
[1]	WATSON, Edwin s/o John & Louisa Watson	01-02-??	03/12/1869 -	05/21/1870
[1]	WATTS, Catharine	75-05-00		10/12/1851
(G) [1]	WAECHTER, Joh. Georg "An elder in the Evangelical Lutheran Congregation here. Born in Liedolfheim, Wurtenberg. His parents who are deceased were Joh. Michael & Elizabeth."	71 y.11 m. 2 wks.	04/23/1731 -	04/09/1803
(G) [1]	WÄCHTER, Catharina NEE Weidman	61-00-04	03/06/1746 -	03/10/1807
(G) [1]	WÄCHTER, Friederich	53-11-24	09/25/1763 -	12/23/1817
(G) [1]	WÄCHTER, Anna Maria NEE Wolfe	45-04-04	05/28/1771 -	10/02/1816
(G) [1]	WÄCHTER, Johannes	48-06-21	10/01/1765 -	04/22/1814
(G) [1]	WECHTER, Georg	67-06-24	10/17/1769 -	05/11/1837
(G) [1]	WACHTER, Margaret NEE Elsere w/o Georg Wachter	47-08-06	01/26/1776 -	10/02/1823
[1]	WECHTER, Elizabeth d/o George & Margratha Wechter	63-07-15	04/30/1808 -	12/15/1871
(G) [1]	WECHTER, Elisabeth NEE Wohlfart w/o Johannes Wechter	76-06-08	07/16/1772 -	01/24/1849
(G) [1]	WAECHTER, Jacob (Stone is very worn.)	01-??-??	07/04/1781 -	08/21/1782
[1]	WECHTER, John	39-09-22	06/24/1798 -	04/16/1838
[1]	WECHTER, Mary w/o John Wechter	57-02-19	01/03/1802 -	03/22/1859
(G) [1]	WECHTER, George	79-06-07	03/31/1792 -	10/08/1871
(G) [1]	WECHTER, Sallie w/o George Wechter	82-11-00	09/15/1802 -	08/15/1885
(G) [1]	WECHTER, Elisabeth d/o Georg & Salome Wechter	00-03-09	07/14/1821 -	10/23/1821
(G) [1]	WECHTER, Elias	43-03-10	04/12/1811 -	07/22/1854
(G) [1]	WECHTER, Susanna NEE Oberl(in) w/o Elias Wechter	31-09-24	06/08/1821 -	04/02/1853
(G) [1]	WECHTER, John C. s/o Elias & Susanna Wechter	19-07-06	05/27/1842 -	01/03/1862
(G) [1]	WEACHTER, Catharine	48-07-12	03/11/1812 -	10/26/1860
[1]	WEACHTER, Isaac G.	70-10-29	06/16/1826 -	05/15/1897
[1]	WEACHTER, Eliza w/o Isaac G. Weachter	76-06-04	09/28/1831 -	04/02/1908
[1]	WEACHTER, John C.	67-09-03	05/15/1841 -	02/18/1909
(G) [1]	WEIDMAN, Jacob	66-09-08	03/12/1736 -	12/20/1802
(G) [1]	WEIDMAN, Barbara NEE Huber w/o Jacob Weidman	88-06-25	02/15/1740 -	09/08/1820
(G) [1]	WEIDMAN, Jacob w/o Jacob & Barbara Weidman	53-02-14	10/28/1762 -	01/11/1816
(G) [1]	WEIDMAN, Elisabeth NEE Zimmerman w/o Jacob Weidman	73-08-05	07/14/1774 -	03/19/1848
(G) [1]	WEIDMAN, Anna Maria d/o Jacob & Elisabeth Weidman	07-06-11	02/07/1791 -	08/18/1798
(G) [1]	WEIDMAN, Martin s/o Jacob & Barbara Weidman	27-08-01	01/15/1776 -	09/16/1803
(G) [1]	WEIDMAN, Johan George	74-06-01	11/25/1760 -	05/26/1835
(G) [1]	WEIDMAN, Barbara w/o Georg Weidman	41-08-07	12/30/1767 -	09/07/1809
(G) [1]	WEIDMAN, Elisabeth d/o Georg & Barbara Weidman	30-05-11	03/05/1790 -	08/21/1820
(G) [1]	WEIDMAN, Sussana d/o Geo G & Barbara Weidman	3 y. 3 m. 1 w.6 d.	10/18/1798 -	02/02/1802

		NAME	AGE	BORN	DIED
(G)	[1]	WEIDMAN, Elizabeth NEE Hinny w/o John George Weidman	67-09-24	11/09/1786 – 09/03/1854
(G)	[1]	WEIDMAN, Jacob s/o Georg & Elisabeth Weidman	14-01-08	10/28/1816 – 12/06/1830
(G)	[1]	WEIDMAN, Johannes F.	79-01-11	08/16/1764 – 09/27/1843
(G)	[1]	WEIDMAN, Anna Maria NEE Mayer w/o Johann	67-10-06	01/26/1771 – 12/02/1838
(G)	[1]	WEIDMAN, Catharina d/o Johannes & Anna Maria Weidman (Age & Dates as carved on Stone)	22-03-02	04/29/1803 – 01/27/1825
(G)	[1]	WEIDMAN, Martin	05-03-05	04/12/1770 – 07/17/1775
(G)	[1]	WEIDMAN, Samuel (Age & Dates as carved on stone.)	61-08-12	06/20/1778 – 04/02/1840
(G)	[1]	WEIDMAN, Christina w/o Samuel Weidman	80-06-06	08/13/1787 – 02/19/1868
(G)	[1]	WEIDMAN, Peter	86-10-28	12/09/1780 – 11/07/1867
(G)	[1]	WEIDMAN, Christina NEE Schnierer w/o Peter Weidman	65-03-28	06/05/1783 – 10/03/1848
	[1]	WEIDMAN, Elizabeth (Stone reset-death dates buried and F.E. Schnerer date used.)		05/24/1784 – 02/21/1796
(G)	[1]	WEIDMAN, David s/o Christoph & Elisabeth Weidman	07-11-19	12/28/1794 – 12/09/1802
(G)	[1]	WEIDMAN, William	59-08-24	08/02/1792 – 04/26/1852
(G)	[1]	WEIDMAN, Elisabeth NEE Ried w/o William Weidman	47-05-29	08/16/1798 – 02/15/1846
(G)	[1]	WEIDMAN, Mary d/o William & Elisabeth Weidman	15-10-10	11/26/1831 – 10/06/1847
(G)	[1]	WEIDMAN, Israel s/o Wilhelm & Elisabeth Weidman	02-11-00	02/22/1826 – 01/21/1829
(G)	[1]	WEIDMAN, Margaretha d/o William & Eliabe^t Weidman	78-04-16	05/22/1839 – 10/08/1847
(G)	[1]	WEIDMAN, George	38-04-25	08/28/1806 – 01/22/1845
	[1]	WEIDMAN, Susanna	82-10-11	02/19/1809 – 12/30/1891
	[3]	WEIDMAN, George	86-08-09	02/20/1809 – 10/29/1895
	[3]	WEIDMAN, Mary w/o George Weidman	77-04-09	03/20/1813 – 07/29/1890
(G)	[1]	WEIDMAN, David	50-01-07	04/28/1811 – 05/31/1861
	[1]	WEIDMAN, Elizabeth w/o David Weidman	67-11-28	08/14/1819 – 08/12/1887
(G)	[1]	WEIDMAN, Jacob s/o David & Eabl. Weidman	00-02-02	03/14/1844 – 05/16/1844
	[1]	WEIDMAN, George K. w/o David & Elizabeth Weidman	22-04-04	07/01/1850 – 11/05/1872
(G)	[1]	WEIDMAN, Maria d/o David & Elizabeth Weidman	09-02-19	10/20/1852 – 01/08/1862
(G)	[1]	WEIDMAN, Priscilla d/o David & Elizabeth Weidman	06-07-05	03/13/1855 – 12/16/1861
(G)	[1]	WEIDMAN, Samuel s/o David & Elizabeth Weidman (Age and dates as carved on stone.)	04-03-07	12/22/1857 – 12/28/1861
	[3]	WEIDMAN, Margaret	76-07-13	08/17/1810 – 04/30/1887
	[1]	WEIDMAN, Daniel	94-09-26	07/15/1811 – 05/11/1906
(G)	[1]	WEIDMAN, Martha NEE Stober(in) w/o Daniel Weidman	20-03-25	01/15/1816 – 05/10/1836
	[1]	WEIDMAN, Fianna w/o Daniel Weidman	72-09-05	04/10/1820 – 01/15/1893
(G)	[1]	WEIDMAN, Henrietta d/o Daniel & Fianna Weidman	18-11-03	02/01/1842 – 01/03/1861
	[1]	WEIDMAN, Joseph	79-00-06	12/17/1813 – 12/23/1892
(G)	[1]	WEIDMAN, Hannah w/o Joseph Weidman	39-08-24	01/04/1823 – 09/28/1862
	[1]	WEIDMAN, Harrietta d/o Joseph & Hannah Weidman	10-03-12	08/27/1849 – 12/23/1859
	[1]	WEIDMAN, Martin w/o Joseph & Hanna Weidman	00-06-10	10/29/1859 – 05/08/1860
(G)	[1]	WEIDMAN, Joseph s/o Joseph & Hannah Weidman	00-02-11	07/27/1862 – 10/09/1862
	[5]	WEIDMAN, Isaac	72-02-20	02/01/1821 – 04/21/1893
	[5]	WEIDMAN, Lydia w/o Isaac Weidman	61-00-01	07/30/1848 – 08/01/1901
	[1]	WEIDMAN, Catharine	75-09-18	01/08/1822 – 10/26/1897
	[1]	WIDEMAN, Louisa d/o David & Catharina Wideman	25-00-18	07/27/1845 – 08/15/1870
	[3]	WEIDMAN, Peter	76-05-03	01/17/1822 – 06/20/1898
	[3]	WEIDMAN, Lydia NEE Wechter	75-05-14	03/19/1826 – 09/03/1901
	[1]	WEIDMAN, Emanuel	67-01-03	10/06/1825 – 11/09/1892
	[1]	WEIDMAN, Lavina w/o Emanuel Weidman	69-11-11	04/02/1831 – 03/13/1901
	[1]	WEIDMAN, Amanda d/o Emanuel & Lavina Weidman	19-05-22	02/18/1857 – 08/10/1876
	[1]	WEIDMAN, Franklin s/o Emanuel & Lavina Weidman	01-08-06	08/01/1859 – 04/07/1861
	[1]	WEIDMAN, Catharine w/o Joel Weidman d/o Sam'l. & Catharine Hershberger	23-03-28	05/14/1830 – 09/12/1853
	[1]	WEIDMAN, Lewis s/o Joel & Catharine Weidman	02-00-07	09/02/1849 – 09/09/1851

	NAME	AGE	BORN		DIED
[1]	WEIDMAN, Obed	27-11-06	09/21/1836	-	08/27/1862
[1]	WEIDMAN, Israel "CO. G. 195 REGT. PA. VOL."	74-07-13			10/11/1910
[1]	WEIDMAN, Amelia B. w/o Israel Weidman	54-01-27			02/26/1897
[1]	WEIDMAN, Myers Geary s/o Israel & Amilia Weidman	00-01-11	06/08/1867	-	07/19/1867
[1]	WEIDMAN, Rebecca w/o Joseph Weidman d/o Benjamin and Susanna Britigam	31-10-03	08/05/1841	-	06/08/1873
[1]	WEIDMAN, Henry W. "Erected by his Grandsons"		09/04/1843	-	03/20/1924
[1]	WEIDMAN, Franklin	72-03-11	02/16/1845	-	05/27/1917
	Sarah	73-06-01	02/04/1846	-	08/05/1919
[1]	WEIDMAN, Emma d/o Franklin & Sarah Weidman	18-04-21	08/07/1867	-	12/28/1885
[1]	WEIDMAN, Infant s/o Franklin & Sarah Weidman				11/22/1870
[1]	WEIDMAN, William Z.	74-08-11	06/24/1846	-	03/05/1921
[1]	WEIDMAN, Lizzie S. w/o Wm. Weidman	48-00-04	01/14/1844	-	01/18/1892
[1]	WEIDMAN, Infant s/o William & Lizzie Weidman	00-00-06	05/14/1879	-	05/20/1879
[3]	WEIDMAN, Andrew	48-02-27	05/10/1846	-	08/07/1894
[3]	WEIDMAN, Anna E. NEE Stauffer w/o Andrew Weidman	75-09-12	03/25/1849	-	01/07/1925
[3]	WEIDMAN, Mary E. d/o Andrew & Anna Weidman	18-10-08	12/01/1869	-	10/09/1888
[3]	WEIDMAN, Anna d/o Andrew & Anna Weidman	01-01-26	11/18/1886	-	01/14/1888
[1]	WEIDMAN, Elias	73-04-24	12/05/1849	-	04/29/1893
(G) [1]	WEIDMAN, Jacob s/o Henry & Maria Weidman	01-10-28	07/22/1847	-	06/18/1849
[3]	WEIDMAN, Hiram	44-02-01	02/02/1855	-	04/03/1899
[3]	WEIDMAN, Sallie Z.		01/15/1853	-	02/06/1931
[3]	WEIDMAN, Adaline A. w/o Hiram Weidman	26-05-15	10/22/1857	-	04/07/1884
[1]	WEIDMAN, George W.		09/18/1857	-	09/07/1938
	Bella B.		10/26/1856	-	09/02/1930
[3]	WEIDMAN, Albert		1866	-	1948
	Kate, his wife		1866	-	1937
[2]	WEIDMAN, Clarence s/o Albert & Kate Weidman	02-09-18	12/15/1892	-	10/03/1895
[3]	WEIDMAN, Abraham B.		02/22/1870	-	12/24/1926
	Ella B., his wife		03/29/1871	-	05/05/1927
[2]	WEIDMAN, Aernum "Father"	50-08-19	01/17/1870	-	10/06/1920
[2]	WEIDMAN, Sidney "Mother"	74-00-27	11/11/1871	-	12/08/1945
[3]	WEIDMAN, Philip S. "Brothers"		1872	-	1954
	Kate W.		1871	-	1947
	John S.		1880	-	1958
	Lizzie P.		1878	-	1939
[3]	WEIDMAN, Cora d/o J.S. & Lizzie Weidman				08/23/1901
[5]	WEIDMAN, Wilson A.		02/07/1875	-	03/19/1949
	Ida E.		10/29/1870	-	08/10/1947
[1]	WEIDMAN, Lillie L. NEE Moyer		08/24/1878	-	04/07/1967
[2]	WEIDMAN, Milton L.		11/20/1878	-	07/08/1958
	Susan		08/02/1881	-	10/17/1957
[1]	WEIDMAN, Milton G.		09/29/1881	-	09/20/1939
[2]	WEIDMAN, Isaac S.		1883	-	1970
	Mahala H.		1883	-	1932
[2]	WEIDMAN, Isaac S.		1883	-	1963
	Dora K.		1004	-	1962
[2]	WEIDMAN, William C. s/o Isaac S. & Dora K. Weidman		08/02/1906	-	08/02/1906
[3]	WEIDMAN, Aaron A.		07/05/1885	-	11/21/1949
	Amy C. NEE Ramsey		03/01/1892	-	09/21/1965
[1]	WEIDMAN, Wayne H.		08/13/1888	-	12/25/1968
[5]	WEIDMAN, Albert Z.	62-03-15	02/24/1888	-	06/09/1950
	Anna K.	45-05-24	03/24/1892	-	09/17/1937
[3]	WEIDMAN, Harry B.		1892	-	1961
	Ellen R.		1895	-	1972

	NAME	AGE	BORN	DIED
[2]	WEIDMAN, Ellsworth M.		1901 –	
	Emma D.		1904 –	1969
	Betty J.		1926 –	1926
	Carl E.		1939 –	1940
[2]	WEIDMAN, Victor E.	01-07-13		02/17/1908
[2]	WEIDMAN, Clarence K.		07/04/1908 – 11/06/1977	
	Kathleen E.		10/21/1914 – 11/22/1975	
[2]	WEIDMAN, Dora E.	20 days		02/12/1942
[2]	WEIDMAN, Susan E.	28 days		06/21/1949
[2]	WEIDMAN, Margie	00-10-29		09/13/1909
[2]	WEIDMAN, Joseph B.		1910 –	
	Ruth C.		1920 –	
[3]	WEIDMAN, Luther E.		09/24/1920 –	
	Marian M. NEE Miller		09/04/1927 – 09/29/1973	
[1]	WEIDMAN, Mark M.		1922 –	1956
	Pauline T.		1924 –	
[2]	WEIDMAN, Marshall		03/12/1924 – 05/08/1924	
[2]	WEIDMAN, Infant d/o Beatrice Weidman	Stillborn	04/07/1936	
[8]	WEIDMAN, Alberta (No dates for any of these names.)			
	Katie			
	Norman			
	James			
[3]	WEIDERS, Harry Z.		1881 –	1958
[3]	WEIDERS, Lizzie	33-01-16		02/16/1916
[3]	WEIDERS, Katie G.		1893 –	1972
[3]	WEIDERS, Mabel	05-05-11		12/28/1911
[3]	WEIDERS, Harry L.		1909 –	1932
(G) [1]	WEIMAN, Georg		05/14/1714 – 06/18/1788	
(G) [1]	WEIMEN(IN), Catharina NEE Bock(en) (The stones of George and		08/19/1714 – 05/09/1787	
	Catharina were reset. Death dates from earlier list.)			
(G) [1]	WEIMAN, Georg	73-06-17	01/20/1785 – 07/03/1859	
[7]	WEINHOLD, Mary Jane "Mother"		08/27/1947 – 01/11/1981	
[2]	WEITZEL, Isaac H.	76-03-17	04/15/1860 – 08/02/1936	
	Amanda K.	75-05-04	01/01/1859 – 06/05/1934	
[2]	WEITZEL, Elisabeth E.		12/16/1881 – 08/15/1950	
[2]	WEITZEL, Sallie H. d/o John & Lizzie Reider	23-04-21	06/05/1895 – 10/26/1918	
(G) [1]	WEMER(IN), Anamaria		1729 – 10/20/1787	
[8]	WENRICH, Jacob		08/03/1906 –	
	Minnie		08/22/1906 – 10/24/1970	
[1]	WHITCRAFT, George	63rd yr.	1742 – 09/22/1805	
[8]	WHITCRAFT, Daniel D.	77-05-19	06/04/1857 – 11/23/1934	
	Annie R.	83-01-04	05/22/1865 – 06/26/1943	
[1]	WHITCRAFT, John J.		1885 –	1960
	Ida D.		1889 –	1958
	Ronald T. "Son"		1933 –	1959
[1]	WHITCRAFT, Sons of John J. & Ida D. Whitcraft			
	Ralph			1909
	Daniel			1910
(G) [1]	WEITH, Johan P.	74-06-23	09/17/1774 – 04/11/1849	
[1]	WHITE, Elizabeth w/o Peter White (As carved)	88-01-03	02/02/1795 – 03/05/1885	
(G) [1]	WEITH, Heinrich s/o Johan Peter & Elesabeth	36-00-19	09/08/1813 – 09/27/1849	
(G) [1]	WEIT, Maria w/o Henry Weit married a second time to			
	Edward Ditzler	71-08-28	11/27/1814 – 06/25/1886	
[1]	WHITE, Peter husband of Hannah White	71-06-27	09/13/1810 – 04/10/1882	
[1]	WHITE, Hannah Sharp w/o Peter White	85-10-19	06/11/1814 – 04/30/1900	

		NAME	AGE	BORN	DIED
	[1]	WEIT, George	50-11-07	06/23/1818 – 05/30/1869
(G)	[1]	WEIT, Mary w/o George Weit	32-07-10	09/06/1825 – 04/16/1857
	[2]	WEIT, Samuel	47-02-19	04/12/1828 – 07/01/1875
	[2]	WEIT, Catharine w/o Samuel Weit	87-03-28	10/08/1820 – 02/06/1908
	[2]	WEIT, Minnie H. "Daughter"		1891 – 1971
	[1]	WEITH, Lydia	53-05-20	02/11/1834 – 07/31/1887
	[3]	WEIT, Henry W.		10/01/1850 – 01/13/1923
		Emeline C. Ulrich, his wife		09/08/1854 – 01/19/1934
	[3]	WEIT, Mary U. "Daughter"		07/15/1877 – 10/13/1947
	[3]	WEITE, Emeline U. d/o Henry & Emeline "Baptized 6/9/1889"		10/04/1887 – 06/06/1892
	[7]	WEIT, Elias G.		07/14/1849 – 03/25/1932
		Christianna		08/03/1852 – 12/09/1934
	[2]	WEIT, Nathaniel K.		1857 – 1944
		Emma B.		1859 – 1945
	[2]	WEIT, Edwin K.		1861 – 1949
		Lizzie B. Hartranft, his wife		1864 – 1947
	[2]	WEIT, Weyne s/o Edwin & Lizzie Weit	00-01-13	07/18/1883 – 09/01/1883
	[2]	WEIT, Samuel H.		1907 – 1910
	[7]	WEIT, Martin G.		08/13/1877 – 07/01/1963
		Lizzie Z.		11/01/1878 – 07/20/1927
	[7]	WEIT, Elva d/o Martin G. & Lizzie Z. Weit	00-08-03	12/21/1897 – 08/24/1898
	[2]	WEIT, Phares J.		11/06/1879 – 01/17/1967
		Mary		04/10/1884 – 09/11/1972
	[2]	WEIT, Alvin N. s/o Phares & Mary Weit	00-02-14	05/20/1903
	[2]	WHITE, Lizzie M. "Mother"		05/13/1881 – 11/01/1912
	[2]	WHITE, Clarence E. "Son"		06/17/1899 – 11/24/1916
	[2]	WEIT, Lincoln		1894 – 1965
		Carrie L.		1898 – 19__
		Jean M.		1937 – 1938
		Richard F.		1938 – 1939
		Margaret A.		1942 – 1943
	[6]	WHITE, George A. "CPL. CO. I 113TH INF."		1915 – 1980
		Kathryn A.		1915 –
	[9]	WHITE, Jody Sue d/o Richard & Bonnie White		11/07/1969 – 11/27/1969
	[5]	WHITMAN, Adam		01/20/1849 – 03/11/1916
		Sarah NEE Miller		06/15/1855 – 09/26/1931
	[5]	WHITMAN, Susie C. d/o Adam & Sarah A. Whitman	01-09-09	06/03/1880 – 03/12/1882
	[5]	WHITMAN, Clayton M. s/o Adam & Sarah A. Whitman	06-10-14	05/27/1876 – 04/11/1883
(G)	[1]	WIELAND, Heinrich	73-01-15	05/12/1769 – 06/27/1842
(G)	[1]	WIELAND, Elisabeth NEE Haushalter w/o Henrich	73-08-26	01/06/1768 – 10/02/1841
(G)	[1]	WIELAND, Johannes	63-08-26	07/28/1783 – 03/24/1847
(G)	[1]	WIELAND, Catharina w/o Johannes Wieland	57-08-04	05/27/1783 – 01/01/1841
	[1]	WIELAND, Salome d/o John & Catharine Wieland	74-08-28	01/12/1808 – 10/10/1882
(G)	[1]	WIELAND, Maria d/o John & Catharine Wieland	69-01-25	01/15/1810 – 03/10/1879
(G)	[1]	WIELAND, Samuel s/o Johanes & Catharina Wieland	21-04-06	07/28/1811 – 12/04/1832
(G)	[1]	WIELAND, Susanna	70-01-23	07/31/1780 – 09/23/1850
(G)	[1]	WIELAND, Georg	51-04-14	02/11/1806 – 06/25/1867
	[1]	WEALAND, Catharine	84-10-06	12/06/1816 – 10/12/1901
(G)	[1]	WEACH, Johan Adam	70-10-16	02/15/1770 – 01/01/1841
(G)	[1]	WEACK, Catharina w/o Johan Adam Weack	87-06-25	01/15/1774 – 09/09/1861
	[2]	WIKE, Peter	76-11-11	07/16/1893
(G)	[1]	WIKE, Mary w/o Peter Wike	39-10-08	09/13/1820 – 07/21/1859
	[3]	WIKE, Sally w/o Samuel Wike	78-02-20	03/22/1822 – 06/12/1900
	[3]	WEIK, Urias s/o Samuel & Sarah Weik	22-01-03	12/22/1853 – 01/25/1876
	[2]	WIKE, Emma Elizabeth d/o Henry H. & Laura Wike	12-11-03	10/27/1868 – 10/03/1881
	[2]	WIKE, Zackarias T. (This stone looks the same as Laura Stamm's.)		1874 – 1942

	NAME	AGE	BORN	DIED
[1]	WIKE, Monroe E.	01-04-08		04/01/1887
[1]	WIKE, Marlin O.		07/09/1906 - 07/11/1975	
	Margaret A.		02/24/1917 - 10/31/1980	
[5]	WEIK, Henry		05/30/1917 -	
	Helene S.		10/29/1929 - 06/22/1985	
[1]	WILLIAMS, Lewis	72-10-20	02/27/1793 - 01/19/1866	
[1]	WILLIAMS, Peter	48-06-15	02/22/1822 - 09/06/1870	
[2]	WILLIAMS, Joseph K.		02/22/1861 - 02/27/1939	
	Amanda U.		07/05/1857 - 08/12/1933	
[2]	WILLIAMS, Robert		1886 - 1893	
[2]	WILLIAMS, Clayton "T/SGT. 86AAFBU WW I WW II"		03/11/1897 - 10/11/1979	
	Mary M. NEE Scott		03/14/1907 - 04/09/1978	
[1]	WILLIAMSO_, Lewis	25-04-21	12/19/1832 - 05/11/1857	
[3]	WILSON, James P. "PVT CO D 162ND INFANTRY 41ST DIV WW I"		08/01/1895 - 02/26/1981	
	Mabel M.		02/22/1894 - 12/23/1982	
[1]	WISE, Rachel w/o Peter Wise d/o Benjamin &			
	Elizabeth Balmer	46-06-18	11/29/1810 - 06/16/1857	
[7]	WITHERS, Curtis S. (Shares stone with Ned		1883 - 1961	
	Stella K. and Clara Hammer)		1885 - 1978	
	Esther M.		1913 -	
[8]	WITMER, Beulah I.		06/26/1920 - 05/17/1924	
(G) [1]	WOHLFART, Margaret NEE Heges(in)	88-00-16	04/30/1734 - 05/16/1822	
(G) [1]	WOHLFART, Martin	55-09-27	06/16/1759 - 04/13/1815	
(G) [1]	WOLF, Samuel	26-05-26	06/27/1785 - 12/22/1811	
(G) [1]	WOLF, George s/o Michael & Elizabeth Wolf	84-01-17	03/23/1781 - 05/09/1865	
(G) [1]	WOLF, Maria d/o Michael & Elizabeth Wolf	72-06-17	04/18/1792 - 11/05/1864	
(G) [1]	WOLF, Regina d/o Michael & Elizabeth Wolf	78-01-23	03/13/1799 - 05/05/1877	
(G) [1]	WOLF, Johan Jacob "born in Wurtemberg"	40-03-17	10/16/1791 - 02/02/1832	
(G) [1]	WOLF, Henry	75-09-13	05/13/1791 - 02/26/1870	
[1]	WOLF, Catharine w/o Henry Wolf	83-04-17	11/20/1807 - 04/07/1891	
[1]	WOLF, Jacob	52-08-20		04/11/1893
[5]	WOLF, Samuel H.	86-08-24		03/20/1931
[5]	WOLF, Annie w/o S.H. Wolf	62-01-19		03/14/1903
[5]	WOLF, Melinda D. d/o Samuel H. & Anna Wolf	19-02-28	01/22/1867 - 04/20/1886	
[5]	WOLF, Henry s/o Samuel & Anna Wolf	02-00-14	05/06/1869 - 05/20/1871	
[5]	WOLF, Harvey D. "Son"	71-03-24		01/20/1945
[5]	WOLF, Adaline d/o Samuel & Anna Wolf	00-02-08	12/03/1875 - 02/11/1876	
(G) [1]	WOODS, Barbara NEE Schaefer w/o John Woods		02/20/1789 - 02/03/1858	
[1]	YEAKEL, Franklin M.	82-09-14		04/22/1936
[1]	YEAKEL, Fianna M.	54-04-24		07/12/1920
[1]	YEAKEL, Jacob H. s/o F.M. & Fianna Yeakel	16-01-13	07/29/1886 - 09/12/1902	
[1]	YEAKEL, George L.H. s/o Frank & Fianna Yeakel	01-06-??	09/12/1890 - 04/01/1891	
[1]	YEAKEL, Byron H. s/o Frank & Fianna Yeakel		Born & Died 06/11/1891	
[1]	YEAKEL, Abram (Roseboro Funeral Home marker)		1892 - 1984	
[5]	YOUNG, Obed	65-02-15	05/20/1829 - 08/05/1894	
[5]	YOUNG, Mary w/o Obed Young	77-00-14	01/06/1834 - 01/20/1911	
[5]	YOUNG, William s/o Obed & Mary Young	08-04-24	10/21/1862 - 03/15/1871	
[5]	YOUNG, George s/o Obed & Mary Young	06-03-23	11/20/1864 - 03/23/1871	
[5]	YOUNG, Peter s/o Obed & Mary Young	02-01-05	02/09/1869 - 03/14/1871	
[1]	YOUNG, Catharine d/o Daniel & Sarah Young	00-02-00	09/27/1852 - 11/27/1852	
[5]	YOUNG, Samuel E.		1871 - 1954	
	Nora E.		1881 - 1938	
[5]	YOUNG, Obed S. s/o Samuel & Nora E. Young	03-??-??	03/28/1898 - 05/??/1901	
[5]	YOUNG, Samuel S. "Son"		06/13/1902 - 06/26/1955	
[5]	YOUNG, Paul S. s/o Samuel E. & Nora E. Young	18-02-17	09/19/1904 - 12/06/1922	

		NAME	AGE	BORN	DIED
	[5]	YONG, Verna (This stone was not carved by a 'stone cutter'.)		11/09/1913 - 05/04/1914	

INITIAL STONE: [1] M.Z.

		NAME	AGE	BORN	DIED
	[3]	ZANDER, Elam E.		1898 -	1964
		Mabel M.		1902 -	1980
	[1]	ZARTMAN, Large monument with the following inscription: "In grateful memory of Alexander Zartman and his wife Ann Catharina Zartman who came to America in 1728. Erected by many descendants. A.D. 1913"			
	[1]	ZARTMAN, Red sandstone Date Stone with the following inscription: "Built by D & F Zartman 1883"			
(G)	[1]	ZARTMAN, Allexander	72-04-03	07/29/1731 - 12/02/1803	
(G)	[1]	ZARTMAN, Michael	70-10-28	05/03/1754 - 04/01/1825	
(G)	[1]	ZARTMAN, Alexander	63-00-04	03/19/1756 - 03/23/1819	
(G)	[1]	ZARTMAN, Maria Barbara	72-07-08	08/20/1760 - 03/28/1833	
(G)	[1]	ZARTMAN, Margaretha	75-00-11	08/21/1763 - 09/02/1838	
(G)	[1]	ZARTMAN, Elisabeth (Stone reset. Age and Death from earlier list.)	75-03-08	08/05/1781 - 11/13/1856	
(G)	[1]	ZARTMAN, Catharina	60-02-18	10/09/1783 - 12/27/1843	
(G)	[1]	ZARTMEN(EN), Elisabeth "Taufzeigen waren Alexander Zartman und sei Ehfrau Barbara." (Sponsors were Alexander and Barbara Zartman)	3 y.3 w. 5 d.	03/16/1785 - 08/11/1788	
	[1]	ZARTMAN, John	85-01-19	09/25/1788 - 11/14/1873	
	[1]	ZARTMAN, Regina	78-08-13	03/29/1794 - 12/11/1872	
(G)	[1]	ZARTMAN, Johannes	58-09-12	12/07/1794 - 09/19/1853	
(G)	[1]	ZARTMAN, Sarah w/o John Zartman	75-07-03	06/02/1799 - 01/05/1874	
	[1]	ZARTMAN, Samuel s/o John & Sarah Zartman (Stone reset and death date buried)		10/15/1834 - ??	
(G)	[1]	ZARTMAN, Sarah d/o Johan & Sarah Zartman	03-11-14	10/01/1829 - 09/17/1833	
(G)	[1]	ZARTMAN, Margaretha	56-10-10	10/29/1796 - 09/08/1853	
(G)	[1]	ZARTMAN, Georg	19 days	09/16/1799	
(G)	[1]	ZARTMAN, Catharina		10/29/1799 - 04/04/1800	
	[1]	ZARTMAN, David	85-05-22	06/06/1800 - 11/28/1885	
(G)	[1]	ZARTMAN, Elisabeth NEE Bender w/o David Zartman	46 yrs. less 3 d.	11/01/1809 - 10/29/1855	
(G)	[1]	ZARTMAN, Jacob	7 m.1 w. 5 d.	01/15/1804 - 08/27/1804	
(G)	[1]	ZARTMAN, Willhelm s/o Jacob & Elisabeth Zartman	01-04-11	08/14/1813 - 12/25/1814	
	[2]	ZARTMAN, Israel	83-04-24	11/07/1817 - 03/31/1901	
	[2]	ZARTMAN, Catharine w/o Israel Zartman	79-11-12	12/04/1816 - 11/16/1895	
(G)	[3]	ZARTMAN, William	29-09-08	11/25/1823 - 09/13/1853	
(G)	[3]	ZARTMAN, Mary d/o Willm & Anna Zartman	00-09-25	10/16/1847 - 08/11/1848	
(G)	[1]	ZARTMAN, John	32-05-01	08/29/1827 - 01/30/1860	
	[1]	ZARTMAN, Mary w/o John Zartman	60-07-21	U6/22/1824 - 02/12/1005	
(G)	[1]	ZARTMAN, Samuel s/o John & Mary Zartman	00-11-13		01/04/1850
(G)	[1]	ZARTMAN, Adaline d/o John & Mary Zartman	01-09-08	12/08/1851 - 09/16/1853	
	[1]	ZARTMAN, Peter	81-07-26	08/05/1832 - 04/01/1914	
		Sarah NEE Wechter	81-06-18	03/27/1840 - 10/14/1921	
	[1]	ZARTMAN, Fianna d/o Peter & Sarah Zartman	03-06-06	10/30/1858 - 05/05/1862	
	[1]	ZARTMAN, Amanda d/o Peter & Sarah Zartman	06-05-27	05/08/1873 - 11/03/1879	
	[2]	ZARTMAN, David	65-08-06	03/15/1834 - 11/21/1899	
	[2]	ZARTMAN, Fianna w/o David Zartman	71-11-18	08/13/1838 - 08/01/1910	

	NAME	AGE	BORN	DIED
[3]	ZARTMAN, Benjamin	70-06-25		02/23/1906
[3]	ZARTMAN, Elizabeth	69-00-15		09/18/1905
[3]	ZARTMAN, William s/o Benjamin & Elizabeth Zartman	00-06-07	10/21/1869 - 04/28/1870	
[5]	ZARTMAN, William	72-08-13	09/11/1841 - 05/24/1914	
[5]	ZARTMAN, Anna w/o William Zartman	79-03-08	05/20/1842 - 08/28/1921	
(G) [1]	ZARTMAN, Infant s/o William & Anna Zartman		10/28/1861	
(G) [1]	ZARTMAN, Infant s/o William & Anna Zartman		07/27/1862	
[1]	ZARTMAN, Lizzie Ann d/o William & Anna Zartman	07-03-??	10/28/1869 - 02/13/1877	
[2]	ZARTMAN, Addison W.	80-10-04	08/30/1841 - 07/04/1922	
	Leventine C.	80-10-12	01/18/1845 - 11/30/1926	
[2]	ZARTMAN, Martin W.	81-10-26	11/29/1844 - 10/25/1926	
	Mary A.	76-03-05	10/31/1847 - 04/06/1923	
[2]	ZARTMAN, Hiram s/o Martin & Mary Zartman	00-08-12	01/18/1887 - 09/30/1887	
[3]	ZARTMAN, Addison R.	54-11-05	06/28/1850 - 06/03/1905	
[3]	ZARTMAN, Alta Catharine d/o Addison R. & Mary I. Zartman	06-01-09	12/11/1890 - 01/20/1897	
[1]	ZARTMAN, John G.	43-04-07		09/05/1903
[1]	ZARTMAN, Delila M.		1861 -	1937
[1]	ZARTMAN, Mary d/o John & Delilah Zartman	01-02-10	08/29/1883 - 11/09/1884	
[1]	ZARTMAN, William s/o John & Delilah Zartman	00-09-20	08/27/1881 - 06/17/1882	
[3]	ZARTMAN, John H.		1858 -	1896
	Mary B., his wife		1860 -	1922
[2]	ZARTMAN, John E. "Father"	78-09-06	01/26/1861 - 11/01/1939	
	Susanna NEE Stober "Mother"	88-11-07	10/22/1864 - 09/29/1953	
[2]	ZARTMAN, George H.		1869 -	1954
	Ida G.		1874 -	1955
[2]	ZARTMAN, Monroe I.		1869 -	1947
	Cora S.		1875 -	1962
	Minerva L.		1898 -	
[3]	ZARTMAN, Wayne K.		05/12/1871 - 04/17/1951	
	Lydia H.		01/09/1872 - 04/14/1935	
	Catharine		10/06/1898 - 05/05/1946	
[7]	ZARTMAN, Eli		1873 -	1941
	Sarah Forry		1878 -	1937
	Martin		1908 -	1909
[7]	ZARTMAN, Martin K. s/o Eli & Sarah Zartman	00-02-26		02/03/1909
[3]	ZARTMAN, Phares K.	71-00-06	07/15/1876 - 07/21/1947	
	Clara E.	93-06-21	04/15/1879 - 11/06/1972	
[3]	ZARTMAN, Clayton K.		07/18/1880 - 10/10/1956	
[5]	ZARTMAN, Aaron	27-06-21	08/12/1883 - 03/03/1911	
[2]	ZARTMAN, Clayton S.		03/04/1884 - 08/21/1959	
	Ella M.		06/13/1882 - 09/30/1952	
[2]	ZARTMAN, Violet d/o Clayton & Ella Zartman	2 days		05/07/1914
[3]	ZARTMAN, David J.		1888 -	1969
	Maggie M.		1891 -	1964
[3]	ZARTMAN, Infant d's/o David J. & Maggie M. Zartman			
	Pauline	3 mnths.		1922
	Grace L.	4 days		1930
[7]	ZARTMAN, Israel B.		06/20/1895 - 03/17/1964	
	Annie		02/17/1897 -	
[1]	ZARTMAN, Phares S.		04/29/1896 -	
	Annie E.		10/09/1893 -	
[7]	ZARTMAN, Ira F.		1899 -	1981
	Edythe G.		1901 -	1960
	Evan N.		1913 -	

		NAME	AGE	BORN	DIED
	[3]	ZARTMAN, Levi H.		1901 –	1978
		Esta M.		1905 –	
	[3]	ZARTMAN, Nancy Jane		08/13/1940 –	08/14/1940
	[3]	ZARTMAN, Roy B.		1903 –	1967
		Naomi		1908 –	1950
	[5]	ZARTMAN, John B.		09/18/1910 –	05/07/1986
		Bertha		12/23/1909 –	
	[7]	ZARTMAN, E. Forry		11/07/1908 –	
		Esther M.		05/16/1910 –	
	[3]	ZARTMAN, Lillian S.	00-01-18		10/12/1916
	[7]	ZARTMAN, Charles "SEAMAN 2ND CLASS CO. NO. 162"		11/03/1926 –	04/14/1945
	[3]	ZARTMAN, Virginia Adele			1932
	[3]	ZARTMAN is carved on the back of Henry A. & Frances L. Heiland's stone.			
	[1]	ZEIGLER, Sarah d/o John & Margaret Zeigler	16-03-17	07/13/1849 –	10/31/1865
(G)	[1]	ZELLER, Peter	47-04-24	02/08/1780 –	07/03/1827
	[1]	ZELLER, John	76-03-04	10/14/1788 –	01/18/1864
(G)	[1]	ZELLER, Lydia w/o John Zeller	62-01-11	09/22/1796 –	11/03/1858
	[1]	ZELLER, Levi "Father"	61-01-01	05/20/1820 –	06/21/1881
	[1]	ZELLER, Catharine w/o Levi Zeller "Mother"	72-08-12	02/17/1820 –	10/29/1802
(G)	[1]	ZELLER, Ann Maria, little d/o Levi & Cathara Zeller	00-01-08	08/13/1862 –	09/21/1862
(G)	[1]	ZELLER, Levina	01-08-01	11/13/1820 –	07/14/1822
	[5]	ZELLER, John	57-09-29		06/20/1910
	[5]	ZELLER, Susan F.	62-10-05		02/20/1922
	[5]	ZELLER, Edgar I.	71-10-17		08/02/1967
	[5]	ZELLER, Alice B. d/o John & Susan Zeller	08-11-10	04/09/1879 –	03/19/1888
	[9]	ZELLER, Anna S. (Shares stone with Alverta Z. Mentzer.)		1883 –	1973
	[7]	ZELLER, Levi L. (Shares stone with Martin & Ella G. Helen Hollinger.)		1886 – 1886 –	1942 1971
	[8]	ZENTMYER, Rosa Ann (See Long-Doster Monument.)	78-03-28	10/05/1860 –	02/03/1939
	[1]	ZERBE, Larry Ray s/o Lester & Mabel Zerbe		Born & Died	12/20/1942
(G)	[1]	ZIEGER, Elizabet	19-07-??	01/16/1765 –	09/15/1784
(G)	[1]	ZIGER(N), Barbara NEE Weidman	26 yrs.	12/14/1758 –	12/07/1784
		(The above stone is slate and upper portion has broken away in layers. Name and birth month and day are from F.E. Schnerer list.)			
	[2]	ZIMMERMAN, Martin S.		06/05/1907 –	08/31/1977
		Elizabeth M.		11/23/1908 –	
	[8]	ZOOK, Moses K.		02/26/1923 –	
		Grace H. NEE Keller		01/18/1920 –	
(G)	[1]	ZUG, Margaretha	25-03-28	08/23/1803 –	12/22/1828
	[3]	ZWALLY, Franklin L.		1897 –	1961
		Mary K.		1897 –	1980
		Elizabeth A.		1925 –	
	[7]	ZWALLY, Eugene F.		10/11/1904 –	04/06/1982
		Helen T.		05/25/1909 –	

Transcribed November 1987 by Martha Xakellis

HAMMER CREEK MENNONITE CEMETERY #3

This cemetery is located in Elizabeth Township at the intersection of Hammer Creek and Brunnerville Roads. It is surrounded by a pipe fence and has a driveway thru it. The Hammer Creek Mennonite Church is located across Brunnerville Road on the corner and the date stone indicates that the church was built in 1819 and rebuilt in 1913.

	NAME	AGE	BORN	DIED
	ALTHOUSE, Barbara H. w/o John W. Althouse	30-03-00	02/05/1857 - 05/05/1887	
	ADAMS, Josiah K. "Father"	26-04-02	06/17/1892 - 10/19/1918	
	ADAMS, Miriam E.		1919 -	
	Ivan C., Jr.		1918 -	1971
	ADAMS, Bernetha S.		1910 -	1976
	Ira. W.		1907 -	1986
	ADAMS, Alvin W.		1901 -	1971
	Clara E.		1903 -	1965
	Shirley		1935 -	1935
	AIRES, Anna H.		1906 -	
	Ray G.		1902 -	1971
	BARTSCH, John H.		01/08/1910 - 10/23/1930	
	BEYER, Russell R.		03/10/1907 -	
	Mary H.		06/12/1911 - 03/07/1982	
	BEYER, John W. s/o Russell & Mary Beyer		03/19/1935 - 03/26/1936	
	BEYER, Arlene W. d/o Russell & Mary Beyer		08/12/1944 - 05/22/1946	
	BENEDICT, Harry B.		1905 -	1973
	BITTNER, Elizabeth	73-11-13		03/14/1906
	Abraham	86-03-05		07/20/1922
	BITTNER, Jacob H. "Father" (On front of stone)		1862 -	1940
	Howard Zook (back of stone)		03/21/1889 - 05/06/1976	
	BLESSING, George B.		1900 -	1953
	Mazie N.		1908 -	1971
	BLESSING, Infant s/o Geo. & Mazie Blessing			11/06/1931
	BLESSING, Mary Ann d/o Geo. & Mazie Blessing	00-03-18		1938
	BLESSING, Clyde E.		11/28/1943 - 07/28/1981	
	Lena S.		04/07/1947 -	
(G)	BRUBAKER, John	86-03-17	01/10/1797 - 02/27/1884	
(G)	BRUBAKER, Susan w/o John Brubaker	82-00-05	01/16/1804 - 01/21/1886	
(G)	BRUBAKER, Isaac s/o Johannes & Susan	00-10-00	10/25/1846 - 08/24/1847	
	BRUBAKER, Jonas	49-08-23	06/16/1837 - 03/09/1887	
	BRUBAKER, Susanna B.	20-00-04	08/14/1840 - 08/18/1860	
	BRUBAKER, Henry E.	84-02-20	02/01/1815 - 04/21/1899	
	BRUBAKER, Mary NEE Hershey	83-00-09	09/19/1820 - 09/28/1903	
	BRUBAKER, Jacob E.	76-08-05	06/14/1821 - 02/19/1898	
	BRUBAKER, Elizabeth w/o Jacob E. Brubaker	65-11-21	06/04/1825 - 05/25/1891	
	BRUBAKER, John H.	67-06-26	07/02/1825 - 01/28/1893	
	BRUBAKER, Fanny H. w/o John H. Brubaker	74-10-15	11/25/1826 - 10/10/1901	
(G)	BRUBACHER, Elias s/o John H. & Fanny Brubacher	21-04-11	09/17/1850 - 01/28/1872	
(G)	BRUBACHER, Nathan s/o John H. & Fanny Brubacher	01-05-01	12/20/1868 - 05/21/1869	
	BRUBAKER, Henry S.	69-05-27	06/02/1828 - 11/29/1897	
	BRUBAKER, Elizabeth w/o Henry S. Brubaker	73-05-26	11/24/1830 - 05/20/1904	
	BRUBACHER, Jacob H.	40-11-16	05/10/1832 - 04/26/1873	
(G)	BRUBACHER, Anna NEE Brubacher w/o Jacob Brubacher	25-01-10	10/07/1841 - 11/18/1866	
	BRUBACHER, Infant d/o J. & A. Brubacher			09/04/1864
	BRUBACHER, Infant s/o J. & A. Brubacher			11/09/1866
	BRUBACHER, Martin s/o Jacob & Anna Brubacher	03-05-13	No Dates	

NAME	AGE	BORN	DIED
BRUBAKER, Infant s/o J. & H. Brubaker (This stone is with the five previous stones. Could be second wife's.)			01/06/1870
BRUBAKER, Isaac	63-03-05	10/17/1839 - 01/22/1903	
BRUBAKER, Maria B. w/o Isaac Brubaker	51-02-20	12/14/1838 - 03/04/1890	
BRUBAKER, Jacob H.	In his 48th year.	03/14/1846 - 01/26/1894	
BRUBAKER, Elizabeth H.	In her 63rd year.	02/01/1844 - 08/31/1906	
BRUBAKER, David S. s/o Elizabeth H. & Jacob H. Brubaker	In his 2nd year.	02/03/1877 - 08/31/1878	
BRUBAKER, Abram H.	73-08-06		04/21/1920
Susan B., his wife	81-09-27		07/08/1934
BRUBAKER, Benjamin B. s/o Abraham H. & Susan B. Brubaker		08/08/1872 - 08/06/1895	
BRUBAKER, Christian B.		04/04/1853 - 10/08/1940	
Mary K.		07/07/1856 - 08/24/1925	
BRUBAKER, Amilla d/o Christian & Mary Brubaker	02-09-09	02/01/1880 - 11/10/1882	
BRUBAKER, Harry H.		03/28/1855 - 01/06/1937	
Fanny Kreider w/o Harry H. Brubaker		08/18/1857 - 02/19/1927	
BRUBAKER, Daughters of Harry H. & Fanny Brubaker			
Elizabeth K.		1881 -	1939
Anna K.		1877 -	1963
BRUBAKER, John H.	78-08-28	1855 -	1933
Adeline G.	86-01-23	1856 -	1942
BRUBAKER, Peter H.	64-10-13	09/25/1857 - 08/08/1922	
BRUBAKER, Lizzie w/o Peter H. Brubaker	50-03-09	05/18/1861 - 08/27/1911	
BRUBAKER, Levi B.		1859 -	1923
BRUBAKER, Menno H.	73-04-11	02/26/1857 - 07/07/1930	
Catharine B. w/o Menno H. Brubaker	61-04-28	08/10/1860 - 01/08/1922	
BRUBAKER, Children of Menno H. & Catharine B. Brubaker			
Katie May	06-08-27	05/12/1882 - 02/08/1889	
Menno B.	05-10-12	10/22/1893 - 09/04/1899	
BRUBAKER, Reuben H.	70-03-10	06/30/1860 - 10/10/1930	
Susan	56-06-05	12/03/1865 - 06/08/1922	
BRUBAKER, Amanda H.	65-03-11	01/13/1867 - 04/24/1932	
Mary H.	62-07-05	05/26/1871 - 12/31/1933	
BRUBAKER, Harry B.		01/01/1884 - 12/06/1971	
Edith I. NEE Turner		07/02/1894 - 01/11/1963	
BRUBAKER, Nathan (Son)	09-03-17	1878 -	1889
Cora E. (Daughter)	03-05-16	1885 -	1889
(This looks to be a replacement stone and does not give parents names.)			
BRUBAKER, Levi B.		1888 -	1930
Mabel S.		1890 -	1968
BRUBAKER, Edith d/o Levi & Mabel Brubaker	00-05-21	09/16/1909 - 03/07/1910	
BRUBAKER, John B.	73-04-02	09/16/1896 - 01/18/1970	
Mary H. NEE Burkholder w/o John B. Brubaker	21-10-02	07/02/1902 - 05/04/1924	
BRUBAKER, R. Harold s/o John & Lizzie Brubaker	00-00-10		1931
BRUMBACH, Morris C.	75-04-10	01/08/1862 - 05/18/1937	
Susan S., his wife	60-08-26	02/17/1862 - 11/13/1922	
BRUMBACH, Peter s/o Morris C. & Susan Brumbach	00-04-10	04/20/1890 - 8/30/1890	
BRUMBACH, Sarah d/o Morris & Susan Brumbach	00-00-05		06/17/1891
BRUMBACH, Infant s/o M.C. & Susan B. Brumbach	00-00-11		02/03/1898
BRUMBACH, Hiram S.		1890 -	1969
Elizabeth W.		1893 -	1961
Morris J.		1930 -	1930
Arlene J.		1931 -	1931
BRUMBACH, Isaac "CO. G 11TH INF."		01/25/1894 - 03/20/1965	

NAME	AGE	BORN	DIED
BRUMBACH, Harry S.		1896 –	1973
Elsie M.		1901 –	1984
BRUMBACH, Grace Irene d/o Harry & Elsie Brumbach	10-08-19	07/03/1919 –	03/22/1930
BRUMBACH, Helen Marie d/o Harry S. & Elsie Brumbach	00-03-16	05/21/1921 –	09/06/1921
BRUMBACH, Daniel S.		1899 –	1944
Lucy s/o Daniel S. Brumbach		1899 –	1952
BRUMBACH, Elmer S.		08/04/1904 –	02/27/1951
Emma W.		02/14/1901 –	05/05/1981
BRUMBACH, Elizabeth M.		1917 –	1986
BOLLINGER, Phares	99-01-03	10/17/1866 –	11/30/1965
Kate H.	61-08-09	09/13/1865 –	06/22/1927
BOLLINGER, Katie B. d/o Phares & Kate Bollinger		06/05/1892 –	04/18/1951
BOLLINGER, Infant s/o Phares & Kate H. Bollinger	00-00-02		02/06/1901
BUCHER, Jonas W.	76-04-10	08/09/1828 –	09/19/1904
BUCHER, Anna B. w/o Jonas W. Bucher	75-07-12	09/27/1832 –	05/09/1908
BUCHER, Emeline d/o Jonas & Ann Bucher	01-11-21	08/23/1850 –	08/13/1852
BUCHER, Samuel s/o Jonas & Anna Bucher	04-11-12	09/11/1852 –	08/29/1857
BUCHER, Jonas s/o Jonas & Anna Bucher	14-10-11	02/20/1860 –	12/31/1874
BUCHER, Christian s/o Jonas & Anna Bucher	00-04-00	05/30/1867 –	09/30/1867
BUCHER, Jacob s/o Jonas & Anna Bucher	00-04-01	04/14/1871 –	08/13/1872
BUCHER, Sarah d/o Jonas & Anna Bucher (As carved)	00-00-17	09/22/1872 –	10/11/1872
BUCHER, Joseph R.	82-11-19	05/26/1848 –	05/15/1931
Barbara H., his wife	76-01-12	06/26/1848 –	08/08/1924
BUCHER, Phares D.		02/12/1855 –	10/24/1932
Annie M.		01/03/1855 –	06/15/1930
BUCHER, Infant s/o Phares B. & Annie M. Bucher		Born & Died	07/31/1878
BUCHER, Amos M. s/o P.B. & Annie M. Bucher	05-10-04	04/25/1885 –	03/09/1891
BUCHER, John B. "Minister"		1858 –	1942
Maggie B. Risser, his wife		1861 –	1943
BUCHER, David B. s/o John B. & Magda B. Bucher	00-04-03	05/13/1884 –	09/16/1884
BUCHER, Hiram B. (New stone-earlier list dates are 4/3/1862-11/22/1902)		1862 –	1902
BUCHER, Benjamin B.	60-05-26	09/17/1864 –	03/13/1925
Emma L.	81-01-01	08/23/1863 –	09/24/1944
BUCHER, Henry W.		10/13/1883 –	06/20/1966
Mabel S.		06/19/1884 –	07/23/1945
BUCHER, Elmer B.		1890 –	1976
Maria M.		1889 –	1970
BUCHER, Ella Barbara		1895 –	1968
BUCHER, Norman H.		1901 –	
Velma C.		1898 –	
Claude I.		1930 –	1943
BUCHER, Elmer C. s/o Lloyd C. & Sarah Bucher			05/29/1944
BURKHOLDER, David L.		1866 –	1939
Emma W.		1865 –	1956
Mary A.		1900 –	1981
BURKHOLDER, Samuel H. s/o David L. & Emma W. Burkholder	13-04-28	11/29/1893 –	04/27/1907
BURKHOLDER, Warren W. s/o David L. & Emma W. Burkholder	15-00-17	10/29/1895 –	11/15/1910
BURKHOLDER, Robert N. s/o David L. & Emma W. Burkholder	00-01-15		10/07/1913
BURKHOLDER, Jacob P. "Husband"		08/10/1874 –	09/20/1945
Alice B. "Wife"		11/12/1875 –	02/23/1963
BURKHOLDER, Willis "Father"		1938 –	1982
Ruth Z. "Mother"		1939 –	
Charles M. "Son"		1965 –	1982
CALDWELL, Lloyd S.		08/30/1909 –	02/06/1985
Edith Hess		09/07/1912 –	

	NAME	AGE	BORN		DIED
	CALDWELL, Samuel N.		03/04/1878	-	05/14/1926
	Minnie M.		10/16/1879	-	04/08/1959
	EARHART, Harry G.		1888	-	1969
	Emma S., his wife		1890	-	1947
	EBERLY, Henry	74-01-07	04/06/1805	-	05/13/1879
	EBERLY, Sabina w/o Henry Eberly	76-06-12	12/11/1815	-	06/23/1892
	EBERLY, Henry B.	37-08-17	06/29/1848	-	03/16/1886
	EBERLY, Susan	60-06-22			09/07/1916
	EBERLY, Harry A. s/o Henry B. & Susan Eberly	00-00-02	No Dates		
	EBERLY, John B.	46-05-18	10/04/1853	-	03/20/1900
	Fannie S.	71-05-01	12/11/1857	-	05/12/1929
	EBERLY, Bertha S.	55-10-29	09/23/1889	-	08/22/1945
	EBY, Christian	80-02-09	02/05/1787	-	04/14/1867
	EBY, Catharine w/o Christian	83-11-23	08/21/1789	-	08/17/1873
	ENCK, Samuel M.		1892	-	1953
	Salome K., his wife		1893	-	1982
	Samuel J. "Our Son"		1916	-	1952
	ENCK, Chester S., Jr. (Spacht Funeral Home Marker)		1957	-	1961
(G)	ERB, Daniel	77-05-25	04/04/1760	-	09/29/1837
(G)	ERB, Maria NEE Lang	65-10-08	07/02/1766	-	05/10/1832
(G)	ERB, Daniel s/o Daniel & Elizabeth Erb	77-03-01	06/18/1794	-	09/19/1871
	ERB, Benjamin H.	73-09-02	07/19/1850	-	04/21/1924
	Lizzie S.	73-03-00	02/21/1859	-	05/21/1932
	ERB, Mary B.	04-07-23	06/04/1879	-	01/27/1884
	ERB, John B.	24-07-03	04/22/1883	-	11/25/1907
	ERB, Israel B.	30-09-24	02/15/1888	-	12/09/1918
	Fannie B. NEE Brubaker	82-00-29	08/16/1889	-	09/15/1971
	ERB, Olive S.		02/05/1917	-	01/13/1968
	ESHELMAN, Elizabeth		1883	-	1975
	ESHLEMAN, J. Henry		02/19/1892	-	10/26/1973
	Maria B.		03/09/1895	-	11/28/1982
	FASNACHT, Samuel B. Father	75-05-05	12/11/1841	-	05/16/1917
	FASNACHT, Sallie A. NEE Meiskey Mother	71-11-25	01/31/1844	-	01/25/1916
	FASNACHT, Susanna d/o S.B. & Sarah Fasnacht	04-05-10	09/16/1869	-	02/26/1871
	FASNACHT, Ellen d/o Samuel B. & Sallie Fasnacht	00-00-19	10/03/1876	-	10/22/1876
	FASNACHT, Jacob s/o Samuel B. & Sallie Fasnacht	03-05-10	09/18/1877	-	02/28/1882
	FASNACHT, Edwin s/o Samuel B. & Sallie Fasnacht (Stone badly worn)		??/??/1879	-	??/??/1883
	FASNACHT, Louisa d/o Samuel B. & Sal. Fasnacht (Stone badly worn)		??/??/1882	-	??/??/1883
	FLORY, Elam s/o Daniel & Catherine Flory (Stone reset)	??-??-??	12/19/1868	-	08/14/1870
	FOX, Bernell Z. s/o Harvey & Mary Ann Fox		Born & Died		08/09/1975
	FREY, Harry C.	30-03-23			08/01/1926
	Alice M.	80-00-14			12/31/1974
	FREY, Beatrice S.	00-00-09			10/21/1918
(G)	FURRY, Joseph s/o Jacob & Elizab. Furry	00-00-19	04/09/1867	-	04/28/1867
	GEISSINGER, Howard S.	62 08-00	1900	-	1962
	Kathryn M.		1905	-	
	Anna H.		1942	-	
	GERTZLER, Wayne Eugene		09/03/1939	-	01/12/1940
	GERTZLER, Robert Lee		07/12/1942	-	09/09/1942
	GOCHENAUR, Annie B. NEE Risser		12/17/1891	-	12/28/1931
	GOOD, Ira M. "Ordained Minister - 1955)		1914	-	
	Ruth W.		1915	-	

NAME	AGE	BORN	DIED
GRAYBILL, Joseph L.		1838 -	1928
Lizzie H. Erisman, his wife		1843 -	1912
GRAYBILL, Wayne E.		05/13/1889 -	10/11/1967
Jennie K.		07/12/1888 -	08/17/1967
GROFF, Charles D.		09/12/1908 -	
Stella E.		04/01/1913 -	10/19/1983
INITIAL STONES: H.H.			
(G) HABECKER, Daniel	68-11-22	02/19/1760 -	02/10/1829
HABECKER, Christian G.	47-07-25	11/15/1879 -	07/10/1927
Elizabeth S.	80-00-26	05/05/1892 -	05/31/1972
HACKMAN, Grandfather "Erected by A. Hackman 1914"		1700 -	1800
HACKMAN, Grandmother "Erected by A. Hackman 1914"		1700-	1800
(G) HACKMAN, Maria NEE Musselman	45-11-18	09/04/1791 -	08/22/1837
HACKMAN, J.B.	73-09-21	03/26/1825 -	01/20/1899
HACKMAN, Maria w/o J.B. Hackman	66-08-13	08/26/1830 -	05/09/1897
HACKMAN, Hiram s/o Jacob & Maria Hackman	01-11-05	11/08/1853 -	10/13/1855
HACKMAN, Annmary d/o Jacob B. & Maria Hackman	00-04-12	01/01/1861 -	05/13/1861
HACKMAN, Joseph L. s/o Jacob B. & Maria Hackman	11-10-24	12/18/1864 -	11/12/1876
HACKMAN, Lane L. s/o Jacob B. & Maria Hackman	06-06-20	05/01/1870 -	01/21/1876
(G) HACKMAN, Anna, infant d/o David & Susana Hackman		11/27/1829 -	04/10/1830
HACKMAN, Reuben C.		12/21/1855 -	11/09/1929
Anna M.		01/16/1859 -	02/26/1937
HACKMAN, Ezra W. s/o Reuben & Anna M. Hackman	08-02-01	01/08/1886 -	03/03/1894
HACKMAN, infant s/o Reuben & Anna Hackman		Born & Died	10/03/1887
HACKMAN, Andrew L. Father	74-09-29	03/18/1858 -	01/17/1933
Amanda B. Mother	79-04-18	03/09/1856 -	07/27/1936
HACKMAN, Samuel L. s/o Andrew L. & Aman. Hackman	00-07-26	01/14/1886 -	09/09/1886
HACKMAN, Joseph N.	78-03-05	07/13/1883 -	10/18/1961
Amelia E.	59-05-10	01/15/1881 -	06/25/1940
HACKMAN, Adam N.		04/17/1895 -	02/28/1961
Martha W.		12/05/1895 -	05/19/1982
HACKMAN, Rhoda L. d/o Adam & Martha Hackman	12-11-21	07/03/1921 -	06/24/1934
HACKMAN, Martin L.	01-08-18		02/23/1910
HALDEMAN, Charles R.		1888 -	1958
Annie S.		1880 -	1942
HALDEMAN, Hiram H. s/o Charles & Annie Haldeman		06/20/1910	
HALDEMAN, Clarence H. s/o Charles & Annie Haldeman		04/29/1920	
HALDEMAN, J. Charles s/o David & Carrie Haldeman		12/04/1941 -	07/20/1953
HALDEMAN, Nancy A. d/o David & Carrie Haldeman		01/27/1945 -	03/20/1945
HALDEMAN, Paul D. s/o David & Carrie Haldeman		03/24/1946 -	06/10/1953
HALDEMAN, Larry G. s/o David & Carrie Haldeman		11/11/1950 -	06/06/1951
HARTRANFT, Mary A.		1869 -	1962
John W.		1868 -	1940
George H. Brother (earlier list shows: s/o Henry & Catharine)	1875 -		1882
HEVERLING, Polly H.	70-08-07		02/28/1912
HEBERLING, Solomon R.	77-01-22		06/03/1927
HEBERLING, Harvey S.	64-11-29	08/30/1874 -	08/29/1939
HEVERLING, Caroline	38 yrs.		02/18/1915
Herold son	7 mo.	No Dates	
HEDERICK, Winfield Scott	About 55 yrs.		01/24/1916
HEISER, John S.	69-10-08	03/23/1826 -	02/01/1896
HEISER, Amanda E.	76-04-14	12/01/1826 -	04/15/1903
HEISER, Franklin M. s/o John S. & Amanda E. Heiser	03-04-04	09/22/1872 -	01/26/1876

NAME	AGE	BORN	DIED
HELLER, John	65-04-17	10/08/1828 - 02/25/1894	
HELLER, Sarah	90-03-07	11/08/1834 - 02/15/1925	
HELLER, Harlan B.		08/25/1891 - 04/03/1986	
Florence N.		08/03/1893 - 10/27/1972	
HELLER, James G. s/o Parke M. & Charity Heller		03/10/1945 - 08/16/1948	
HELLER, Jay Mark s/o Parke M. & Charity G. Heller		11/02/1949 - 08/29/1950	
HERNLEY, Sam B.		1866 - 1947	
Barbara B.		1867 - 1941	
HERNLEY, Katie W. d/o Sam B. & Barbara Hernley	06-09-07	09/20/1898 - 06/27/1905	
HERNLEY, Samuel s/o Sam & Barbara Hernley	02-02-27	06/22/1900 - 09/19/1902	
HERNLEY, Katie d/o Jonas R. & Ella M. Hernley	01-01-14	08/10/1889 - 09/24/1890	
HERNLEY, Jonas s/o Jonas R. & Ella M. Hernley	01-04-09	09/03/1891 - 01/12/1893	
HERNLEY, Levi W.		1897 - 1978	
Mary K.		1896 - 1960	
HERNLEY, J. Risser		06/19/1898 - 09/18/1927	
HERSHEY, J. Harry (share stone with John C. & Ada M. Mellinger)		1895 - 1965	
Ella Mae		1902 -	
HERSHEY, Elwood D. "World War II"		1917 -	
Ruth B.		1919 -	
HERTZLER, Jacob B.		06/05/1848 - 11/07/1920	
Catharine H.		09/04/1848 - 06/23/1930	
(G) HESS, Johannes	39-10-06	09/24/1791 - 07/30/1831	
(G) HESS, Elizabeth	85-01-29	01/24/1794 - 03/23/1879	
(G) HESS, Esther d/o Johannes & Elizabeth Hess	01-06-28	03/16/1825	
HESS, Jacob R.	60-07-11	07/11/1816 - 02/22/1877	
(G) HESS, Mary NEE Schenck w/o Jacob R. Hess	38-01-10	11/15/1825 - 12/25/1863	
(G) HESS, Johannes s/o Jacob & Mary Hess	00-10-24	11/02/1847 - 09/26/1848	
(G) HESS, Susana d/o Jacob & Maria Hess	00-00-04	12/??/1851	
HESS, John R. "Our Father"	69-01-02	10/13/1828 - 11/15/1897	
HESS, Anna "Our Mother"	72-05-20	03/25/1832 - 09/15/1904	
HESS, Albert s/o John & Anna Hess	00-11-25	03/04/1855 - 02/29/1856	
HESS, Amanda d/o John & Anna Hess	03-08-01	08/24/1867 - 04/25/1870	
HESS, Samuel R.	75-08-25	07/27/1830 - 04/22/1906	
HESS, Martha NEE Wissler	82-10-09	06/28/1832 - 05/07/1915	
HESS, Susan B. d/o Samuel P. & Martha Hess	25-09-13	01/25/1855 - 11/08/1880	
HESS, Lizzie Eda d/o Samuel R. & Martha Hess	12-00-07	12/10/1863 - 12/17/1875	
HESS, Sarah Amelia d/o Samuel R. & Martha Hess	04-02-00	04/13/1872	
HESS, Elias s/o Samuel & Martha Hess	00-03-09	No Dates	
HESS, Israel W.	24-05-13	02/10/1853 - 07/22/1877	
HESS, Samuel A.	75-10-25	1857 - 1933	
Mary F.	49-02-03	1858 - 1908	
HESS, Maggie L. d/o Sam'l. A. & Mary Hess	00-00-26	06/06/1881	
HESS, Mary A.	56-10-00	04/02/1859 - 02/02/1916	
HESS, Jacob W.	18-11-08	09/22/1860 - 08/30/1879	
HESS, Benjamin F.	65-08-09	01/18/1863 - 09/27/1928	
Anna K., his wife	67-09-01	02/14/1864 - 11/15/1931	
HESS, Bertha Mae d/o Benj. F. & Anna Hess	08-01-20	06/09/1902 - 07/29/1910	
HESS, Menno W.		1874 - 1950	
Magdalena S.		1876 - 1968	
HESS, Harry L.		12/18/1888 - 08/27/1965	
Minnie B.		09/21/1889 - 02/02/1975	
HESS, Howard C.		1892 - 1974	
Elva Brubaker, his wife		1892 - 1944	
Anna Mae Adair		1911 -	

NAME	AGE	BORN	DIED
HESS, Infant d/o S. Walter & Minnie M. Hess		01/20/1910	
HESS, Paul B.		01/22/1916 -	11/30/1978
Emma E.		01/25/1915 -	
HESS, Harold B.		10/14/1917 -	
Wanda S.		10/05/1917 -	
Harold Glenn		12/04/1947 -	
Dennis Lamar		10/11/1955 -	11/19/1968
HETSER, Mary w/o Anthony Hetser	74-07-28	06/12/1805 -	02/10/1880
HUBER, Henry s/o Levi & Fanny Huber	01-10-11	10/31/1866 -	09/15/1868
HUBER, Jacob G.		1870 -	1948
Sabina L.W., his wife		1864 -	1945
HUBER, Landis	56-07-03	1877 -	1934
Ellen	80-11-08	1880 -	1961
HUBER, Sadie B. "Daughter"	00-02-11		1904
HUBER, Paul B. s/o Landis & Ellen Huber		12/10/1922 -	12/18/1922
HUBER, Ira B.		1902 -	1976
Elizabeth B.		1903 -	
HUBER, Dale Lamar s/o Ira & Elizabeth Huber	00-01-11		1937
HUBER, Willis B.		09/20/1909 -	01/18/1984
Beulah		07/10/1906 -	
Melvin		1933 -	1933
HUBER, P. Elmer		1915 -	
Mabel E.	65 yrs.	1917 -	1983
HUBER, B. Landis		1917 -	
Anna R.		1918 -	
HUFFMAN, Morris J. s/o Franklin & Sarah Huffman	00-11-12	09/16/1854 -	08/18/1855
HUNT, William H.	41-01-02	04/09/1879 -	05/11/1920
Emma B., his wife	82-10-19	06/02/1881 -	04/21/1964
HURST, Noah W. "Ordained Minister 1925"		01/29/1877 -	11/27/1964
Lydia Z.		12/20/1877 -	02/02/1970
HURST, Roy M.	40-01-27	11/22/1911 -	01/19/1952
Emily Walter, his wife		09/13/1914 -	
KAUFFMAN, Norman N.		1892 -	1969
Stella S.		1895 -	1978
(G) KELLER, Samuel	51-01-10	10/31/1816 -	12/10/1867
KELLER, Susan NEE Huber	72-10-21	09/15/1819 -	08/06/1802
KISINGER, Henry	71-00-25	08/15/1820 -	09/10/1891
KISINGER, Sarah w/o Henry Kisinger	51-03-17	11/03/1835 -	02/20/1887
(G) KLASSEN, Margaretha Arron "Born in Russland"		07/23/1887 -	10/27/1967
(The above stone is carved in old style script letters)			
KRAATZ, Infant d/o J. & E. Kraatz			06/12/1853
KRAATZ, Infant d/o J. & E. Kraatz			04/21/1854
KRAATZ, Infant s/o J. & E. Kraatz			04/22/1856
KRAATZ, Infant d/o J. & E. Kraatz			07/15/1857
KREIDER, Jacob E.		08/20/1878 -	05/17/1964
Lizzie E.		12/09/1880 -	12/24/1960
Christian B.		1908 -	1908
KREIDER, Christian B. s/o Jacob & Lizzie Kreider (Old Stone)		01/17/1908 -	08/02/1908
KREIDER, Elvin E. "PVT. 86TH STA. HOSP. MED. DEPT."		09/15/1898 -	02/12/1955
Anna H.		03/27/1899 -	06/27/1965
KREIDER, Benjamin S.		08/14/1902 -	08/02/1954
Lizzie B.		09/04/1904 -	

NAME	AGE	BORN	DIED
KREIDER, Tina Marie d/o Harry E. & Darlene R. Kreider		05/27/1968 - 05/29/1968	
LANDIS, Susanna	70-06-25	06/08/1834 - 01/03/1905	
LANDIS, David E.		03/24/1869 - 06/22/1952	
Mary B.		08/12/1871 - 08/29/1938	
LANDIS, Amos N.		1869 - 1944	
Amanda B. Snyder, his wife		1872 - 1956	
John S., our son		1896 - 1902	
LANDIS, John s/o John & Magdalena Landis	00-05-15	11/18/1871 - 05/06/1872	
LANDIS, Richard J.		08/29/1907 - 07/05/1960	
LANTZ, Rosanne S. d/o Sam K. & Esther L. Lantz	00-00-06	07/07/1907 - 07/10/1985	
LONG, Charles W.		1893 - 1957	
Mamie S.		1899 - 19__	
LONG, Wilmer H. "Father"		06/07/1925 -	
Ada N. "Mother"		05/23/1930 -	
Eugene L. "Son"		03/01/1953 - 09/19/1985	
LOOSE, John W.		06/01/1896 - 12/10/1961	
Marie B.		08/31/1901 -	
John, Jr.		12/05/1929 -	
LEHN, Joseph	94-08-10	01/06/1798 - 09/16/1892	
(G) LEHN, Elizabeth NEE Erb s/o Joseph Lehn	73-00-25	07/25/1792 - 08/19/1865	
(G) LEHN, Henry (Stone badly worn. Earlier list shows dates of 8/1/1809-4/4/1875)			
(G) LEHN, Esther w/o Henry Lehn	67-00-01	03/10/1816 - 03/11/1883	
(G) LEHN, Emanuel s/o Henry & Hetty Lehn	21-10-16	06/16/1838 - 05/01/1860	
(G) LEHN, Henrich E.	39-03-00	03/26/1823 - 06/26/1862	
(G) LEHN, Joseph E.	25-04-19	04/15/1829 - 09/04/1854	
LANE, Abram E.		01/28/1864 - 11/28/1920	
Alice O. NEE Wissler		09/02/1862 - 01/19/1921	
MARTIN, Aaron N. (Spacht Funeral Home marker)		1904 - 1987	
MARTIN, Harvey H.		05/11/1910 -	
Vera H.		05/26/1913 -	
MARTIN, Mildred H. d/o Harvey & Vera Martin		Born & Died 02/06/1943	
MARTIN, Gladys Arlene d/o Allen K. & Lydia Martin	07-00-00	1945 - 1952	
MARTIN, John Eby		05/25/1949 - 02/11/1984	
Ivy Jo		07/10/1949 -	
MARTIN, Infant s/o Eugene K. & Carol A. Martin		10/11/1968 - 10/12/1968	
MARTIN, Darnell Ray s/o Eugene K. & Carol A. Martin		06/28/1976 - 06/30/1976	
MARTIN, Derl Richard s/o Earl & Joyce Martin		06/03/1974	
MELLINGER, John C. (Shares stone with J. Harry		1869 - 1963	
Ada M. and Ella M. Hershey)		1875 - 1960	
MELLINGER, John R. s/o John C. & Ada Mellinger	00-06-20	03/11/1914	
METZLER, John H.	73-04-21	09/24/1849 - 02/15/1923	
Mary N.	69-07-01	02/13/1854 - 09/14/1923	
MILLER, Israel		1879 - 1935	
Emma, his wife		1885 - 1952	
MILLER, Phares K. (Shares stone with Henry S. Stauffer)		1900 -	
Fanny S.		1895 -	
MILLER, John S.	00-09-04	01/14/1923	
MILLER, Dorothy S. d/o Phares & Fanny Miller		10/16/1924 - 01/18/1928	
MORT, Charles E.		1916 -	
Dorothy J.		1924 -	
Dennis E.		1955 - 1962	

NAME	AGE	BORN	DIED
MOSEMAN, Michael	64-02-14	11/11/1822 - 01/25/1887	
MOSEMAN, Maria	80-10-27	02/25/1831 - 01/22/1912	
MUSSER, Fanny H. (Earlier list shows dates of 9/7/1871-8/20/1923)		1871 -	1923
David G.		1880 -	1966
Lena M.		1891 -	1959
Vera B.		09/27/1902	
David		04/20/1908	
John		06/22/1908	
Infant Daughter		06/06/1925	
MUSSER, Martin W.		1870 -	1948
Katie E.		1875 -	1967
MUSSER, Ellen Risser		1874 -	1945
NESSINGER, Isaac	80-00-10	05/12/1845 - 05/22/1925	
Harriet	79-01-17	11/12/1845 - 12/29/1924	
NOLT, Phares H.		01/24/1881 - 09/14/1947	
Alma B.		02/25/1884 - 01/01/1930	
Anna H.		09/13/1910 - 12/11/1910	
Dora H.		01/17/1912 - 04/26/1930	
Infant Daughter		Stillborn 01/01/1930	
NOLT, John Jacob		1885 -	1972
Emma Martin		1886 -	1971
NOLT, David M.		08/23/1900 -	
Hattie H.		12/23/1901 -	
OBERHOLTZER, J. Melvin		03/13/1899 - 07/03/1975	
Suey W.		07/14/1901 -	
OBERHOLTZER, Lois Jane d/o Isaac H. & Ellen A.		09/25/1932 - 10/20/1932	
PAUL, Henry Edwin			1908
PAUL, Jay Marvin		1911 -	1912
PAUTZ, Ephraim	73-10-19	02/20/1820 - 01/09/1894	
PFAUTZ, Lydia d/o Christian & Catharine Eby			
w/o E. Pfautz	41-06-17	01/19/1825 - 08/06/1869	
PFAUTZ, Lizzie d/o Ephraim & Lydia Pfautz	10-11-15	08/29/1861 - 07/15/1872	
PFAUTZ, Mary w/o Ephram Pfautz	72-09-07	07/18/1829 - 04/25/1902	
INITIAL STONES: C.R., B.R., H.R., M.R.			
(G) RACK, Infant d/o George & Lidia Rach	00-00-02		11/22/1843
REIST, Eugene N.		1893 -	1961
Suley E., his wife		1902 -	
John H.		1927 -	1939
(G) RISSER, Christian	82-11-24	02/24/1799 - 02/18/1882	
(G) RISSER, Maria NEE Sneyder w/o Christian Risser	78-01-21	04/08/1800 - 05/29/1878	
(G) RISSER, Maria	02-07-17	05/01/1829 - 12/18/1831	
(G) RISSER, John	72-05-27	05/23/1801 - 11/20/1873	
(G) RISER, Elisabeth NEE Hesz(in) w/o Johan Riser	31-02-24	11/19/1807 - 02/12/1839	
(G) RISER, Barbara NEE Martin w/o Johan Riser	37-10-21	05/28/1813 - 04/19/1851	
(G) RISSER, Peter	72-07-28	09/24/1823 - 05/22/1896	
RISSER, Fannie NEE Stauffer w/o Peter Risser	59-04-02	01/02/1826 - 05/04/1885	

	NAME	AGE	BORN	DIED
(G)	RISSER, Mary An, Infant d/o Peter & Fanny Risser	01-00-08	10/15/1850 -	10/23/1851
(G)	RISSER, Fanny d/o Peter & Fanny Risser	08-04-05	01/05/1859 -	05/10/1867
	RISSER, Christian S.	84-11-23	05/27/1825 -	05/20/1910
	RISSER, Katie L. w/o Christian S. Risser	69-00-22	03/24/1831 -	04/16/1900
	RISSER, Henry	80-10-03	04/25/1827 -	02/28/1908
	Barbara	86-02-18	08/08/1838 -	10/26/1924
	RISSER, John H.	75-08-07	07/09/1829 -	03/16/1905
	RISSER, Eliza Ann w/o John H. Risser	71-09-11	05/16/1832 -	02/27/1904
	RISSER, Phares B. s/o John H. & Eliza Ann Risser	02-09-03		07/05/1857
	RISSER, Amos B. s/o John H. & Eliza Ann Risser	01-03-07		06/19/1857
	RISSER, Infant d/o John H. & Eliza Ann Risser		05/23/1866	
	RISSER, Abner B.	77-10-27	06/29/1851 -	05/26/1929
	Susan B.	68-02-28	10/03/1856 -	12/31/1924
	RISSER, Wayne M. s/o Abner B. & Susan B. Risser	08-07-23	05/16/1881 -	01/09/1890
	RISSER, Infant d/o Abner & Susan Risser		02/--/1889	
	RISSER, Harry S.		09/10/1852 -	02/21/1926
	Magdalena, his wife		08/28/1865 -	02/17/1943
	RISSER, Kate L. w/o Harry S. Risser (Badly worn)		08/05/1848 -	01/10/1888
	RISSER, Greybill, Infant s/o Harry & Kate L. Risser		01/07/1888	
	RISSER, Reuben L.	63-01-13		11/13/1915
	Emma B.	62-11-28		10/02/1918
	RISSER, Katie M. d/o Reuben & Emma Risser	02-03-01	05/15/1876 -	08/16/1878
	RISSER, Emma M. d/o Reuben & Emma Risser	00-09-24	07/15/1877 -	05/09/1878
	RISSER, Clayton M. s/o Reuben & Emma Risser	00-11-18	09/06/1878 -	08/02/1879
	RISSER, Susan M. d/o Reuben & Emma Risser	00-11-21	10/11/1880 -	10/05/1881
	RISSER, Elmer M. s/o Reuben & Emma Risser	00-04-26	06/06/1891 -	10/02/1891
	RISSER, Fanny d/o Jacob & Fanny Risser	01-01-17	06/25/1857 -	08/11/1858
	RISSER, Elizabeth d/o Jacob & Fanny Risser	00-11-08	03/30/1861 -	03/08/1862
	RISSER, Jacob E. s/o Jacob & Fanny Risser	00-03-25	10/03/1864 -	01/28/1865
	RISSER, Infant d/o Jacob & Fanny Risser		11/15/1866	
	RISSER, Christian B.		1857 -	1939
	Lizzie I.		1858 -	1941
	Jacob W.		1884 -	1973
	Edna M.		1889 -	1947
	RISSER, Christian W. s/o Christian B. & Lizzie I. Risser	00-06-25	06/12/1899	
	RISSER, Levi B.		08/27/1857 -	02/19/1940
	Lizzie B.		06/14/1859 -	07/27/1942
	RISSER, Amos L.	83-09-26	08/01/1859 -	05/27/1943
	Susan G. NEE Eberly	53-00-23	11/23/1866 -	12/16/1919
	RISSER, Henry L.		04/01/1864 -	01/04/1956
	Lizzie M. Oberlin, his wife		06/20/1867 -	09/04/1930
	Alma Grace, our daughter		10/16/1895 -	01/31/1980
	RISSER, Infant d/o Henry L. & Eliza Risser		12/19/1892	
	RISSER, Christian L.		1865 -	1951
	Mary E.		1874 -	1941
	RISSER, Jacob B.	43-07-12		07/29/1911
	RISSER, Susan G.	54-03-13		11/09/1920
	RISSER, Victor H.	18-02-19		06/23/1914
	RISSER, Barbara d/o Jacob B. & Susan G. Risser	00-06-15	03/16/1898 -	10/01/1898
	RISSER, Elizabeth B.		1870 -	1930
	RISSER, John M.	30-00-13		08/10/1906
	RISSER, Reuben M.		1888 -	1952
	RISSER, Tillman M.	49-09-14	1886 -	1936
	Anna S.		1888 -	1983

NAME	AGE	BORN	DIED
RISSER, Harry H.		1892 -	1940
Elsie M.		1899 -	1960
Beatrice M.		1918 -	1921
RISSER, Peter M.		1893 -	1961
Susanna w/o Peter Risser (1), w/o Allen Keller (2)		1897 -	1979
RISSER, Jacob H.			10/17/1920
RISSER, Barbara H.	00-00-06		01/17/1924
RISSER, Anna H.			01/02/1925
RISSER, Christ S.		04/16/1895 -	
Anna W.		05/04/1891 -	11/22/1969
RISSER, Ruth H.	00-01-10		08/26/1918
RISSER, David M.		01/20/1896 -	12/18/1940
RISSER, Mabel L. w/o David M. Risser	25-03-13	10/21/1895 -	02/04/1921
RISSER, Jonas E., D.C. "WW I CO. K. 316 INF 79 DIV"		02/01/1894 -	04/28/1985
RISSER, Norman E. "WW II"		06/08/1900 -	
RISSER, Edna M.		1916 -	
RISSER, Jacob W. s/o Jacob W. & Edna M. Risser		05/17/1921 -	05/17/1935
RISSER, Evelyn B.			04/08/1915
SAUDER, Aaron B.		01/23/1914 -	09/08/1968
Edna H.		10/14/1915 -	
SAUDER, Infant s/o Aaron B. & Edna H. Sauder		05/22/1947	
SCHAEFFER, John	86-03-20	10/02/1817 -	01/22/1904
SCHAEFFER, Nancy d/o Jacob Shirk w/o John Schaeffer	50-06-02	07/26/1824 -	01/28/1875
SCHAEFFER, Adam s/o John & Nancy Schaeffer		09/15/186? -	12/30/187?
SCHAEFFER, Milton S.	79-02-25	01/14/1855 -	04/08/1934
Ann Maria	80-08-14	07/06/1856 -	03/20/1937
SHOEMAKER, Peter	69-06-00	11/19/1810 -	05/19/1880
Hannah w/o Peter Shoemaker	75-09-24	03/19/1813 -	01/13/1889
SCHOEMAKER, Cora Eliza (Stone badly worn, reset and most of inscription is buried. Earlier list shows dates as 10/19/1866-11/12/1867)		??/??/1866 -	??/??/????
SHIRK, Todd Andrew s/o Neal M. & Carla M. Shirk		12/23/1980 -	03/31/1981
SIELING, Elizabeth May d/o Dr. J.H. & Katie H. Sieling		05/10/1884 -	10/18/1887
SNAVELY, Benj. H.	88-06-20	03/22/1833 -	10/12/1921
Elizabeth B.	81-06-03	08/11/1844 -	02/14/1926
SNAVELY, Elias s/o B.H. & Elizabeth Sanvely	00-06-25	02/06/1880 -	08/31/1880
SNAVELY, David H.		06/12/1838 -	02/24/1923
Annie S. Gingrich, his wife		11/25/1851 -	08/27/1932
SNAVELY, Ella G. "Daughter"		12/11/1877 -	11/21/1881
SNAVELY, Henry B.	62-04-20	04/03/1863 -	08/23/1925
SNAVELY, Mary R. w/o Henry B. Snavely	46-05-09	08/13/1864 -	01/22/1911
SNAVELY, John B.		07/03/1871 -	05/25/1945
Sarah B.		03/06/1875 -	04/09/1957
SNAVELY, Israel O. s/o John B. & Sarah Snavely	00-04-22	05/05/1897 -	09/27/1897
SNAVELY, Ada O. d/o John & Sarah B. Snavely	00-02-00	05/24/1900	
SNAVELY, Benjamin B.		1872 -	1946
Cora E.		1872 -	1943
Elias , Son		1895 -	1895
SNAVELY, Elias s/o B.B. & Cora Snavely (Small old stone)	00-01-27		04/07/1895
SNAVELY, Samuel "Father"	24-01-15	03/29/1875 -	05/04/1899
SNAVELY, Elmer S.		08/23/1890 -	04/20/1977
Edna R.		01/01/1895 -	12/21/1971

NAME	AGE	BORN	DIED
SANVELY, Ben S. "Father"		1895 -	1979
Mabel "Mother"		1899 -	
Helen W. "Daughter"		1926 -	
SNAVELY, Milton Eberly		01/11/1896 -	
Ida Miller Risser		01/12/1896 - 03/14/1977	
SNAVELY, Harvey E.		07/10/1899 - 11/30/1965	
Sallie R.		03/17/1900 - 03/15/1977	
Paul S., our son		1920 -	1920
SNAVELY, Mary A.		08/20/1904 - 11/25/1984	
SNAVELY, J. Warren		01/02/1909 -	
D. Marie		04/08/1915 -	
SNAVELY, Carl Risser		09/05/1930 -	
Dorothy Kendig Keener		04/15/1931 -	
SNAVELY, Lois Jane d/o Warren & Marie Snavely		1938	
SNYDER, Simon B.	71-05-00	01/05/1836 - 06/05/1907	
SNYDER, Fannie S. w/o Simon B. Snyder	69-03-17	10/07/1841 - 12/24/1910	
SNYDER, Ella d/o S____ & Fanny Snyder (Stone badly worn) 04-??-??		??/??/1868 - ??/??/1872	
SNYDER, Jacob E.		12/31/1893 - 07/14/1975	
Jennie B.		04/05/1889 - 04/06/1985	
SPANGLER, Earl H.		1902 -	1966
Mabel M.		1908 -	
STATLER, Kenneth F.		1975 -	1975
(G) STAUFFER, Benjamin	64-00-18	07/08/1799 - 07/26/1863	
(G) STAUFFER, Anna w/o Benjamin Stauffer	73-00-28	11/14/1801 - 12/12/1874	
(G) STAUFFER, Maria L. d/o Benjamin & Anna Stauffer	25-05-00	07/24/1843 - 12/24/1870	
STAUFFER, John L.	46-07-17	08/30/1824 - 04/17/1871	
STAUFFER, Anna H. w/o John L. Stauffer	79-05-28	08/13/1829 - 02/11/1909	
STAUFFER, Peter L.	73-11-22	01/27/1831 - 01/19/1905	
STAUFFER, Sarah L. w/o Peter L. Stauffer	58-06-24	07/23/1841 - 02/17/1900	
STAUFFER, Benjamin L.	52-05-22	10/27/1834 - 04/19/1887	
STAUFFER, Fannie S. w/o Benj. L. Stauffer	63-02-14	02/11/1835 - 04/25/1898	
STAUFFER, Jacob L.	42-03-26	01/14/1837 - 05/10/1879	
STAUFFER, Adam L.	65-10-05	01/16/1839 - 11/21/1904	
STAUFFER, Leah M. w/o Adam L. Stauffer	81-04-13	04/26/1843 - 09/09/1924	
STAUFFER, Susanna	73-05-09	08/15/1850 - 01/24/1924	
STAUFFER, John H.	67-08-11	08/26/1858 - 05/07/1926	
STAUFFER, Annie w/o John H. Stauffer	44-04-21		07/04/1905
STAUFFER, Christian H.		02/04/1877 - 11/29/1964	
Fannie B.		04/16/1877 - 07/27/1962	
Lizzie S. Witmer		01/16/1908 -	
STAUFFER, Ada S. d/o John H & Annie R. Stauffer	00-00-31	08/12/1883 - 09/11/1883	
STAUFFER, Benjamin S. s/o John H. & Annie R. Stauffer	00-00-24	10/11/1884 - 11/06/1884	
STAUFFER, Stella S. d/o John H. & Annie R. Stauffer	02-01-19	01/24/1893 - 03/15/1895	
STAUFFER, Benjamin B.	61-03-29	04/15/1863 - 08/14/1924	
STAUFFER, Anna H. w/o Benj. B. Stauffer	45-05-29	07/24/1864 - 01/23/1910	
STAUFFER, Infant d/o B.B. & Anna H. Stauffer (Stone reset and inscription is buried)			
STAUFFER, Peter B.	66-01-13	08/14/1864 - 09/27/1930	
STAUFFER, Barbara N. w/o P.B. Stauffer	34-04-13	11/17/1865 - 03/30/1900	
STAUFFER, Benjamin M. s/o P.B. & Barbara Stauffer	15-09-13	09/11/1888 - 06/24/1904	
STAUFFER, Alvin M. s/o Peter & Barbara Stauffer	00-00-07		08/17/1894
STAUFFER, Isaac B.		12/15/1865 - 05/10/1945	
Annie H. Metzler, his wife		11/02/1867 - 12/22/1948	
Peter M.		03/06/1900 - 09/16/1900	
STAUFFER, Henry S. (Shares stone with Phares K. & Fanny S. Miller)		1885 -	1968

NAME	AGE	BORN	DIED
STAUFFER, Sarah B.	37-11-17	03/16/1889 -	03/03/1927
STAUFFER, Evan S.		12/15/1890 -	04/08/1960
Barbara B.		03/07/1894 -	10/28/1956
STAUFFER, Infant s/o Evan S. & Barbara B. Stauffer		Stillborn	01/08/1925
STAUFFER, Clarence W.		08/27/1902 -	08/20/1964
Minnie S.		07/27/1900 -	
STEELY, Martin W.		1874 -	1941
Susan K.		1874 -	1937
STEFFY, George N.		1897 -	
Elizabeth I.		1893 -	1970
Lois R., our daughter		1925 -	1925
STONER, Samuel N.	68-06-14	11/03/1865 -	05/17/1934
Kate B.	90-03-09	10/22/1866 -	01/31/1957
STONER, Fanny S. d/o Samuel N. & Kate Stoner	00-02-10	02/15/1890 -	04/25/1890
STONER, Katie S. d/o Samuel N. & Kate Stoner	01-11-19	03/30/1896 -	03/19/1898
STONER, Lavina S. d/o Samuel N. & Kate B. Stoner	17-11-06	06/18/1902 -	05/24/1920
STONER, Jacob S.		10/24/1899 -	
STRAUSS, George W.		10/24/1859 -	04/12/1944
Mary Ann, his wife		08/14/1863 -	04/15/1951
STRAUSS, Elmer		04/23/1902 -	12/08/1973
Helen D., his wife		05/24/1911 -	01/30/1971
SWEIGART, Donald E.		11/21/1964 -	02/15/1981
SWEIGART, Infant d/o Roy S. & Edith R. Sweigart		Stillborn	01/13/1971
WEACHTER, Infant d/o Johannes & Maria Weachter		02/14/1835	
WEACHTER, George M.	51-07-20	1878 -	1930
Katie A.	66-08-09	1880 -	1947
WEAVER, Paul M.		03/08/1917 -	
Alice N.		05/31/1919 -	
WEAVER, James L.		01/23/1948 -	08/29/1977
Carolyn		05/10/1949 -	
WEAVER, Dean S. (Beck Funeral Home Marker)			1968
WEIDMAN, Elizabeth H. w/o Henry Weidman	67-02-20	04/03/1844 -	06/23/1911
WEIDMAN, Katie B. d/o A.B. & Ella B. Weidman	11-04-13	10/10/1894 -	02/23/1906
WEIDMAN, Infant d/o Abram & Ella Weidman	00-00-03	07/13/1900	
WEIDMAN, Lloyd		1903 -	1981
Anna Snavely		1908 -	
WEIl, Elmer H.		1904 -	1981
Elizabeth W.		1903 -	
Helen M.		1927 -	
WHITE, G. Lester		1904 -	
Anna M.		1903 -	1932
Lester		1932 -	1932
Mary Ann		1900 -	
WIDDERS, Reuben B.		07/29/1892 -	09/18/1958
Bertha M.		11/10/1892 -	04/19/1958
WIEST, Lemon B.	86-06-06		03/11/1946
Sarah B.	64-10-06		01/03/1929
WIEST, Ada d/o Lemon & Sarah Wiest	00-01-15	04/04/1890 -	05/19/1890
WISE, Baby Girl		No Date	
WISE, Baby Girl		No Date	
WISE, Baby Girl		No Date	
(G) WISSLER, Jacob	76-05-15	11/12/1776 -	04/27/1853

	NAME	AGE	BORN		DIED
(G)	WISSLER, Anna d/o Christian Eby w/o Jacob Wissler	51-07-16	09/09/1777	–	04/25/1829
(G)	WISSLER, Jacob	52-03-23	04/10/1803	–	10/03/1855
(G)	WISSLER, Barbara NEE Bomberger w/o Jacob Wissler	66-10-24	07/31/1805	–	06/24/1872
	WISSLER, Christian	73-09-27	01/14/1805	–	11/11/1878
	WISSLER, Anna w/o Christian Wissler	88-00-21	08/28/1807	–	09/19/1895
	WISSLER, Ezra	82-05-27	05/06/1809	–	11/03/1891
	WISSLER, Mary w/o Ezra Wissler	78-00-28	07/25/1808	–	08/22/1886
(G)	WISSLER, Catharine	52-11-19	11/10/1812	–	10/29/1865
	WISSLER, Levi	61-06-11	01/03/1817	–	07/14/1881
	WISSLER, Fanny w/o Levi Wissler	67-05-16	09/07/1827	–	02/23/1895
	WISSLER, Christian s/o Levi & Fanny Wissler	00-00-04	08/29/1855	–	09/02/1855
	WISSLER, Hannah H. d/o Levi & Fanny Wissler	17-03-20	03/20/1869	–	07/20/1886
	WISSLER, Jacob B.	83-07-24	09/04/1828	–	04/28/1912
	WISSLER, Anna R. w/o Jacob B. Wissler	76-11-10	01/16/1837	–	12/26/1913
	WISSLER, Samuel B. s/o Jacob B. & Ann B. Wissler	01-02-25	04/21/1855	–	07/15/1856
	WISSLER, Christian B. s/o Jacob B. & Ann B. Wissler	00-05-17			08/07/1861
	WISSLER, Susan B. d/o Jacob B. & Ann R. Wissler	08-01-24	09/06/1881	–	10/30/1889
	WISSLER, John B.		05/30/1836	–	11/18/1913
	WISSLER, Caroline C. d/o Henry & Sabina Eberly w/o John B. Wissler	61-10-11	07/29/1836	–	05/10/1898
	WISSLER, Mary C. d/o John B. & Caroline C. Wissler	17-07-18	07/17/1853	–	03/04/1876
	WISSLER, Infant s/o John B. & Caroline C. Wissler	00-00-29	09/21/1859	–	10/23/1859
	WISSLER, Aaron	73-05-21			02/15/1906
	WISSLER, Leah	85-11-07			08/13/1921
	WISSLER, Benjamin	77-07-20	10/05/1838	–	05/25/1916
	WISSLER, Susanna	74-11-17	07/21/1839	–	07/07/1914
	WISSLER, Ella E. d/o Benjamin & Susan Wissler	24-04-26	09/30/1864	–	02/26/1889
	WISSLER, John H.	61-08-13	04/06/1850	–	12/19/1911
	WISSLER, Mariah H. d/o Jacob & Elizabeth Brubaker w/o John H. Wissler	29-06-14	05/08/1850	–	04/22/1880
	WISSLER, Levi H.	77-10-24	02/07/1852	–	01/01/1930
	Martha M. NEE Kreiter	64-07-14	05/18/1860	–	01/02/1925
	WISSLER, James s/o Levi H. & Martha M. Wissler	03-01-07	10/20/1886	–	11/27/1889
	WISSLER, Joseph B.	52-08-13	05/12/1856	–	01/25/1909
	WISSLER, Lizzie I.	70-07-24	02/14/1859	–	10/08/1929
	WISSLER, Minnie B. d/o Joseph B. & Lizzie I. Wissler	14-07-22	05/11/1877	–	01/03/1892
	WISSLER, Jacob B. "Son"		1879	–	1945
	WISSLER, Roy B. "Son"		1898	–	1952
	WISSLER, Christian		11/07/1866	–	07/14/1957
	Emma E.		01/13/1869	–	11/17/1945
	WISSLER, Howard T. s/o Christ F. & Emma E. Wissler	00-00-01			06/25/1909
	WISSLER, Elva M. Fogleman "Sister"		01/01/1883	–	07/01/1967
	Hanna K. Wissler "Sister"		07/26/1884	–	09/07/1978
	WISSLER, John N.		1888	–	1977
	Sue B. Hess w/o John N. Wissler		1890	–	1957
	Anna B. Hess "Sister"		1889	–	1979
	Earl H.		1913	–	1978
	WISSLER, Ruth W. w/o Earl H. Wissler		No Dates		
	WISSLER, David K. "Brother"		03/26/1895	–	05/13/1982
	WISSLER, J. Kevin		1962	–	1981
	WITMER, Lizzie S. (On Christian H. & Fannis B. Stauffer stone)		01/16/1908	–	
	ZANDER, Frederick	71-03-26	03/04/1815	–	08/30/1886
	ZIMMERMAN, Joseph s/o Isaac & Barbara Zimmerman	03-08-24	10/17/1873	–	08/11/1877

<u>Miscellaneous</u>

Stone located between Christian Risser (1799-1882) and aElmer M. Risser s/o Reuben & Emma
    Risser (1891-1891) is not readable.

Stone between Anna Wissler w/o Jacob (1777-1829) and Christian Wissler s/o Levi & Fanny
    (1855-1855) has 'Sie war 9 jahr 8 monate' and nothing else can be read.

Stone between Daniel Habecker (1760-1829) and Nancy w/o John Schaeffer [Adam - Sept 15, 18_1-
    Decem 30 186_) can be read. This matches up with Adam s/o John & Nancy Schaeffer,
    1861-1866 from an earlier list.

                              Transcribed by Martha Xakellis
                              November 1986

COLEMAN MEMORIAL CHAPEL CEMETERY #5

Surrounded by a low wall and located behind the church, this small cemetery has only two apparent graves. The one is a large box-like tomb with two small stones, one at the top right and one at the bottom right of the tomb. At the back wall there is a small headstone and a still smaller footstone.

The tomb is inscribed as follows:

Sacred to the memory of
John Matthews SNR.
Born in Ireland May 12, 1769
Came to Elizabeth Furnace
November 2, 1790
Where he departed this Life the 22nd
of April A.D. 1852
Aged 82 years 9 months
and 10 days

Rebecca Matthews
wife of
John Matthews
Departed this life the 21st of
September A.D. 1854
Aged 85 years

The small stone which has the top left corner broken is inscribed as follows:

"___ memory of Jane infant daughter of David & Margaret Care"

There are no dates but there is a footstone with the initials- J.C.

Transcribed April 1986 by Martha Xakellis

SAHM/KUNZI #9

This very small triangle is in a sharp right turn of what was once a road but is now a farm lane. If you were not looking for it specially, you would miss it. It is full of ground hog diggings and brambles. There were three (3) one foot by 2 foot red sandstones with no markings as well as several gray limestones that looked as though they were shaped by someone's hand to serve as markers, but again there were no inscriptions. One small red sandstone, about one foot wide and two feet long, was marked with D. K.*   There was also a bottom section of a larger sandstone with a portion of the funeral text, but no top portion was found.

NAME	AGE	BORN	DIED
SAHM, Heinrich	02-11-19	03/28/1839 - 03/08/1842
SAHM, Jacob	00-07-10	11/12/1842 - 06/22/1842

* In an earlier record of these stones there was also a stone for
   David Kunzi   56-06-26   03/24/1769 - 12/15/1827

Transcribed May 1985 by Martha Xakellis

LEXINGTON/KAUFFMAN CEMETERY #10

Located in Elizabeth Township on Bomberger Road just off Lexington Road at it's intersection with Route 501. There is an abundance of initial stones in this small plot. Three initials were used on some of the stones and they could be paired as footstones to some of the head stones. Because they were not located in the proper position for a footstone, I will list them all by last initial in their proper alphabetical category. Also because there seems to be no match for some of these initial stones, I believe that some head stones may be missing.

NAME	AGE	BORN	DIED
Initial Stones: C.A., A.			
ADAMS, Infant s/o John & Ellen Adams			12/18/1888
Initial Stone: A.M.B.			
BARDEL, Catarina NEE Reichweine	88-00-13	03/23/1737	- 04/06/1846
BOLL, Anna Maria w/o Mathias Boll	53 yrs.		07/15/1865
BOOKS, Levi	48-00-26	02/08/1839	- 03/04/1887
BOOKS, Lydia	39-00-22	12/12/1847	- 01/04/1887
CARPENTER, Gabriel	87-08-17	12/25/1814	- 09/12/1902
CARPENTER, Leah w/o Gabriel Carpenter	64-09-03	12/29/1816	- 10/02/1881
EITNIER, Abraham	01-06-05	02/07/1861	- 08/12/1862
Initial Stones: F., A.F.			
FETTER, Infant children of Sam'l. & Maria Fetter		No Dates	
FETTER, Allison s/o Samuel & Maria Fetter	01-02-13	01/16/1882	- 04/03/1883
Initial Stones: L.G., A.G., A.G., G.G., A.G.			
GINGRIG, Georg	86-07-16	03/08/1760	- 10/24/1846
GINGRICH, Barbara w/o George Gingrich	86-07-13	05/27/1777	- 11/14/1863
GORDON, Amos C. s/o Jacob & Catharine Gordon	01-00-03	02/16/1862	- 02/19/1863
GORDON, Infant d/o Jacob & Catharine Gordon		Born & Died	06/15/1863
Initial Stones: E.H., J.H., E.H.			
HACKMAN, Betty Louise d/o Martha Hackman		11/18/1935	- 01/25/1936
HELMAN, Jacob	70-07-14	05/18/1784	- 01/02/1855
HELMAN, Elizabeth w/o Jacob Helman	71-03-21	08/01/1788	- 11/22/1863
HELMAN, Elizabeth w/o Daniel Helman	??	02/15/1832	- 04/01/1882
Initial Stones: L.K., M.K., K., K., J.C.K.			
KAUFFMAN, Lightner	44-07-11	12/07/1851	- 07/18/1896
KAUFFMAN, Mazie d/o Lightner & Sallie Kauffman		03/18/1891	- 03/27/1891
KAUFFMAN, Infant d/o Lightner & Sallie Kauffman		Born & Died	04/11/1892
KAUFFMAN, Infant d/o Lightner & Sallie Kauffman		Born & Died	10/08/1893
KAUFFMAN, Benj.	75-01-01	10/13/1820	- 11/14/1895
KAUFFMAN, Hannah w/o Benj. Kauffman	70-00-27	04/01/1829	- 04/28/1899
KAUFFMAN, Elizabeth d/o Benjamin & Hannah Kauffman	06-02-26	01/27/1853	- 03/24/1859
KAUFFMAN, Aaron s/o Benjamin & Hannah Kauffman	01-06-07	02/02/1855	- 09/04/1857
KAUFFMAN, Amanda d/o Benjamin & Hannah Kauffman	08-06-19	09/12/1868	- 03/31/1877
KISSINGER, Charles Henry	00-10-00	12/27/1848	- 10/26/1849
KREIDER, Charles	15-05-29	12/12/1824	- 06/11/1870
KRIDER, John C. s/o Charles & Louise Krider	04-10-16	05/14/1856	- 04/01/1861
Initial Stones: H.A.L., E.L., S.L., H.L.			
LUTZ, Samuel (Stone worn)	??-01-18	01/22/1850	- 03/10/1855

NAME	AGE	BORN	DIED
LUTZ, Henry	07-03-04	12/31/1847 - 04/04/1855	
H.A.L., Infant of H.A.L. (Nothing else inscribed)			
Initial Stones: A.N.M., J.M., A.M., O.M., S.M., L.M., E.M., J.M.			
MARKLEY, Leonard	73-01-10	09/21/1785 - 01/31/1859	
MARKLEY, Salome w/o Leonard Markley	63-05-27	No Dates	
MARKLEY, Jacob	80-04-06	12/17/1823 - 04/23/1904	
MARKLY, Hette U. w/o Jacob Markly	64-02-24	11/09/1826 - 02/03/1891	
MARKLY, Elmira d/o Jacob & Hette Markly	15-??-??	12/10/1856 - 04/07/1872	
MARKLEY, Anna Mary w/o Abraham Markley	59-02-29	03/02/1827 - 07/31/1886	
MARKLEY, Oliver	62-10-25	02/17/1851 - 01/12/1914	
MARKLEY, Jno. "CO. H 118TH PA. INF." "GAR 1861-1865"		No Dates	
MEILEY, I.M. "CO. H 4TH PA. CAV." "GAR 1861-1865"		No Dates	
MEILY, Infant d/o Addison & Elizabeth Meily		Born & Died 04/03/1855	
MEILY, Darious s/o Addison & Elizabeth Meily	00-04-10	09/28/1862 - 02/07/1863	
OEHME, Jacob Elias	02-05-06	08/23/1847 - 01/29/1850	
Initial Stones: H.R., C.R., J.R.			
ROTH, John	77-05-00	01/03/1809 - 06/03/1886	
ROTH, Cassia w/o John Roth d/o Wm. Matlem	55-16-23	12/23/1813 - 11/16/1869	
ROTH, Henry s/o John & Cassia Roth	14-10-11	10/14/1850 - 08/25/1865	
Initial Stones: M.S., A.S., S., W.S., A.S., H.S., J.S., A.S., M.S., E.H.S.			
SCHENCK, Anna S. d/o Jacob & Mary Ann Schenck	00-09-01	10/27/1858 - 07/28/1859	
SCHENCK, Edward Henry s/o Jacob & Mary Ann Schenck		06/17/1861 - 06/03/1862	
SCHENCK, Twin sons of Jacob & Mary Ann Schenck		1863	
SHCANCK, Mary E. d/o Jacob & Mary Ann Schanck	00-11-00	08/20/1865	
SHREINER, William	86-11-04	02/01/1775 - 01/05/1862	
SCHREINER, Wilhelm	77-02-17	12/08/1803 - 02/25/1881	
SCHREINER, Anna w/o Wilhelm Schreiner	65-01-30	12/09/1800 - 02/08/1866	
SHREINER, Henry	26-02-18	12/04/1825 - 02/22/1852	
SCHREINER, Susanna w/o Elias Schreiner		06/05/1824 - 01/13/1865	
SHRINER, Jacob s/o Elias & Susanna Shriner	00-08-05	01/02/1851	
SHRINER, Amanda d/o Elias & Susanna Shriner	00-05-23	08/18/1859 - 02/11/1860	
SHRINER, Amanda d/o Jacob & Catharina Shriner	04-08-13	08/08/1852 - 04/21/1857	
SCHREINER, Mary d/o George & Anna Schreiner	01-06-08	09/29/1860 - 04/06/1862	
SHARP, Anna " Nº 469º, ANNA SHARP, hor : W;;ic " (Nothing else inscribed)			
STEFFY, Solomon	77-04-13	04/14/1817 - 08/29/1894	
STEFFY, Ellen C. d/o Solomon & Mariah Steffy	02-04-01	06/26/1854 - 08/01/1856	
STUBER, Sallie	66-06-11	03/01/1860 - 09/12/1926	
ULRICH, Barbara K.	35 yrs.	08/22/1857 - 07/13/1893	
Samuel N.	65 yrs.	08-07-1851 - 06/06/1917	
Initial Stone: M.P.W.			
WITMAN, Michael		1845 -	1921
WITMAN, Fianna E. w/o Michael Witman	51-04-28	09/06/1858 - 02/04/1910	
WITMAN, Milton P. s/o Michael & Fianna Witman	??	06/01/1882 - 08/26/1885	
WITMAN, Lizzie P. d/o Michael & Fianna Witman	07-05-12	02/17/1880 - 08/29/1887	
WITMAN, Elizabeth w/o Michael Witman		1842 -	1928
WITMAN, Henry R. s/o Henry P. & Katie Witman	00-00-10	12/31/1916	

MISCELLANEOUS

Two small shaped field stones with no markings.

Narrow short white stone with no markings.

One small red sandstone with no markings.
Small red sandstone with date of 1833 and initials P.B.

Transcribed August 1985 by Martha Xakellis

BRUBAKER/BAR GRAVEYARD #11

Location: Elizabeth Township on the south side of Brubaker Valley Road just west of
Reifsnyder Road. The stones are set in curbstone like bases and there are three rows surrounded by a pipe fence that is partially broken down.

NAME	AGE	BORN	DIED
BÄR, Ephrahim	12-00-08	08/30/1810 - 09/07/1822	
BÄR, Samuel	39 and about		
	10 mnths.	1788 - 04/08/1828	
BÄR, Johanes	51-07-26	06/09/1750 - 02/05/1802	
BÄR, Maria	71-00-06	07/06/1756 - 07/12/1827	
BÄR, Johannes	46-08-21	12/10/1776 - 09/01/1822	
BÄR, David	02-08-18	12/28/1819 - 09/21/1822	
BÄR, Twin sons of Samuel & Barbara Bär			
Isaac	01-01-24	02/04/1829 - 03/28/1829	
Samuel	00-09-03	02/04/1829 - 11/07/1829	
BRUBACHER, Johannes	84 yrs.	1719 - 04/09/1804	
BRUBACHER, Maria w/o Johannes Brubacher, born in	30 yrs.	1720 - 1750	
Deutschland.			
BRUBACHER, Maria	73-08-18	10/03/1728 - 06/21/1802	
BRUBACHER, Jacob	35-1-2w.		
	6 d.	06/11/1758 - 08/31/1793	
BRUBACHER, Susanna nee Erb	81-10-05	03/17/1762 - 01/22/1844	
BRUBACHER, Jacob	72-06-03	01/27/1782 - 07/30/1854	
BRUBACHER, Maria w/o Jacob Brubacher	76-06-04	10/12/1787 - 04/16/1864	
BRUBACHER, Elisabeth d/o Jacob & Maria Brubacher	26-10-26	12/01/1826 - 10/27/1853	
BRUBACHER, Johannes		09/2?/1783 - 11/18/1792	
BRUBACHER, Henrich	52-06-04	10/21/1785 - 04/26/1839	
BRUBACHER, Andrew s/o Jacob & Elizabeth	06-10-22	03/08/1853 - 01/30/1860	
BRUBACHER, Jacob s/o Jacob & Elizabeth Brubacher	00-07-12	07/29/1855	
BRUBACHER, Ephraim s/o Henry & Mary Brubacher	01-00-06	07/19/1859 - 07/27/1860	

Transcribed November 1985 by Martha J. Xakellis

EBY GRAVEYARD #12

This graveyard is located north of Snavely Mill Road on the hill and is visible from the road. It is enclosed by a wrought iron fence and is very well kept.

NAME	AGE	BORN	DIED
EBY, Theodorus This is a Memorial Stone inscribed as follows:			

OUR IMMIGRANT FOREFATHER
THEODORUS EBY
1663 - 1727
BORN IN SWITZERLAND AND BURIED
ON HIS HOMESTEAD IN LEACOCK
TOWNSHIP LANCASTER COUNTY PA
WE THANK THEODORUS FOR COMING TO THIS
GREAT COUNTRY WHERE HIS DESCENDANTS
HAVE BEEN ABLE TO PRACTICE RELIGIOUS
FREEDOM

The base has the following inscription:

ERECTED BY A GRATEFUL POSTERITY

NAME	AGE	BORN	DIED
EBY, I Christian (This is a newer stone)		1698 -	1756
Elizabeth M.		c1708 -	1787
EBY, II Christian (This is a newer stone)		1734 -	1807
Catherine B.		1743 -	1810
(G) EBY, Christian	60-10-13		08/27/1824
(G) EBY, Veronica	52-02-15		02/04/1826
(G) EBY, Johannes	77-07-02	10/23/1767 -	05/25/1845
(G) EBY, Maria	83-00-04	08/25/1773 -	08/29/1856
EBY, G. (Roughly shaped red sandstone, crudely carved)			1793
(G) EBY, Sem s/o Benjamin & Veronica Eby	03-06-12	02/10/1829 -	08/22/1832
(G) EBY, little s/o Benjamin & Veronica Eby		09/27/1831	
(G) EBY, Henry W. s/o Benjamin & Veronica Eby	11-11-19	10/09/1840 -	09/28/1852
EITNIER, Jacob	70 yrs.		06/21/1844
EITNIER, Maria NEE Hoffer w/o Jacob Eby	88-08-08		06/21/1871
EITNIER, Abraham	77-06-20	02/22/1811 -	09/12/1888
EITNIER, Elizabeth	75-09-20	06/18/1815 -	04/08/1891
(G) EITNIER, Simon A. s/o Abraham & Elizabeth Eitnier	17-01-26	11/30/1834 -	01/26/1852
EITNIER, Elias C. s/o Abraham & Elizabeth Eitnier	15-07-19	03/30/1837 -	11/19/1852
EITNIER, Anna B. d/o Abraham & Elizabeth Eitnier	13-02-15	04/06/1849 -	06/21/1862
EITNIER, Aaron s/o Abraham & Elizabeth Eitnier	01-05-06	06/02/1860 -	11/08/1861
EITNIER, Martha C.	78-01-15	09/05/1847 -	10/20/1925
Allen C.	33-07-03	10/08/1851 -	05/11/1885
EITNIER, Willie s/o Allen C. & Martha Eitnier	00-01-02		07/07/1878
(G) FRANK, Michael	78-09-29	05/10/1757 -	03/08/1836
FRANK, Mary w/o Michael Frank	84-05-27	07/12/1770 -	01/09/1855
NIES, Justina	00-04-01		09/02/1862
SPOONHOWER, Catharine	79-04-17	11/10/1811 -	03/27/1891
SPOONHOWER, Henry	70-04-14	04/13/1017 -	08/27/1887
(G) WITWER, Jonas	82-02-18	02/24/1763 -	05/12/1845
(G) WITWER, Veronica	79-02-08	04/17/1763 -	06/25/1842

Initial Stones: H.W.E., J.E., M.E., A.E., E.E., S.A.E., E.C.E., A.B.E., A.E., M.F., J.N., J.W.

MISCELLANEOUS: There were six roughly cut limestones. On one of them there was A.E. carved.
On another one was C + H. There was nothing decipherable on the rest.
There was also a larger light colored sandstone with a decorated top too badly worn to
read.

Arpil 1986 by Martha Xakellis

STEINMETZ
CEMETERY
RESTORED BY
BARON STIEGEL
LIONS CLUB
1979

STEINMETZ CEMETERY #13

This cemetery is located north of Brubaker Valley Road near its junction with Route 322. A small sign states that is was restored in 1979 by the Baron Stiegel Lions Club and is in good condition. It is enclosed by a pipe fence and has a gate in the southwest corner.

NAME	AGE	BORN	DIED
(G) BAMBERGER, Moses	64-10-25	09/04/1776 - 07/30/1841	
(G) BAMBERGER, Catharine w/o Moses Bamberger	81-02-07	06/30/1779 - 09/07/1860	
(G) BAMBERGER, Johanes	03-05-20	04/16/1815 - 10/16/1818	
(G) BENTZ, Cecelia d/o Mar^t. & Cath. Bentz	03-10-??	06/30/1846 - 05/12/1850	
(G) BENTZ, Israel s/o Mart. & Cath. Bentz		08/26/1848 - Unreadable	
BERGELBACH, Catharine	76-11-29	11/14/1741 - 11/13/1819	
(G) BRUBAKER, Christian	65-04-26	09/18/1787 - 02/14/1853	
(G) BRUBAKER, Elizabeth NEE Shenck w/o Christian Brubaker	83-07-05	09/01/1789 - 04/05/1873	
BRUBAKER, Susan	88-01-19	10/08/1810 - 11/27/1898	
BRUBAKER, Jacob S.	74-01-19	12/06/1812 - 01/25/1887	
BRUBAKER, Priscilla NEE Dillman	39-00-25	02/10/1829 - 03/06/1868	
BRUBAKER, Infant d/o J. & P. Brubaker		No Dates	
BRUBAKER, Infant d/o J. & P. Brubaker		No Dates	
BRUBAKER, Infant s/o J. & P. Brubaker		No Dates	
(G) BRUBACHER, Johannes	05-09-17	12/08/1816 - 09/25/1820	
(G) BRUBAKER, Abraham	29-02-22	04/13/1823 - 07/05/1852	
BRUBAKER, Elizabeth	67-07-22	03/08/1830 - 10/30/1897	
DISSINGER, Amanda d/o Danial & Eliza Dissinger	13-00-11	03/04/1856 - 03/15/1869	
(G) DULEBAN, Mar?red		09/09/1743 - 08/29/1827	
(G) EBERLE, Johannes	63-10-20	12/24/1780 - 11/25/1844	
(G) EBERLE, ??dia	64-04-23	08/28/1780 - 10/21/1844	
(G) EBY, Peter	77-00-02	11/11/1742 - 11/24/1819	
(G) EBY, Barbara w/o Peter	42 yrs.	1764 - 1806	
(G) EBY, Catharina w/o Abraham (Broken portion of stone)		08/26/1777 - 02/06/1851	
(G) ERB, Johannes	54-00-02	10/05/1756 - 12/03/1810	
(G) ERB, Judith w/o Johannes Erb	79-05-24	12/26/1759 - 06/19/1839	
(G) ERB, Elisabeth w/o Daniel Erb	33-02-00	07/15/1770 - 09/15/1803	
(G) ERB, Jacob	32-00-14	01/15/1783 - 01/29/1815	
ERB, John (Broken portion of stone)		11/03/1786	
ERB, John (Replacement for above stone)	75-07-22	11/03/1786 - 06/25/1862	
ERB, Barbara	80-08-24	09/14/1788 - 06/08/1869	
(G) ERB, Susana	00-09-02	06/12/1792 - 04/06/1793	
ERB, Anna d/o Christian Erb		12/02/1797 - ??/28/1807	
(G) ERB, Christian	00-02-04	07/01/1798 - 11/05/1798	
(G) ERB, Josua	16-00-03	11/01/1800 - 11/04/1816	
(G) ERB, Anna	00-10-08	06/07/1812 - 04/15/1813	
ERB, Leah w/o John B. Erb	42-01-17	04/26/1816 - 09/12/1858	
ERB, John K. s/o John B. & Leah Erb	16-10-01	07/19/1840 - 05/23/1857	
ERB, Elvina d/o Josua & Sarah Erb	02-00-27	02/15/1841 - 03/14/1843	
ERB, Infant d/o Hiram L. & Celinda Erb		06/04/1866	
(G) ILLIG, Catharina		06/04/1773 - ??/??/1848	
ILLIG, George s/o Johannes & Catharina Illig	36-07-18	10/25/1796 - 02/07/1833	
(G) SCHENCK, Martin	75-08-11	06/30/1737 - 03/11/1813	
(G) SCHENCK, Anna	87th yr.	12/--/1740 - 08/08/1827	
(G) SCHENK, Christian	68-04-16	12/22/1760 - 05/07/1829	

	NAME	AGE	BORN	DIED
(G)	SCHENCK, Johannes (Most of stone buried)		08/06/1763	??/??/1805
(G)	SCHENCK, Susanna	57-05-13	09/11/1768	02/24/1826
(G)	SCHENCK, Elisabeth NEE Tulipan	60-04-11	01/14/1770	05/25/1830
(G)	SCHENCK, Johanes	28-06-12	08/27/1790	03/11/1819
(G)	SCHENCK, Anna	16-06-00	02/06/1793	08/06/1809
(G)	SCHENCK, Christian s/o Johanes Schenck		04/10/1791	??/26/1793
(G)	SCHENCK, Maria	27-00-15	02/13/1795	02/28/1822
(G)	SCHENCK, Susana "Born in Elisabeth Township"	32-03-02	07/16/1795	10/18/1827
(G)	SCHENCK, Christian	29-00-11	12/19/1795	12/30/1824
(G)	SCHENCK, Abraham	21 less 4 days	03/07/1800	03/03/1821
	SHENCK, Samuel "was intermarried to Lydia Shirk d/o John Shirk"	71-11-17	06/26/1800	06/13/1872
	SHENCK, Lydia w/o Samuel Shenck	80-05-11	01/31/1805	07/12/1885
(G)	SCHENCK, Anna	25-10-19	02/10/1803	01/01/1829
(G)	SCHENCK, Hanna	4 less 1 day	01/15/1817	01/14/1821
(G)	SNYDER, Joseph	51-05-26	08/11/1807	02/05/1859
(G)	SNYDER, Veronica w/o Joseph Snyder	47-05-18	10/09/1812	04/27/1859
	SNYDER, Esther K.	69-02-18		03/24/1904
	SNYDER, Moses B.	66-03-17		04/17/1902
	SNYDER, Ada L.	00-08-25	06/29/1869	03/24/1870
	STEHLE, Johannes	37-02-19	11/27/1775	02/16/1833
	STEINMETZ, Reuben	40-08-04	02/21/1829	10/25/1869
	STEINMETZ, Susan w/o Reuben Steinmetz	81-09-19	03/12/1835	12/31/1916
	STEINMETZ, Atline d/o Reuben & Susan Steinmetz	00-09-12	11/06/1859	08/18/1860
	STEINMETZ, Martin s/o Reuben & Susan Steinmetz	12-00-02	05/12/1863	06/06/1875
	STEINMETZ, Grant S.		02/04/1868	03/16/1925
	Mary L. w/o Grant S. Steinmetz		12/01/1863	04/07/1953
	STEINMETZ, Elvira d/o Grant & Mary Steinmetz	00-11-27		07/24/1894
	STEINMETZ, Etna d/o Grant & Mary Steinmetz		03/01/1897	
	STINEMAN, Eliza	60-11-17	04/02/1828	03/13/1889
(G)	WITMER, (Broken off) d/o Abraham & Catharina Cassel	69-06-00	02/01/1769	08/01/1838
	WITMER, Catharine (Replacement stone for above)	69-06-00	02/01/1769	08/01/1838
(G)	WOLF, John (Portion of stone)-death date from earlier record)		03/13/1777	03/27/1855
(G)	WOLF, Margaretha w/o Absalom Wolf	36-00-05	01/20/1817	01/25/1853

MISCELLANEOUS

Along one side of this cemetery is a concrete pad that has imbedded in it fragments and portions of stones probably left from the restoration in 1979. There are duplicate stones in this cemetery and I have noted those that were standing. The following is a list of the fragments.

    J.E., B.E. - Probably footstones
    BARB][1788 - Barbara Erb, 1788-1869
    Hier Ruhet _Catharin_ - Top of Witmer, d/o Abraham & Catharina Cassel
    Barbara][mber 1-, 1771][__AR 1_, 1851] -
    UND ST___ SEPT][75-03-05 - Could not identify.
    UND 11 TAG - Could not identify.
There was an upright stone with the top broken off which duplicates the dates of Catharine
    Bergelbach.
And finally there were the following initial stones:
    E.E. - 1803 (Elizabeth Erb?), E.B., R.I., E.S.
From earlier record are the following:
    Barbara Heinecke, 12/18/1771 - 01/12/1851
    Susanna Stahle Wolf w/o Johannes Wolf, 05/23/1780 - 03/27/1833.
    John Wolf, 05/01/1817 - ??/??/1831.   April 1986

BRUBAKER GRAVEYARD #14

Located between Blantz and Weber Roads in the middle of a field, this graveyard was maintained at one time but not lately. There is no extensive brush growth but the iron pipe fence is starting to collapse and the gate is broken off. The one gate post has the date 1890 on it. Some of the stones are starting to lean at alarming angles. There are two large monuments with stones imbedded in them. They seem to be recuttings of the original stones as I found six duplicates carved in an older style. The recut stones have No. 1, No. 2, No. 3, and No. 4 on them which seem to number the generations.

LARGE MONUMENT

No. 1 John Brubaker and wife Anna from Switzerland buried at Rohrerstown.
No. 2 Daniel Brubaker born about 1726, died when quite young, had 2 sons, John & David.
       Foronica wife of Daniel Brubaker, born about 1727. She was a daughter of Michael Doner.
No. 3 John Brubaker   69-00-07   11/07/1759 - 11/14/1828
       Elizabeth Bomberger Brubaker   83-11-06   02/24/1758 - 01/30/1842

LARGE MONUMENT

No. 4 Christian Brubaker   40-06-25   03/18/1781 - 10/13/1821
No. 4 Elizabeth Brubaker Wenger   48-07-26   10/22/1798 - 06/16/1847
No. 4 Elias Brubaker   57-10-21   07/20/1789 - 06/10/1847
No. 4 Maria Brubaker   70-11-24   07/01/1787 - 06/24/1858

OTHER STONES

NAME	AGE	BORN	DIED
(G) BRUBACHER, Elisabeth	84-11-06	02/24/1758 - 01/30/1842	
(G) BRUBACHER, Johannes	69-01-07	11/07/1759 - 11/14/1828	
(G) BRUBACHER, Christian	40-06-24	03/18/1781 - 11/13/1821	
(G) BRUBACHER, Maria	70-11-24	07/01/1787 - 06/24/1858	
(G) BRUBACHER, Elias	57-07-21	07/20/1789 - 06/10/1847	
(G) BRUBACHER, Peter	69-01-04	03/09/1794 - 04/13/1863	
(G) BRUBACHER, Anna NEE Hursh w/o Peter Brubacher	82-01-11	01/28/1787 - 03/11/1869	
(G) BRUBACHER, Abraham	76-09-14	11/02/1811 - 08/16/1888	
(G) BRUBACHER, Anna NEE Hess w/o Abraham Brubacher	63-08-27	12/31/1817 - No Date	
(G) BRUBACHER, Peter s/o Abraham & Anna Brubacher	16-05-02	11/13/1852 - 03/15/1869	
(G) BRUBACHER, Barbara d/o Abraham & Anna Brubacher	13-10-26	12/04/1848 - 10/31/1862	
BRUBAKER, Henry s/o John H. & Fanny Brubaker	00-11-02	06/07/1853 - 05/09/1854	
(G) WENGER, Elisabeth NEE Brubacher	48-07-09	10/22/1792 - 06/01/1841	

Initial Stones: C.B., M.B., P.B., A.B., A.B., B.B., H.B., E.W., R.B.

Transcribed April 1986 by Martha Xakellis

FORMER BADORF/SAHM GRAVEYARD   #15

A 1942 description locates a 25 by 25 feet graveyard "in the center of a wheat and potato field surrounded by a wire fence on wooden posts with a gate in the southwest corner. There is an oak tree growing in the center of the little graveyard." It went on to state that "there were 19 head and 2 foot stones." The oak tree is still there but now the gate leans against the tree and the stones are piled haphazardly around the tree with the field plowed quite close to the tree. Among the stones are a few old locust fence posts, quite possibly the posts in the 1942 description. What few stones and pieces were there are listed here.

	NAME	AGE	BORN	DIED
	ADAIRE, Leander	00-03-09		04/04/1864
(G)	BADARF, Catharine d/o Benjamin & Catharine Badarf	21-01-17	02/17/1837 - 04/04/1858	
	(The above stone is in at least two pieces.)			
(G)	BADARF, Enoch s/o Benjamin & Catharine Badarf	00-00-03		04/28/1843
(G)	BADARF, a d/o Benjamin & Catharine Badarf			12/04/1844
(G)	SAHM, George	59-02-20	07/28/1767 - 10/18/1826	
(G)	SAHM, Elisabeth (Stone in two pieces)	30 y.-7 m.	03/--/1771 - 10/13/1821	
(G)	SAHM, Henry	34-02-00	04/12/1802 - 06/12/1836	

Initial Stones: C.B., C.B.

FRAGMENTS:
   (G) Catharine ehefrau von - From an earlier record this would be Catharine Badarf wife of Benjamin Badarf, born 01/06/1810, died 08/29/1850.

STONES IN EARLIER LIST THAT ARE NOT THERE NOW.

NAME	AGE	BORN	DIED
Adaire, Jacob s/o James & Susanna Adaire	5 dys.		10/13/1853
Adaire, Henry s/o James & Susanna Adaire	04-05-02		04/15/1859
Adair, Allen s/o James & Susanna Adair	01-11-29		05/09/1862
Adaire, Wilson	02-02-02		04/19/1874
Adaire, Susanna	00-03-19		01/29/1875
Badarf, Noah s/o Benjamin & Catharine Badarf	1 day		03/15/1839
Badarf, d/o Benjamin & Catharine Badarf	3 dys.	01/10/1847	
Badarf, Margaret d/o Benjamin & Catharine Badarf	6 dys.		12/13/1845
Badard, Aaron s/o Benjamin & Catharine Badarf	6 dys.	03/17/1848	
Badarf, s/o Benjamin & Catharine Badarf			08/22/1850
Heinicke, d/o Beniamin & Vronica Heinicke			02/23/1853 - 05/23/1853

Transcribed April 1986 by Martha Xakellis

STAUFFER GRAVEYARD #16

This family graveyard is located in Elizabeth Township on the north side of Evans Road which is unpaved. It is up on the hill in the middle of the fields. Surrounding it is a four foot high galvanized pipe barrier. I say barrier because there is <u>no gate</u>. It is approximately 20 ft. square and full of ground hog diggings. In 1985 the area along the north side was used as a dead animal dump.

NAME	AGE	BORN	DIED
RUDY, Eliza "Born in Manheim Township, Lancaster County"	19-11-17	07/18/1815 - 07/04/1835	
STAUFER, Christian	72 yrs.	Died in the year	1808
STAUFFER, Anna	81 yrs.	Died in July of	1826
STAUFFER, Magdalena With footstone M.S.	73-02-05		09/05/1846
STAUFFER, Jacob (stone is mostly buried, inscription taken from earlier listing)	30th yr.		1805
STAUFFER, Peter With footstone P.S.	67-06-26	07/07/1783 - 02/03/1851	
STAUFFER, Magdalena w/o Peter Stauffer	71-02-00	07/16/1784 - 09/16/1855	
STAUFER, Anna d/o Henry & Maria Staufer	buried	11/27/1837 - 11/29/1839	
STAUFFER, John s/o Henry & Maria Stauffer		Born & Died 12/05/1852	

(This stone is from an earlier list. It's not there now.)

Transcribed May 1985 by Martha Xakellis